W9-CPX-561

THE NEW INTERNATIONAL
WEBSTER'S POCKET
THESAURUS
OF THE ENGLISH LANGUAGE

◆ ◆ ◆

TRIDENT PRESS
INTERNATIONAL

Published by

Trident Press International

1997 EDITION

Cover Design Copyright © Trident Press International
Text Copyright © 1997 J. Radcliffe

ISBN 1-888-777-16-8 Deluxe Edition
ISBN1-888-777-26-5 Hardcover Edition
ISBN1-888-777-34-6 Paperback Edition

All Rights Reserved

Printed in the United States of America

aback *adv.* **BACKWARD:** back, behind, rearward; **UNEXPECTED:** suddenly, unawares, unexpectedly

abandon *n.* **ENTHUSIASM:** impetuosity, spontaneity; **IMMORALITY:** shamelessness, wantonness

abandon *v.* **GIVE UP:** forgo, forswear, quit, relinquish; **DESERT:** forsake, leave, resign, vacate

abandonment *n.* abdication, renunciation, repudiation, resignation, surrender

abase *v.* debase, degrade, disgrace, dishonor, humble, humiliate

abased *adj.* degraded, disgraced, dishonored, humbled, humiliated, lowered

abasement *n.* degradation, deterioration, disgrace, dishonor, groveling, humiliation, lowering, shame

abash *v.* confound, confuse, disconcert, embarrass, humble, humiliate, mortify, shame

abashed *adj.* ashamed, chagrined, confused

abasing *adj.* abusive, insulting, offensive

abate *v.* **LESSEN:** decline, decrease diminish, ease, ebb, fade, lower, moderate, slacken, relieve, slow; **DISCOUNT:** allow, deduct, rebate, remit, subtract

abatement *n.* **LESSENING:** alleviation, decrease, mitigation, slackening, subsidence; **ENDING:** cessation, remission, suppression, termination

abbreviate *v.* abridge, condense, contract, cut, reduce, shorten, truncate

abbreviation *n.* abridgement, brief, compendium, condensation, shortening, truncation

abdicate *v.* abandon, cede, disavow, disclaim, disown, relinquish, renounce, resign, secede

abdomen *n.* belly, breadbasket, gut, midsection, paunch, potbelly, stomach, tummy

abduct *v.* capture, kidnap, seize, shanghai

abecedarian *n.* beginner, novice

abed *adj.* asleep, resting

aberrant *adj.* DEVIATING: divergent, errant, irregular, straying; ODD: abnormal, peculiar, queer, strange, unnatural, unusual, weird

aberrational *adj.* curious, odd, peculiar, strange

abet *v.* advance, aid, assist, back, condone, favor, further, help, promote, sanction, second, support

abettor *n.* accessory, accomplice, ally, associate, cohort, confederate, conspirator

abeyance *n.* cessation, deferral, discontinuance, hiatus, moratorium, suspension

abhor *v.* despise, detest, disgust, hate, loathe

abhorrence *n.* aversion, disgust, dislike, distaste, hatred, loathing, horror, repugnance

abhorrent *adj.* abominable, despicable, detestable, disgusting, loathsome, offensive, nauseating, odious, repugnant, repulsive, revolting, shocking, vile

abidance *n.* compliance, continuance

abide *v.* DWELL: inhabit, live, reside, stay; WAIT: attend, await, remain, stay, tarry; ENDURE: allow, bear, remain, stand, suffer

abiding *adj.* enduring, lasting, permanent, steadfast

ability *n.* aptitude, bent, capability, capacity, competence, dexterity, expertise, facility, faculty, knack, proficiency, qualification, skill, skillfulness, talent

abject *adj.* base, contemptible, degrading, despicable, disheartening, ignominious, miserable, poor, sorry

abjection, abjectness *n.* churlishness, degradation, humiliation, meanness, nastiness

abjuration *n.* abnegation, denial, disavowal, rejection, renouncement, renunciation

abjure *v.* forswear, recant, recall, renounce, retract, withdraw

ablaze *adj.* **BURNING:** aflame, blazing, fiery, flaming; **FERVENT:** ardent, eager, excited, exhilarated, intense

able *adj.* **CAPABLE:** adequate, apt, competent, efficient, fit, qualified; **SKILLFUL:** accomplished, adroit, dexterous, expert, gifted, ingenious, proficient, talented

able–bodied *adj.* fit, healthy, robust, strong

abloom *adj.* blossoming, flowering, sprouting

ablution *n.* cleansing, purification, purging, washing

abnegation *n.* abjuration, denial, disavowal, rejection, renouncement, renunciation, self–denial

abnormal *adj.* aberrant, anomalous, curious, deviant, irregular, odd, peculiar, unnatural

abnormality *n.* anomaly, curiosity, irregularity, malformation, nonconformity, peculiarity, perversion

abode *n.* domicile, dwelling, habitat, house, residence

abolish *v.* abrogate, annul, cancel, eliminate, end, eradicate, erase, extinguish, nullify, obliterate

abolishment *n.* annulment, cancellation, elimination, eradication, nullification

abolition *n.* annulment, cancellation, dissolution, elimination, eradication, repeal, revocation

abominable *adj.* abhorrent, contemptible, despicable, detestable, disgusting, hateful, horrible, loathsome, offensive, repugnant

abominate *v.* abhor, despise, detest, hate, loathe

abomination *n.* **HORROR:** loathing, revulsion; **WICKEDNESS:** amorality, depravity, evil, immorality

aboriginal *adj.* domestic, indigenous, local, native, original, primitive

abort *v.* annul, cancel, destroy, fail, interrupt, miscarry, nullify, scrap, stop, terminate

abortion *n.* CESSATION: cancellation, interruption, termination; MONSTROSITY: abnormality

abortive *adj.* fruitless, futile, ineffectual, unavailing

abound *v.* overflow, pour, swarm, swell, teem

abounding *adj.* abundant, lavish, luxuriant, plentiful

about *adv.* CONCERNING: referencing, regarding; APPROXIMATELY: almost, around, close, near, nigh

above *adv.* HIGHER: atop, beyond, over, overhead; GREATER: preeminent, superior, surpassing

aboveboard *adj.* candid, frank, guileless, honest, open, overt, sincere, straightforward

abradant *adj.* annoying, harsh, nasty, offensive

abrade *v.* WEAR: chafe, corrode, erode, grind, rub, scrape; IRRITATE : anger, annoy, bother, gall, irk

abrading *n.* abrasion, attrition, erosion

abrasion *n.* blemish, bruise, cut, scrape, scratch

abrasive *adj.* annoying, exasperating, grating, harsh, jarring, nasty, offensive, rasping, shrill, strident

abreast *adj., adv.* BESIDE: against, aligned; INFORMED: apprised, familiar

abridge *v.* abstract, compress, condense, curtail, cut, decrease, diminish, lessen, reduce, restrict, shorten

abrogate *v.* abolish, annul, cancel, invalidate, nullify, repeal, rescind, revoke, void

abrupt *adj.* SUDDEN: quick, sharp, unexpected; CURT: blunt, boorish, brusque, discourteous, hasty, impatient, rude; STEEP: craggy, hilly, precipitous, sheer

abruptness *n.* brevity, curtness, shortness, terseness

abscessed *adj.* inflamed, painful, ulcerated

abscission *n.* deletion, eradication, excision, removal

abscond *v.* bolt, depart, escape, flee

absconder *n.* charlatan, cheat, rogue, swindler

absence *n.* **LACK:** dearth, default, defect, deficiency, need, want; **AWAY:** nonattendance, truancy

absentee *n.* defector, delinquent, deserter, fugitive, escapee, runaway, truant

absent–minded *adj.* forgetful, oblivious, preoccupied, unmindful

absolute *adj.* **PERFECT:** certain, definite, faultless, ideal, sure, unconditional, unquestionable, utter, whole; **AUTHORITARIAN:** autocratic, despotic, dictatorial, imperious, peremptory, strict, tyrannical

absolution *n.* acquittal, clearance, exoneration, vindication

absolvable *adj.* excusable, forgivable, inconsequential, justifiable, minor, pardonable, permissible, venial

absolve *v.* acquit, clear, discharge, excuse, exonerate, forgive, free, justify, liberate, pardon, release

absorb *v.* **INCORPORATE:** amalgamate, assimilate, consume, devour, engulf; **ENGROSS:** engage, employ, occupy; **UNDERSTAND:** assimilate, grasp, learn, sense

absorbed *adj.* **INCORPORATED:** assimilated, digested, dissolved, permeated; **ENGROSSED:** enthralled, immersed, intent, involved, preoccupied, rapt

absorbent *adj.* permeable, penetrable, porous, spongy

absorbing *adj.* engaging, enthralling, exciting, fascinating, interesting

absorption *n.* absent-mindedness, preoccupation, reflection, reverie

abstain *v.* avoid, decline, eschew, forgo, refrain, shun

abstinence *n.* avoidance, forbearance, moderation, self–denial, sobriety, temperance

abstinent *adj.* abstemious, continent, moderate

abstract *adj.* **THEORETICAL:** conceptual, ideal, hypothetical; **ISOLATED:** apart, separate, special, unrelated; **COMPLEX:** complicated, deep, difficult, obscure

abstract *n.* abridgment, brief, compendium, condensation, digest, distillation, outline, summary

abstract *v.* **REMOVE:** disjoin, dissociate, isolate, separate, withdraw; **CONDENSE:** abbreviate, abridge, digest, distill, edit, outline, summarize

abstruse *adj.* complex, difficult, intricate, involved

absurd *adj.* asinine, foolish, inane, irrational, ludicrous, preposterous, ridiculous, silly

abundance *n.* bounty, extravagance, fullness, profusion, prosperity, wealth

abundant *adj.* abounding, copious, flowing, fruitful, opulent, plentiful, prodigal, profuse, prolific, teeming

abuse *n.* misuse, defilement, desecration, mistreatment, profanation, subversion, violation

abuse *v.* **MISUSE:** attack, desecrate, harm, hurt, injure, maltreat, mistreat, wrong; **BERATE:** assail, denounce, disparage, insult, malign, reproach, revile, scold

abusive *adj.* **AGONIZING:** insufferable, intolerable, painful, unbearable, unendurable; **DISCOURTEOUS:** rude, sarcastic, slanderous, truculent, vituperative

abut *v.* adjoin, border, touch, verge

abysmal *adj.* bottomless, deep, immeasurable, profound, unfathomable

abyss *n.* chasm, gorge, gulf, hole, perdition

academic *adj.* **SCHOLARLY:** collegiate, erudite, learned, lettered, literary, scholastic, schooled; **TRADITIONAL:** conventional, conservative, established, formalistic; **THEORETICAL:** conjectural, speculative, suppositional

academician *n.* intellectual, egghead, scholar

academics *n.* courses, studies

academy *n.* college, conservatory, school

accede *v.* acquiesce, agree, allow, assent, comply, consent, grant, permit, sanction

accelerate *v.* hasten, expedite, quicken, throttle

acceleration *n.* dispatch, hastening, quickening

accent *n.* MODULATION: beat, inflection, emphasis, rhythm; SIGNIFICANCE: importance, prominence

accent, accentuate *v.* emphasize, stress, underscore

accept *v.* RECEIVE: embrace, take, welcome; ACQUIESCE: accede, acknowledge, allow, assent, concede, concur, grant; BELIEVE: affirm, hold, maintain, trust; UNDERSTAND: appreciate, conclude, construe

acceptable *adj.* adequate, agreeable, permissible, pleasant, pleasing, satisfactory, sufficient

acceptance *n.* acknowledgement, agreement, assent, capitulation, concurrence, consent, recognition

accepted *adj.* ACCREDITED: accustomed, acknowledged, allowed, recognized; SETTLED: admitted, affirmed, endorsed

accessible *adj.* approachable, attainable, available, convenient, obtainable, reachable

accessory *adj.* added, contributing, extra

accessory *n.* abettor, accomplice

accident *n.* MISHAP: casualty, misadventure, misfortune, pileup, wreck; CHANCE: coincidence, fortune

accidental *adj.* UNEXPECTED: casual, chance, fortuitous, odd, random, unintentional, unplanned; INCIDENTAL: insignificant, minor, nonessential, secondary, subsidiary

acclaim *n.* applause, approval, enthusiasm, fame,

plaudits, praise, recognition

acclaim *v.* applaud, celebrate, commend, laud, praise

acclamation *n.* acclaim, accolades, applause, approval, jubilation, plaudits, praise

acclimate *v.* accommodate, adapt, adjust, conform

acclimation *n.* adaptation, adjustment, conformity

acclimatize *v.* acclimate, adapt, adjust, conform

acclivity *n.* ascent, incline, slope, upgrade

accolade *n.* acknowledgement, esteem, praise, tribute

accommodate *v.* **AID:** abet, assist, oblige, provide, serve, supply; **ENTERTAIN:** board, house, lodge, quarter; **ADJUST:** adapt, conform, fit, harmonize, reconcile, temper; **RECEIVE:** contain, have, hold

accommodating *adj.* kind, gracious, helpful, neighborly, obliging

accompaniment *n.* addition, accessory, adjunct, appendage, appurtenance

accompany *v.* **ATTEND:** chaperon, convey, escort, follow, join, see, show, usher; **APPEND:** augment, complement, complete, enhance, supplement

accomplice *n.* accessory, affiliate, associate, confederate, conspirator, partner

accomplish *v.* achieve, attain, complete, do, effect, execute, fulfill, make, manage, perform, realize

accomplished *adj.* skillful, able, cultivated, cultured, expert, proficient, refined, talented

accomplishment *n.* achievement, attainment, exploit, feat, fulfillment, success

accord *n.* agreement, conformity, consent, harmony, peace, unanimity

accord *v.* **AGREE:** accommodate, adapt, affirm, assent, coincide, concur, correspond, harmonize, reconcile;

BESTOW: allow, deign, grant, concede, yield

accordance n. accord, agreement, coincidence, concordance, conformity, harmony

accost v. address, approach, confront, face, greet, halt, meet, proposition, solicit, waylay

account n. **NARRATIVE:** anecdote, chronicle, description, explanation, exposé, journal, narration, recital, report, story, tale; **REASON:** consideration, excuse, grounds, motive; **WORTH:** advantage, benefit, consideration, estimation, importance, profit, reputation

account v. **EXPLAIN:** describe, justify, rationalize; **REGARD:** consider, count, credit, deem, estimate, hold, judge, reckon, think

accountable adj. answerable, culpable, liable, responsible

accredit v. certify, endorse, pass, ratify, recognize, sanction, support, uphold, validate, warrant

accrual, accruement n. accumulation, expansion, growth, increase, recovery, return, yield

accumulate v. accrue, amass, collect, cumulate, gather, heap, garner, increase, stockpile, store

accuracy n. exactness, precision, sureness

accurate n. careful, correct, exact, factual, faithful, flawless, precise, proper, right, true, unerring

accursed adj. doomed, bewitched, condemned, damned, haunted, ill–fated

accusation n. allegation, charge, complaint, denunciation, indictment, insinuation, slur, smear

accuse v. arraign, arrest, blame, charge, denounce, implicate, impute, incriminate, indict, involve

accustom v. familiarize, habituate, inure, season

ace n. champion, expert, master, specialist

acerbate *n.* heighten, increase, intensify, worsen
acerbic *adj.* bitter, harsh, rough, sharp, sour
ache *n.* agony, pain, pang, spasm, twinge
ache *v.* hurt, pain, suffer, throb
achievable *adj.* attainable, feasible, obtainable
achieve *v.* accomplish, effect, fulfill, finish, reach, attain, gain, get, realize, secure
achy *adj.* aching, bruised, painful
acid *adj.* biting, cutting, sarcastic, sardonic, satirical, scornful, sharp, vitriolic
acknowledge *v.* admit, agree, allow, appreciate, approve, avow, concede, confess, confirm, declare, endorse, grant, ratify, recognize, reply, respond
acknowledgment *n.* ACCEPTANCE: affirmation, corroboration, recognition; RESPONSE: answer, call, greeting, letter, nod, note, reaction, reply, thanks
acme *n.* apex, peak, summit, top, zenith
acolyte *n.* aide, assistant, helper, subordinate
acquaint *v.* inform, accustom, advise, familiarize, reconnoiter, introduce, present
acquaintance *n.* friend, associate, colleague, companion, crony, pal
acquainted *adj.* conversant, familiar, introduced
acquiesce *v.* assent, accede, accept, agree, bend, comply, concur, consent, rest, submit, yield
acquire *v.* appropriate, attain, earn, gain, get, obtain, procure, secure
acquisitive *adj.* avaricious, grasping, greedy
acquisitiveness *n.* covetousness, greed
acquit *v.* absolve, exonerate, pardon, release
acquittal *n.* absolution, amnesty, deliverance, discharge, dismissal, exoneration, pardon, vindication

acreage *n.* grounds, land, property, spread, terrain

acrid *adj.* astringent, biting, bitter, caustic, harsh

acrimonious *adj.* acerbic, caustic, irascible, testy

acropolis *n.* bastion, citadel, blockhouse, fort, fortification, redoubt, stronghold

across *adv.* athwart, crosswise, over, transversely

act *n.* **EXPLOIT:** accomplishment, deed, feat, performance; **DECREE:** edict, law, order, resolution, statute, writ; **PERFORMANCE:** routine, sketch, stint, turn

act *v.* **DO:** accomplish, conduct, operate; **SUBSTITUTE:** represent, officiate, serve; **PERFORM:** appear, dramatize, impersonate, pretend, play, simulate

acting *adj.* deputy, officiating, surrogate, temporary

acting *n.* depiction, performance, role impersonation

action *n.* **MOTION:** activity, maneuver, movement, performance; **FEAT:** accomplishment, exercise, transaction; **BEHAVIOR:** conduct, response; **MACHINE:** apparatus, contrivance, mechanism; **CONFLICT:** battle, contest, encounter, engagement, skirmish; **LAWSUIT:** case, claim, litigation, proceeding, process, suit

activate *v.* animate, begin, initiate, stimulate

active *adj.* animated, busy, dynamic, energetic, functioning, industrious, lively, living, mobile, moving, operative, spirited, tireless, working

actively *adv.* energetically, spryly, vigorously

activist *n.* agitator, firebrand, malcontent, radical, reformer, revolutionary

activity *n.* action, motion, movement, pastime

actor *n.* artist, entertainer, impersonator, mime, performer, player, thespian, trouper

actual *adj.* **FACTUAL:** certain, definite, genuine, sure, true; **EXISTING:** concrete, material, real, tangible

actually *adv.* indeed, really, truly

actuate *v.* drive, impel, move, propel, push

acuity *n.* discernment, discrimination, insight, perception, perspicacity, sharpness, shrewdness

acumen *n.* cleverness, discernment, insight, intelligence, keenness, sagacity, shrewdness

acute *adj.* **POINTED:** keen, sharp; **IMPORTANT:** critical, crucial, intense, serious; **PERCEPTIVE:** astute, clever, discerning, ingenious, intelligent, keen, penetrating

adage *n.* cliché, maxim, motto, proverb, saying, slogan

adamant *adj.* firm, fixed, insistent, obstinate, resolute, set, steadfast, stubborn, unbending, unyielding

adapt *v.* acclimatize, accustom, adjust, conform, fashion, fit, modify, reconcile, shape, tailor, temper

adaptable *adj.* docile, flexible, pliable, pliant, tractable, versatile

adaptation *n.* **ACCLIMATIZATION:** acculturation, conversion, revising; **DEVICE:** apparatus, appliance, contraption, contrivance, gadget, mechanism

add *v.* **AFFIX:** annex, append, attach, augment, connect, supplement, unite: **CALCULATE:** compute, figure, increase, sum, tally, total

addendum *n.* addition, adjunct, annexation, appendix, attachment, augmentation, codicil, rider

addict *n.* buff, devotee, fan, hound, junkie, lover

addicted *adj.* chronic, dependent, fanatical, fixated, habituated, hooked, inclined, obsessed

addictive *adj.* compelling, irresistible, overpowering

additional *adj.* added, auxiliary, collateral, extra

addle *v.* cloud, confound, confuse, obfuscate

addled *adj.* befuddled, bewildered, confounded, confused, dazed, disconcerted, flustered, muddled

add–on *n.* improvement, modernization, supplement

address *n.* SPEECH: discourse, lecture, oration, sermon; LOCATION: dwelling, house, lodging, residence

adept *adj.* able, capable, competent, expert, proficient, skilled

adequacy *n.* acceptability, plenty, sufficiency

adequate *adj.* ample, enough, satisfactory, suitable

adhere *v.* STICK: attach, cleave, cling, fasten, hold; CONFORM: comply, follow, heed, obey

adherent *n.* advocate, devotee, disciple, fan, follower

adhesive *n.* cement, epoxy, glue, mucilage, tape

adjacent *adj.* abutting, adjoining, bordering, close, contiguous, near, nearby, neighboring, touching

adjoin *v.* abut, append, border, butt, meet, neighbor, touch, verge

adjourn *v.* defer, discontinue, dissolve, recess, interrupt, postpone, suspend

adjournment *n.* break, continuance, deferment, intermission, pause, postponement, recess

adjudicate *v.* arbitrate, decide, mediate, settle

adjudication *n.* determination, judgment, finding, ruling, verdict, sentence

adjudicator *n.* arbiter, judge, mediator, referee

adjunct *n.* accessory, addition, attachment

adjure *v.* ask, appeal, beg, beseech, entreat, implore, petition, plead, request, supplicate, urge

adjust *v.* adapt, alter, calibrate, correct, modify, regulate, tune, temper, truc

adjustable *adj.* flexible, malleable, tractable, variable

adjustment *n.* ALTERATION: calibration, modification, setting; COMPENSATION: allotment, compromise, reconciliation, redress, remuneration, settlement

adjutant *n.* aide, assistant, attaché, deputy, helper

ad–lib *adj.* improvised, spontaneous, unrehearsed

administer *v.* **MANAGE:** control, direct, execute, oversee, supervise; **DISPENSE:** distribute, give, parcel

administrative *adj.* bureaucratic, executive, governmental, jurisdictional, official, managerial

admirable *adj.* commendable, excellent, meritorious, noble, praiseworthy, splendid, superb, worthy

admiration *n.* affection, approbation, awe, esteem, fondness, regard, respect, veneration, wonder

admire *v.* celebrate, esteem, honor, regard, respect, revere, venerate

admirer *n.* **FAN:** devotee, enthusiast, follower, patron, supporter; **BEAU:** adorer, suitor, sweetheart, wooer

admissible *adj.* allowable, lawful, legal, legitimate

admission *n.* **ACCESS:** admittance, entrée, entrance, entry, pass, ticket; **AFFIRMATION:** acknowledgment, confession, confirmation, disclosure, divulgence

admit *v.* **ACCOMMODATE:** allow, grant, permit; **AFFIRM:** concede, confess, disclose, divulge, expose, reveal

admittance *n.* access, admission, entrance

admonish *v.* caution, counsel, exhort, reprove, warn

admonition *n.* **COUNSEL:** advice, caution, warning; **REBUKE:** censure, reprimand, reproach, scolding

ado *n.* bother, bustle, commotion, fuss, stir

adolescence *n.* puberty, pubescence, teens, youth

adolescent *adj.* childish, immature, juvenile, youthful

adolescent *n.* minor, teen, teenager, youth

adopt *v.* **APPROPRIATE:** assume, borrow, espouse, utilize; **RATIFY:** approve, confirm, endorse, sanction

adorable *adj.* charming, cute, darling, delightful, enchanting, lovable, precious, sweet

adoration *n.* devotion, idolatry, veneration, worship

adore *v.* cherish, esteem, idolize, love, revere, venerate, worship

adorer *n.* admirer, beau, suitor, sweetheart, wooer

adorn *v.* beautify, bedeck, decorate, embellish, garnish, festoon, ornament, trim

adroit *adj.* adept, dexterous, expert, handy, quick, resourceful, skillful

adulation *n.* adoration, glorification, laudation, praise, worship

adult *adj.* developed, grown, mature, ripe

adulteration *n.* contamination, pollution, taint

adulterer *n.* debaucher, lecher, libertine, philanderer, rake, reprobate

adulterous *adj.* dissolute, immoral, licentious, lustful

adultery *n.* cuckoldry, fornication, infidelity

adulthood *n.* majority, maturity

advance *v.* **PROGRESS:** go, move, proceed, update, upgrade; **BROACH:** introduce, propose, present, suggest; **PROMOTE:** encourage, foster, propound; **OFFER:** lend

advanced *adj.* aged, elderly, futuristic, precocious, radical, seasoned, unconventional

advancement *n.* betterment, elevation, preference, progression, promotion

advantage *n.* benefit, edge, gain, leverage, profit

adventure *n.* undertaking, experience, exploit

advantageous *adj.* beneficial, expedient, favorable, lucrative, profitable, worthwhile

advent *n.* appearance, arrival, coming

adventure *n.* escapade, experience, exploit, feat, happening, quest, undertaking, venture

adventuresome, adventurous *adj.* bold, courageous,

daring, enterprising, gallant

adversarial *adj.* antagonistic, hostile, unfriendly

adversary *n.* antagonist, enemy, foe, opponent

adverse *adj.* antagonistic, conflicting, contrary, detrimental, hostile, negative, unfavorable, unfriendly

adversity *n.* affliction, distress, hardship, misery, misfortune, sorrow, trouble

advertise *v.* broadcast, communicate, divulge, exhibit, expose, proclaim, promote, publicize, show

advertisement, advertising *n.* blurb, broadside, endorsement, handbill, pitch, poster, plug

advice *n.* counsel, guidance, lesson, suggestion

advisable *adj.* advantageous, desirable, expedient, politic, prudent, sensible, sound

advise *v.* admonish, caution, counsel, consult, forewarn, inform, notify, recommend

advised *adj.* cautious, circumspect, deliberate

adviser, advisor *n.* attorney, consultant, counsel, counselor, elder, expert, guide, instructor, lawyer, mentor, patriarch, teacher, tutor

advocacy *n.* adoption, belief, espousal, promotion

advocate *v.* advance, bolster, champion, further, promote, recommend, support

aesthete *n.* collector, connoisseur, dilettante

aesthetic, aesthetical *adj.* artistic, discriminating, elegant, pleasing, polished, refined, tasteful

afar *adj.* abroad, distant, remote

affable *adj.* agreeable, amiable, civil, cordial, courteous, friendly, gracious, obliging, pleasant, sociable

affair *n.* CONCERN: business, circumstance, pursuit; ROMANCE: liaison, relationship, rendezvous, tryst; GATHERING: event, function, party

affect *v.* **INFLUENCE:** alter, change, modify, sway, stir, transform; **PRETEND:** assume, dissemble, fake, feign
affectation *n.* artificiality, pose, pretense, show
affection *n.* devotion, fondness, friendship, liking, love, regard, respect, tenderness, warmth
affectionate *adj.* attentive, devoted, loving, tender
affianced *adj.* betrothed, pledged, plighted
affidavit *n.* affirmation, deposition, oath, testimony
affiliate *n.* agent, associate, colleague, partner
affiliation *n.* alliance, association, coalition, confederation, connection, federation, pact, union
affinity *n.* **ATTRACTION:** affection, closeness, fondness; **SIMILARITY:** correspondence, likeness, resemblance
affirm *v.* **DECLARE:** assert, claim, maintain, state, swear, testify; **CONFIRM:** approve, endorse, ratify
affirmative *adj.* concurring, confirming, endorsing, supporting
affix *v.* add, append, attach, bind, connect, fasten
afflict *v.* ail, beset, distress, hurt, torment
affliction *n.* distress, hardship, misfortune, suffering
affluence *n.* abundance, prosperity, wealth
afford *v.* allow, grant, permit, provide, sustain
affront *v.* insult, abuse, offend, provoke, slight
aficionado *n.* buff, devotee, fan, hound, lover
afield *adv.* amiss, astray, awry
afoot *adj.* **WALKING:** hiking, marching; **FORTHCOMING:** brewing, happening, hatching, progressing
aforementioned *adj.* earlier, former, preceding, prior
afraid *adj.* anxious, apprehensive, disquieted, fearful, frightened, scared, shocked, terrified
after *adj., adv.* afterward, following, later, subsequent
aftereffect *n.* consequence, outcome, result

afterthought *n.* addendum, addition, appendix

agape *adj.* **ASTONISHED:** aghast appalled confounded dismayed horrified shocked; **AJAR:** open

age *n.* **PERIOD:** eon, epoch, era, generation, time; **STAGE:** adolescence, adulthood, childhood, infancy

age *v.* decline, deteriorate, develop, mature, mellow, ripen, season

ageless *adj.* classic, timeless, traditional

agenda *n.* aims, goals, program, calendar, list, plan

agent *n.* **REPRESENTATIVE:** ambassador, attorney, broker, factor, intermediary, proxy, surrogate; **MEDIUM:** agency, cause, instrument, means, method, vehicle

agglomerate *adj.* clustered, collected, jumbled

agglomerate *v.* amass, concentrate, consolidate

aggrandize *v.* **ENLARGE:** amplify, expand, extend, increase; **ACCLAIM:** boast, exaggerate, extol, praise

aggravate *v.* **WORSEN:** deepen, exacerbate, heighten, increase, intensify; **PROVOKE:** anger, annoy, exasperate, irritate

aggravating *adj.* bothersome, disquieting, disturbing

aggravation *n.* **AFFLICTION :** annoyance, exasperation, irritation; **WORSENING:** deepening, heightening

aggregate *adj.* combined, complete, entire, total

aggressive *adj.* **HOSTILE:** belligerent, combative, contentious, pugnacious; **ASSERTIVE:** determined, dynamic, energetic, enterprising, forward, pushy

aggressor *n.* attacker, intruder, invader, trespasser

aggrieve *v.* disturb, harass, irritate, trouble, worry

aggrieved *adj.* harmed, hurt, injured

aghast *adj.* appalled, astonished, horrified, shocked

agile *adj.* **QUICK:** brisk, deft, lithe, lively, nimble, sprightly, vigorous; **BRIGHT:** clever, keen, smart

agility *n.* dexterity, liveliness, nimbleness

agitate *v.* **STIR:** churn, mix, toss, tumble; **DISTURB:** discomfit, disquiet, fluster, perturb, ruffle, trouble, unsettle, upset; **DEBATE:** argue, dispute

agitator *n.* activist, firebrand, rabble–rouser, radical

agnostic *n.* doubter, non–believer, skeptic, unbeliever

agog *adj.* anxious, breathless, eager, enthusiastic

agonize *v.* struggle, suffer, writhe, toss

agony *n.* anguish, distress, misery, pain, suffering, torment, torture

agree *v.* **CONSENT:** accede, acquiesce, allow, assent, concede; **COINCIDE:** correspond, equal, harmonize, match, suit; **COMPROMISE:** contract, resolve, settle

agreeable *adj.* **PLEASING:** amiable, congenial, gracious, pleasant, polite; **SUITABLE:** acceptable, satisfactory

agreement *n.* **COVENANT:** bargain, compact, contract, deal, pact, settlement, understanding; **ACCORD:** compromise, harmony, peace, unity

ahead *adj., adv.* before, earlier, leading, preceding

aid *n.* **ASSISTANCE:** backing, charity, help, relief, support; **HELPER:** aide, assistant, colleague, supporter

aid *v.* assist, facilitate, help, serve, support, sustain

ailment *n.* illness, affliction, infirmity, sickness

air *n.* atmosphere, breeze; tune; affectation, manner

air *v.* ventilate; announce

alarm *v.* warn; frighten

alert *adj.* ready, aware, attentive, intelligent, wary

alert *v.* caution, inform, warn

alien *adj.* different, foreign, strange, unfamiliar

alienation *n.* animosity, disaffection

allay *v.* calm, alleviate

allegation *n.* accusation, assertion, claim

allege *v.* assert, attest, declare
alleviate *v.* abate, ease, relieve, lessen, soften
alley *n.* byway, lane, street, passageway
alliance *n.* union, treaty, marriage
allocate *v.* allot, designate
allow *v.* approve, grant, let, permit, sanction
allure *v.* tempt, attract
ally *n.* associate, backer, confederate
alms *n.* charity, dole, donation
aloof *adj.* cool, detached, distant, reserved
alter *v.* change, modify, adjust
altercate *v.* contend, oppose, quarrel, bicker
alternate *n.* replacement, substitute
alternative *n.* choice, option
altruism *n.* benevolence, charity, kindness
amateur *n.* beginner, neophyte, novice
amaze *v.* astonish, dumfound, stupefy, surprise
amazement *n.* awe, shock, surprise
ambassador *n.* diplomat, emissary, envoy, minister
ambiguous *adj.* indistinct, puzzling, unclear, vague
ambitious *adj.* determined, industrious, intent
ambivalent *adj.* uncertain, wavering
ameliorate *v.* alleviate, improve, rectify
amenable *adj.* agreeable, docile, pliable, responsive
amend *v.* improve, change, correct
amenity *n.* courtesy, consideration, pleasantness
amiable, amicable *adj.* friendly, affable, agreeable,
  congenial, kindly, genial, sweet, peaceful
amiss *adj.* wrong, faulty, erroneous, imperfect, awry
amity *n.* goodwill, regard, friendliness, affection
amnesty *n.* pardon, liberation, acquittal, reprieve
among *prep.* amid, amongst, amidst

amount *n.* TOTAL: sum, product; PRICE: expense, output, outlay; QUANTITY: bulk, mass, number
ample *adj.* sufficient, plenty, adequate, enough
amplify *v.* increase, augment, magnify
amulet *n.* charm, talisman
amuse *v.* entertain, divert, cheer, enliven
amusement *n.* entertainment, recreation, pastime
analyze *v.* dissect, examine, investigate
anarchy *n.* disorder, turmoil, chaos
ancestor *n.* forebear, progenitor, forefather
ancestry *n.* lineage, heritage, parentage, family
anchor *n.* stay, tie, mooring, support
ancient *adj.* old, antiquated, antique, aged
anecdote *n.* story, tale, incident, episode
anger *n.* ire, wrath, rage, fury, exasperation, irritation
anger *v.* infuriate, annoy, irritate enrage
angle *n.* PLAN: plot, scheme, maneuver; VIEWPOINT: standpoint, outlook, perspective; INTERSECTION: notch, crotch, elbow, fork
angry *adj.* enraged, furious, infuriated, irate, raging, cross, annoyed, displeased, riled, hostile
anguish *n.* pain, wretchedness, agony
angular *adj.* intersecting, crossing, crotched, forked
animate *v.* activate, vitalize, arouse, energize
animosity *n.* hatred, dislike, enmity, displeasure
annex *v.* add, incorporate, append, attach, affix.
annihilate *v.* destroy, demolish, exterminate
annotate *v.* comment, explain, interpret
announcement *n.* declaration, publication, statement, bulletin, notice, communiqué, release
annoy *v.* bother, irritate, pester, trouble
annoyance *n.* irritation, pique, displeasure, nuisance,

discontent, dissatisfaction, impatience,
annul *v.* invalidate, repeal, revoke, cancel
anoint *v.* sprinkle, consecrate
anonymous *adj.* unsigned, nameless, unknown
answer *v.* **REPLY:** respond, retort, acknowledge, refute, react, rebut; **EXPLAIN:** solve, elucidate, clarify
answerable *adj.* responsible, liable
antagonism *n.* hatred, enmity, hostility, opposition
antic *n.* prank, joke, trick, frolic, caper
anticipate *v.* expect, forecast, predict, assume, await
antipathy *n.* aversion, dislike, hatred, repulsion
antiquated, antique *adj.* old, outmoded, out–of–date
antiseptic *adj.* clean, germ–free, sterilized, pure
antithesis *n.* contrasting, reverse
antitoxin *n.* vaccine, antibody, serum
anxiety, anxiousness *n.* concern, trouble, misgiving
anxious *adj.* **APPREHENSIVE:** concerned, dreading troubled; **EAGER:** desirous, fervent, zealous
apathetic *adj.* unemotional, unconcerned, indifferent.
ape *v.* imitate, mimic, copy, impersonate.
aperture *n.* opening, hole, slot
aphorism *n.* motto, proverb, saying
apologetic *adj.* regretful, contrite, remorseful, sorry
appall *v.* horrify, amaze, dismay, shock
apparatus *n.* equipment, appliance, machinery
apparel *n.* clothes, attire, suit, dress
apparent *adj.* open, visible, clear, manifest, obvious
apparition *n.* ghost, manifestation, phantom, spirit
appeal *n.* **PLEA:** request, petition, entreaty, prayer, supplication; **ATTRACTIVENESS:** charm, glamour
appeal *v.* **REQUEST:** beg, urge, petition; **FASCINATE:** attract, interest, engage, tempt

appear *v.* emerge, rise, loom, arrive, recur, materialize, show; seem, resemble
appearance *n.* bearing, demeanor, features
appease *v.* satisfy, do, serve
appeasement *n.* settlement, amends, reparation
append *v.* add, affix, attach, supplement
appendix *n.* supplement, attachment, index, addition
appetite *n.* hunger, thirst, craving, longing, desire
appetizing *adj.* savory, tasty, delectable, delicious
applaud *v.* approve, cheer, clap, acclaim, praise
applicable *adj.* suitable, appropriate, usable, fit
applicant *n.* petitioner, claimant, candidate.
application *n.* USE: employment, utilization; AT-
TENTION: devotion, zeal, diligence; PETITION: entreaty,
appeal; INSTRUMENT: petition, form, requisition
apply *v.* REQUEST: petition, beg; UTILIZE: employ,
practice, exploit; PERTAIN: involve, affect
appoint *v.* name, select, designate, delegate
appointment *n.* DESIGNATION: selection, nomination,
choice; ENGAGEMENT: meeting, rendezvous, date
apportion *v.* distribute, share
appraise *v.* assess, price, assay, rate
appreciable *adj.* considerable, sizable, tangible, large
appreciate *v.* THANK: acknowledge; ESTEEM: honor,
praise, admire
appreciative *adj.* grateful, obliged, satisfied, thankful
apprehend *v.* COMPREHEND: understand, perceive,
grasp; ARREST: detain, seize
apprehension *n.* FOREBODING: trepidation, dread,
misgiving, fear; UNDERSTANDING: comprehension;
ARREST: capture, seizure, detention
apprentice *n.* beginner, student, learner

apprise *v.* notify, teach, warn

approach *n.* **ACCESS:** avenue, path, entrance, gate, way; **PLAN:** method, program, procedure

approbation *n.* approval, regard

appropriate *adj.* suitable proper, suited, fitting, fit

appropriate *v.* **SEIZE:** secure, usurp, take; **SET APART:** allocate, assign, reserve, apportion, budget, allot

appropriation *n.* stipend, grant, fund, allotment, allowance, allocation, contribution, support

approval *n.* **REGARD:** esteem, favor, admiration; **SANCTION:** endorsement, consent, permission

approve *v.* authorize, endorse, ratify, confirm, sanction, legalize, accredit, allow, advocate, pass

approximate *adj.* inexact, imprecise, close

appurtenance *n.* adjunct, accessory

apropos *adj.* applicable, appropriate, befitting

apt *adj.* **APPROPRIATE:** apropos, suitable, fitting; **INCLINED:** probable, prone, liable, likely; **QUICK:** adept, clever, bright, intelligent, talented

aptitude *n.* ability, capability, competence, capacity

arbitrary *adj.* **OPTIONAL:** discretionary, unscientific; **WHIMSICAL:** capricious, fanciful, inconsistent, irrational; **AUTOCRATIC:** willful, tyrannical,

arbitrate *v.* settle, adjust, reconcile, negotiate

arch *n.* arc, curve, vault, bend, arching, archway

archaic *adj.* antiquated, old, obsolete

architect *n.* planner, designer, draftsman, artist

archive *n.* repository, vault, museum, storage

ardent *adj.* fervent, impassioned, zealous, passionate, enthusiastic

arduous *adj.* hard, laborious, difficult, strenuous

argue *v.* dispute, contend, wrangle, bicker, debate

argumentative *adj.* hostile, contentious, factious
arid *adj.* parched, desert, dried, dry, barren
arise *v.* **GET UP:** rise, stand, awaken; **ASCEND:** mount, climb, rise
aristocracy *n.* nobility, elite, gentry, patricians
aristocratic *adj.* noble, refined, well-bred
arm *n.* limb, member, appendage, projection, branch
armistice *n.* treaty, cease-fire, truce
aroma *n.* smell, fragrance, perfume, odor
arouse *v.* awaken, stir, excite, move, stimulate
arraign *v.* accuse, summon
arrange *v.* order, regulate, systematize, organize
arrest *v.* apprehend, capture, imprison, incarcerate
arrival *n.* **ENTRANCE:** appearance, landing, debarkation; **NEWCOMER:** visitor, guest, traveler
arrive *v.* land, disembark, reach, appear, attain
arrogance *n.* insolence, audacity, haughtiness, pride
art *n.* representation, illustration, abstraction, portrayal, design, painting, creation
artery *n.* **BLOOD VESSEL:** aorta, capillary, vein; **MAIN CHANNEL:** highway, line, route, canal, roadway
artful *adj.* crafty, cunning, clever, adroit, ingenious
article *n.* **WRITING:** essay, editorial, commentary; **ITEM:** object, substance, commodity, thing
articulate *v.* **SPEAK:** enunciate, pronounce, verbalize; **JOIN:** combine, connect, link
artifact *n.* antique, heirloom, relic
artifice *n.* ruse, scheme, trick
artificial *adj.* synthetic, counterfeit, false, imitation
artistic *adj.* imaginative, creative, accomplished, cultured, sensitive, elegant, harmonious
artistry *n.* workmanship, skill, proficiency

artless *adj.* innocent, rough, unskilled
arty *adj.* affected, ostentatious
ascend *v.* soar, rise
askance *adv.* suspiciously, disapprovingly
aspect *n.* **APPEARANCE:** looks, countenance, face, features; **VIEW:** perspective, regard, slant, viewpoint
asperity *n.* roughness, harshness
aspiration *n.* desire, yearning, inclination, ambition
assail *v.* assault, attack
assailant *n.* antagonist, foe, enemy, opponent
assassin *n.* murderer, slayer, butcher, killer
assassinate *v.* **MURDER:** kill, slay, slaughter; **SLANDER:** defame, denigrate, libel
assault *n.* **ATTACK:** charge, advance, onslaught
assay *v.* test, analyze
assemble *v.* **CONVOKE:** convene, mobilize, gather, collect; **CONSTRUCT:** erect, join, unite, mold
assent *n.* approval, consent, permission, agreement
assert *v.* state, say, affirm, declare
assertion *n.* affirmation, statement, declaration
assess *v.* **TAX:** charge, exact; **ESTIMATE:** appraise, judge, reckon, guess
asset *n.* property, holdings, possessions, capital
assiduous *adj.* painstaking, diligent
assign *v.* **ALLOCATE:** allot, earmark; **APPOINT:** commission, name, select, deputize, charge, elect
assimilate *v.* **UNDERSTAND:** grasp, learn, sense; **ABSORB:** digest, osmose
assist *v.* aid, support, serve, help
assistance *n.* comfort, support, compensation, help
assistant *n.* aid, deputy, lieutenant, helper, flunky
associate *n.* comrade, peer, colleague, friend, ally,

henchman, confederate, collaborator, teammate
associate *v.* relate, link, connect, join, compare
association *n.* **RELATIONSHIP:** friendship, camaraderie, membership, community; **RECOLLECTION:** impression, remembrance; **ORGANIZATION:** union, club
assortment *n.* variety, combination, group, collection
assuage *v.* alleviate, calm, satisfy
assume *v.* suppose, theorize, presuppose, postulate, hypothesize, guess, conjecture, deem, imagine, surmise, opine, estimate, speculate, deduce, infer
assurance *n.* **GUARANTY:** support, pledge, promise; **CONFIDENCE:** conviction, trust, certainty, faith
assure *v.* **GUARANTEE:** aver, attest; **CONVINCE:** prove, persuade, induce
astonish *v.* shock, amaze, astound, surprise, stun
astonishment *n.* amazement, bewilderment, wonder
astute *adj.* perceptive, shrewd
asunder *adv.* apart, divided, separated, disjoined
athletic *adj.* hardy, robust, vigorous, powerful
atmosphere *n.* sense, impression, taste, character
atone *v.* compensate, pay
atrocious *adj.* cruel, offensive
atrocity *n.* **BRUTALITY:** inhumanity, wickedness, barbarity, cruelty; **OFFENSE:** outrage, horror, crime
attach *v.* **ADHERE:** join, connect, append, add; **ATTRIBUTE:** associate, impute, ascribe, give
attachment *n.* **AFFECTION:** fondness, liking, devotion; **ACCESSORY:** adjunct, annex, addition
attack *n.* **ASSAULT:** raid, onslaught, offensive, siege, invasion, incursion; **LIBEL:** slander, denunciation, blame, **ILLNESS:** seizure, breakdown, relapse
attacker *n.* aggressor, assailant, antagonist, invader

attain *v.* achieve, accomplish, arrive, reach, gain

attempt *v.* endeavor, strike, venture, try

attend *v.* heed; minister; frequent, visit, revisit, haunt

attention *n.* regard, vigilance, heed, alertness, diligence, thoroughness, recognition

attentive *adj.* considerate, thoughtful

attest *v.* testify, certify

attitude *n.* BEARING: air, demeanor; DISPOSITION: inclination, nature, temperament, mood, viewpoint

attorney *n.* lawyer, barrister, counsel

attract *v.* DRAW: pull, drag, bring; ALLURE: entice, lure, charm, fascinate

attraction *n.* ALLUREMENT: magnetism, enticement, appeal; EVENT: spectacle, display, demonstration

attractive *adj.* engaging, beautiful, handsome

attribute *n.* peculiarity, quality, characteristic, trait

attribute *v.* ascribe, impute, give

audacious *adj.* bold, daring, shameless

audible *adj.* perceptible, discernible, distinct

audience *n.* interview; spectators, witness, patrons

audit *n.* checking, scrutiny, inspection, examination

auditorium *n.* hall, theater, playhouse, amphitheater

augment *v.* increase, enlarge, expand, magnify

auspices *n. pl.* protection, aegis, patronage, omen

austere *adj.* stern, harsh, hard, ascetic, severe, plain

authentic *adj.* genuine, real, true, actual

authenticate *v.* verify, confirm, validate, prove

author *n.* writer, journalist, columnist, playwright, poet, novelist, essayist

authority *n.* COMMAND: jurisdiction, power; SPECIALIST: expert, veteran, professional

authorization *n.* sanction, signature, permission

authorize *v.* **ALLOW:** permit, tolerate, suffer; **APPROVE:** sanction, ratify, affirm, endorse

autocratic *adj.* domineering, aggressive, absolute

autograph *n.* signature, handwriting

automatic *adj.* **MECHANIZED:** computerized, self–regulating, automated; **INVOLUNTARY:** instinctive, spontaneous, intuitive

autonomous *adj.* self–governing, independent, free

auxiliary *adj.* **SUBSIDIARY:** secondary, subordinate; **SUPPLEMENTARY:** reserve, supplemental, spare, extra

available *adj.* accessible, convenient, handy, obtainable, practicable, feasible, possible, realizable

avarice *n.* acquisitiveness, greed

aver *v.* assert, claim, declare, swear

average *adj.* ordinary, medium, mediocre, common

averse *adj.* disinclined, opposed

aversion *n.* abhorrence, disgust, dislike, loathing

avocation *n.* hobby, sideline

avoid *v.* evade, shun, elude, dodge, withdraw,

avow *v.* affirm, assert, declare, swear

awake *adj.* alert, attentive, vigilant; conscious

awake, awaken *v.* stir, arise, waken, arouse

award *n.* citation, honor, scholarship, prize, judgment

award *v.* grant, confer, bestow, give

aware *adj.* conscious, knowledgeable, cognizant

awareness *n.* discernment, alertness, keenness, attentiveness, perception, apprehension, appreciation

awe *n.* fright, wonder, reverence

awesome *adj.* striking, moving, exalted, grand

awkward *adj.* clumsy, bungling, gawky, floundering, ungainly, unwieldy, inept, amateurish

axiom *n.* adage, maxim, proverb, saying

babble *n.* chatter jabber, twaddle, nonsense.
babel *n.* bedlam, clamor, commotion
baby *adj.* juvenile, childish, small
baby *v.* pamper, coddle, spoil, caress, nurse, indulge
backlash *n.* repercussion, reaction, recoil
backlog *n.* queue, reserve
badge *n.* marker, symbol, emblem, pin, medal, insignia, shield, medallion, button, crest
baffle *v.* perplex, confuse, puzzle, bewilder
baggage *n.* luggage, gear, trunk, valise, suitcase,
bail *v.* dip, scoop, empty, drain
bait *v.* **LURE:** entice, attract, draw, fascinate; **TEASE:** provoke, torment, anger, nag, bother
balance *n.* **REMAINS:** excess, surplus, residue, remainder; **EQUILIBRIUM:** symmetry, equivalence, parity
balance *v.* equalize, even, compensate, adjust, coordinate, equate, match, harmonize
balcony *n.* gallery, verandah, terrace
baleful *adj.* noxious, harmful
balk *v.* refuse, demur, desist
balky *adj.* contrary, obstinate, perverse, stubborn
ball *n.* **SPHERE:** globe, spheroid, orb, globule, pellet, pill; **DANCE:** promenade, reception, party
ballad *n.* carol, chant, song
ballot *n.* tally, ticket, poll, vote
balm *n.* **OINTMENT:** salve, lotion, dressing, medicine; **SOLACE:** comfort, relief, refreshment, remedy
ban *n.* taboo, prohibition, limitation, refusal
ban *v.* forbid, prohibit, outlaw, prevent
banal *adj.* dull, trite, hackneyed, prosaic, trite
bandage *n.* compress, cast, gauze, dressing
bandage *v.* tie, swathe, truss, bind, fasten.

bandit *n.* highwayman, thief, brigand, robber

bang *n.* **REPORT:** blast, detonation; **BLOW:** hit, cuff, whack; **THRILL:** enjoyment, kick, excitement

banish *v.* exile, deport, expel, expatriate, ostracize, outlaw, extradite, isolate

bank *n.* shore, ledge, embankment, edge

bankrupt *adj.* failed, broke, ruined, insolvent

banner *n.* flag, colors, pennant, emblem; headline

banquet *n.* feast, repast, festivity, dinner

bar *n.* **STICK:** boom, crosspiece, rod; **OBSTRUCTION:** hindrance, obstacle, hurdle, barrier; **SALOON:** tavern, lounge, cabaret, dive, pub; **LAWYERS:** counselors, barristers, solicitors, jurists, attorneys, advocates; **STRIP:** stripe, ribbon, band

bar *v.* **OBSTRUCT:** barricade, blockade, impede; **REFUSE:** ban, forbid, prevent, stop; **CLOSE:** shut, lock, seal

barbarian *n.* savage, brute, beast

barbaric *adj.* inhuman, brutal, fierce, cruel

bare *adj.* **UNCOVERED:** bald, naked; **PLAIN:** unadorned, simple, modest; **EMPTY:** barren, void, unfurnished

bare *v.* divulge, reveal, uncover, expose

bargain *n.* **UNDERSTANDING:** agreement, pact, compact, contract, deal; **DISCOUNT:** reduction, steal, giveaway

bargain *v.* barter, buy, sell, negotiate

barrel *n.* cask, keg, vat, receptacle, container, vessel

barren *adj.* childless, fallow, unproductive, fruitless

barricade *n.* obstacle, obstruction, barrier, blockade

barrier *n.* obstruction, hindrance, obstacle, hurdle, restriction, restraint, impediment, barricade

barrister *n.* advocate, attorney, lawyer, solicitor

barter *v.* trade, bargain, swap, buy, sell

base *n.* **BOTTOM:** footing, foundation; **BASIS:** principle;

bashful

HEADQUARTERS: terminal, harbor, station

bashful *adj.* retiring, reserved, timid, modest, shy

basic *adj.* fundamental, essential, central, primary

basin *n.* bowl, pan, tub, container

basis *n.* foundation, justification, reason, explanation, background, source, authority, principle, grounds

bask *v.* relax, enjoy, wallow

basket *n.* container, bushel, crate, bin

baste *v.* **SEW:** stitch, tack; **MOISTEN:** grease, season

bathe *v.* soap, scour, scrub, wash.

batter *n.* dough, mix, paste

battery *n.* beating, assault, attack, mugging

bauble *n.* ornament, trifle, trinket

bazaar *n.* market, fair

beach *n.* shore, seaside, sand, coast

beached *v.* stranded, marooned, aground, abandoned

beacon *n.* signal, flare, beam

beam *n.* timber, brace, rafter, stringer, stud, joist, girder, support, trestle, post, column, pillar, shaft

beam *v.* **TRANSMIT:** broadcast, send; **SHINE:** radiate, glitter, glare; **SMILE:** grin, laugh, smirk

bear *v.* **TOLERATE:** undergo, endure; **SUPPORT:** sustain

bearable *adj.* endurable, tolerable, sufferable

beard *n.* whiskers, goatee, sideburns

beastly *adj.* brutal, savage, coarse, depraved, loathsome, vile, foul, base, disgusting, vulgar

beat *adj.* weary, fatigued, tired, exhausted

beat *v.* **HIT:** whip, flog, spank, scourge, buffet, bash; **PULSATE:** pound, thump, pulse, throb; **MIX:** whip, knead; **WORST:** overcome, conquer, defeat

beautiful *adj.* lovely, attractive, appealing, charming, enticing, elegant, gorgeous, exquisite, alluring

beckon *v.* summon, signal, motion
becoming *adj.* attractive, handsome, comely, fair
bedlam *n.* pandemonium, clamor, confusion, noise
befall *v.* occur, happen
beg *v.* entreat, implore, beseech, supplicate, solicit, plead, petition, request, ask
beggar *n.* panhandler, moocher, bum
begin *v.* initiate, start, inaugurate, launch, mount, create, institute, introduce, originate, found, establish, commence, arise
beguile *v.* charm, deceive
behavior *n.* conduct, performance
behold *v.* observe, regard, view
belie *v.* deceive, mislead, misrepresent
belief *n.* opinion, feeling, conviction
believable *adj.* trustworthy, creditable, convincing
believe *v.* trust, accept, think
believer *n.* convert, devotee, adherent, apostle, disciple, prophet, follower
bellicose *adj.* hostile, aggressive
belligerent *adj.* warlike, pugnacious, hostile
bellow *v.* howl, call, shout, cry, yell
beloved *adj.* cherished, loved, adored, worshipped, idolized, precious, prized, treasured, favored
beloved *n.* fiancé, sweetheart, lover
below *prep.* BENEATH: underneath, under; INFERIOR: subject, subordinate; IN HELL: damned, condemned
bend *v.* turn, twist, contort, coil, curl, loop, curve
beneficial *adj.* advantageous, helpful, useful
benefit *v.* help, aid, serve, profit
benevolence *n.* altruism, charity, kindness
bent *adj.* curved, warped, crooked, contorted, twisted

bent *n.* leaning, tendency, propensity, inclination
bequeath *v.* grant, give
beseech *v.* ask, implore
best *adj., adv.* first, greatest, finest, incomparable, unrivaled, unequaled, inimitable, foremost
best *v.* overcome, defeat, worst
bestow *v.* bequeath, present, offer, give, endow
betray *v.* **DOUBLE–CROSS:** delude, trick, deceive; **REVEAL:** divulge, disclose
betrayal *n.* treason, treachery, disloyalty, deception
bevy *n.* group, herd, pack, swarm
bewail *v.* complain, gripe, grumble, lament
bewilder *v.* confound, disconcert, puzzle, confuse.
bewildered *adj.* confused, muddled, dazed, puzzled, baffled, disconcerted, adrift, stupefied, befuddled, stunned, electrified, confounded, flabbergasted
bewitch *v.* charm, enchant, fascinate, captivate
bias *n.* prejudice, partiality, preference, inclination
bicker *v.* wrangle, squabble, dispute, argue, quarrel
bid *n.* proposal, proposition, declaration, suggestion
bigoted *adj.* biased, dogmatic, opinionated, prejudiced
bill *v.* dun, solicit, invoice
billow *v.* surge, swell
bind *n.* dilemma, quandary, predicament
bind *v.* **SECURE:** attach, adhere, fasten; **OBLIGATE:** oblige, compel, force; **CONTAIN:** shackle, fetter, leash, restrict, hitch, yoke, tether; **BANDAGE:** dress, treat; **JOIN:** unite, connect
biography *n.* memoir, journal, autobiography, life
bit *n.* **FRAGMENT:** piece, crumb, particle, morsel, speck, flake, scrap; **TRIFLE:** iota, mite, whisker, hair
bite *n.* **MOUTHFUL:** taste, morsel, nibble; **WOUND:** sting,

laceration; **QUICK MEAL:** snack

biting *adj.* **TANGY:** sharp, keen, sour; **SARCASTIC:** caustic, acrimonious, bitter

bitter *adj.* **ACRID:** astringent, acid; **INTENSE:** harsh, severe; **SARCASTIC:** acrimonious, caustic, biting

bizarre *adj.* unusual, unexpected, fantastic, grotesque

blackmail *n.* extortion, tribute, protection, bribe

blackout *v.* **DELETE:** eradicate, erase; **FAINT:** swoon; **DARKEN:** batten, shade

blade *n.* **LEAF:** frond, spear, shoot; **INSTRUMENT:** edge, sword, knife

blame *v.* charge, condemn, denounce, disparage

bland *adj.* insipid, flat, dull, tasteless

blanket *n.* quilt, robe, comforter, featherbed, throw, cloak, covering

blanket *v.* cover, envelop, conceal, bury

blast *v.* explode, dynamite, detonate; denounce

blatant *adj.* clear, obvious, plain

blaze *n.* conflagration, combustion, burning, fire

bleak *adj.* dreary, desolate, bare, cheerless, barren

bleary *adj.* blurred, fuzzy

bleed *v.* hemorrhage, gush, spurt, flow

blemish *n.* flaw, defect, stain, imperfection, dent

blemish *v.* damage, deface, mar

blend *n.* mixture, combination, compound, amalgam

blight *n.* disease, withering, mildew, decay

blind *adj.* **OBTUSE:** unseeing, unaware; **CLOSED:** obstructed, blocked; **RANDOM:** accidental, unplanned, aimless

blindly *adv.* wildly, frantically, heedlessly, carelessly, recklessly, aimlessly, indiscriminately

bliss *n.* joy, rapture, ecstasy, happiness

blithe *adj.* gay, lighthearted, vivacious
blizzard *n.* snowstorm, tempest, blast, gale
block *n.* **CHUNK:** slab, cake, clod, hunk; **BARRIER:** obstruction, hindrance, bar, obstacle
block *v.* **IMPEDE:** prevent, hinder, restrict; **TACKLE:** check, stop
blockade *n.* barrier, barricade, bar, barrier
bloom *n.* **FLOWER:** blossom, floweret; **GLOW:** blush, flush
blossom *n.* flower, bloom, floweret, bud
blot *n.* flaw, spot, stain, smudge, blemish
blotch *n.* stain, blemish
blow *n.* hit, strike, bump, wallop, rap, knock, clout
blow *v.* **PUFF:** blast, fan; **FLUTTER:** waft, whisk, flap, wave, buffet; **PLAY:** pipe, toot, tootle; **SPEND:** waste, squander; **FAIL:** miss, flounder, miscarry
blubber *v.* bawl, cry, sob, weep
blue *adj., n.* despondent, depressed, melancholy, sad
bluff *n.* **BANK:** hill, cliff, precipice, steep, mountain; **DECEPTION:** trick, ruse, delusion
bluff *v.* fool, mislead, trick, deceive
blunder *n.* mistake, lapse, oversight, error
blunt *adj.* **DULL:** unsharpened, unpointed, round; **ABRUPT:** brusque, curt, bluff, rude
bluster *v.* brag, swagger, strut, boast
board *n.* **PLANK:** lath, strip, lumber; **MEALS:** food, fare, provisions; **REGULATORS:** council, cabinet, committee
boast *n.* brag, pretension, self–satisfaction, bravado
boast *v.* gloat, swagger, swell, brag, strut, flaunt
boastful *adj.* bragging, pretentious, bombastic
body *n.* **CHASSIS:** fuselage, hull, skeleton; **GROUP:** society, organization; **COLLECTION:** reservoir, supply,

variety; **HUMAN:** anatomy, physique, figure, trunk, build; **CORPSE:** cadaver, carcass, mummy, remains

bog *n.* marsh, swamp

boil *v.* cook, steep, seethe, stew, simmer

boisterous *adj.* rowdy, uproarious, noisy, loud, rude

bold *adj.* **DARING:** courageous, intrepid, fearless; **IMPERTINENT:** brazen, audacious, presumptuous, rude; **PROMINENT:** strong, clear, plain, definite

boldness *n.* audacity, self–reliance, courage

bolster *v.* reinforce, sustain, support

bombastic *adj.* high–sounding, pompous

bond *n.* **LINK:** attachment, connection, affiliation, friendship, marriage; **DEBENTURE:** security, warranty, certificate; **BAIL:** surety, guaranty, warrant

bonus *n.* reward, compensation, payment, incentive

book *n.* volume, manual, handbook, reference

boom *n.* **SOUND:** roar, blast, blare, noise; **ACTIVITY:** rush, growth, inflation

boor *n.* yokel, lout, clown, bumpkin, churl, oaf, boob

boost *n.* **ASSISTANCE:** aid, help; **INCREASE:** addition, advance, hike

boost *v.* **PUSH UPWARD:** raise, hoist; **INCREASE:** raise, heighten, expand; **SUPPORT:** promote, encourage

booth *n.* stall, counter, nook, corner, stand

bootleg *adj.* illegal, illicit, unlawful

border *n.* **EDGE:** hem, end, trim, decoration, fringe, margin; **BOUNDARY:** frontier, outpost, perimeter

bore *v.* **DRILL:** ream, perforate; **WEARY:** fatigue, tire

boredom *n.* apathy, doldrums, listlessness, monotony, tedium, indifference

borrow *v.* take, sponge, bum, beg, chisel, mooch

botch *v.* bungle, blunder, mishandle, muddle

bottom *n.* underside, base, foot; depths, bed, floor

bough *n.* limb, arm, fork, branch

boulder *n.* stone, slab, crag, rock

boulevard *n.* street, avenue, highway, road

bounce *v.* rebound, ricochet, recoil

bound *adj.* determined, compelled, driven, pressed

bound *v.* **LEAP:** spring, vault, jump; **BOUNCE:** ricochet, recoil; **LIMIT:** restrict, confine, circumscribe

boundary *n.* border, rim, bounds, extremity, perimeter, extent, periphery, limit

boundless *adj.* limitless, endless, unlimited, infinite

bounteous *adj.* abundant, lavish, plentiful

bounty *n.* bonus, inducement, reward; profusion

bouquet *n.* fragrance, aroma, scent, smell

bow *v.* **CURTSEY:** stoop, dip; **YIELD:** submit, surrender, acquiesce, capitulate

bowl *n.* dish, vessel, tureen, pot, saucer, crock

boycott *v.* ostracize, avoid, strike

brace *v.* support, prop, bolster, hold up, steady

brackish *adj.* salty, disagreeable, tainted

brag *v.* boast, swagger, exult, gloat, boast

braggart *n.* blowhard, windbag, swaggerer, strutter

braid *v.* interweave, plait, twine

brain *n.* **INTELLECT:** genius, mentality; **SCHOLAR:** egghead, intellectual

brake *v.* check, dampen, slow, stop

branch *n.* **DIVISION:** office, bureau, extension; **SHOOT:** bough, limb, sprig, twig, arm, fork, growth

brand *n.* mark, scar, welt, earmark, trademark

brand *v.* blaze, stamp, imprint, mark

brandish *v.* wave, flourish, gesture, warn, threaten

brass *n.* boldness, impudence, effrontery, rudeness,

impertinence, audacity

bravado *n.* pretense, bluster

brave *adj.* fearless, daring, dauntless, valiant, intrepid, bold, unafraid, stout, stalwart

brawl *v.* fight, quarrel, squabble

brawn *n.* power, strength

brazen *adj.* bold, brassy, forward, impudent

breach *n.* BREAK: opening, rupture; VIOLATION: infringement, transgression, crime

breadth *n.* largeness, extent, vastness, size, width

break *n.* BREACH: fracture, split, rupture; PAUSE: intermission, interim; LUCK: accident, opportunity

breakthrough *n.* finding, discovery, invention

breath *n.* inhalation, exhalation, gasp, sigh, wheeze

breathe *v.* respire, inhale, exhale, gasp, pant

breed *n.* strain, variety, kind, race, type

breeze *n.* zephyr, flurry, wind

brevity *n.* conciseness, shortness, terseness

brew *v.* make, concoct, ferment, mull, cook, formulate

bribe *v.* corrupt, influence, entice, tempt

bridge *n.* STRUCTURE: viaduct, pontoon, catwalk, trestle; LINK: connection, bond, tie, joint

bridle *n.* halter, leash, restraint

brief *adj.* momentary, fleeting, concise, abrupt

brief *n.* abstract, outline, summary

bright *adj.* QUICK–WITTED: intelligent, clever, alert; CLEAR: sunny, fair; LIVELY: cheerful, vivacious; SHINING: luminous, lustrous, sparkling, illuminated

brighten *v.* lighten, glow; polish, intensify, shine

brightness *n.* shine, luster, illumination, light

brilliant *adj.* SPARKLING: shining, dazzling, gleaming, bright; TALENTED: profound, intelligent

brim *n.* rim, margin, border, edge
bring *v.* transport, convey, bear, carry
brink *n.* edge, limit, brim, rim
brisk *adj.* keen, invigorating, stimulating, active
briskly *adv.* energetically, brusquely, nimbly
bristle *n.* hair, fiber, quill, point
brittle *adj.* fragile, crisp, inelastic, weak
broad *adj.* **COSMOPOLITAN:** cultivated, experienced, cultured; **WIDE:** large, extensive, spacious, expansive, roomy; **TOLERANT:** progressive, unbiased, liberal
broadcast *v.* announce, transmit, air, send
broaden *v.* widen, expand, increase, grow
broad-minded *adj.* tolerant, progressive, unprejudiced, liberal
brochure *n.* handout, circular, pamphlet, folder
broil *v.* cook, sear, bake, roast
broiler *n.* oven, grill, barbecue, appliance
broken *adj.* **INOPERABLE:** busted, faulty; **FRACTURED:** shattered, smashed, damaged, cracked; **SPASMODIC:** erratic, intermittent, irregular; **INCOHERENT:** muttered, mumbled
brood *v.* pine, grieve, fret, sulk, mope, muse, deliberate, worry
brook *n.* stream, creek, streamlet, river
broth *n.* soup, consommé, bouillon, stock
browbeat *v.* intimidate, bully, frighten, threaten
browse *v.* skim, peruse, scan, inspect, examine
bruise *v.* wound, damage, beat, injure, hurt
brush *n.* **THICKET:** undergrowth, cover, shrubbery, grove, hedge, fern, scrub; **TOUCH:** rub, tap, stroke
brush *v.* **CLEAN:** sweep, whisk, wipe; **TOUCH LIGHTLY:** stroke, smooth, graze

brusque *adj.* abrupt, blunt, curt, terse
brutal *adj.* pitiless, harsh, unmerciful, cruel
brutalize *v.* degrade, demean
bubble *v.* froth, foam, gurgle, effervesce, percolate
bucket *n.* container, pail, canister, can, pot
buckle *n.* clasp, clamp, harness, fastening, fastener
budge *v.* stir, shift, move
budget *n.* projection, estimate, allocation, plan, funds
buffet *v.* batter, strike, whip
buffoon *n.* clown, jester, fool, jerk
bug *n.* INSECT: beetle, pest, gnat; MICROORGANISM: bacillus, virus; DEFECT: flaw, fault, annoyance
bug *v.* EAVESDROP: spy, overhear, wiretap; ANNOY: irritate, plague, pester, bother, disturb
build *v.* increase; construct, create, form, erect, make, manufacture, fabricate, fashion, produce, devise
bulb *n.* globe, globule, ball, knob
bulge *n.* swelling, protuberance, bump, prominence
bulk *n.* most, majority
bulk *v.* enlarge, expand
bull *n.* ANIMAL: steer, calf, ox, cow; NONSENSE: balderdash, rubbish, trash
bulletin *n.* report, newsletter, release, notice
bully *n.* ruffian, rowdy, tough, rascal
bully *v.* intimidate, tease, domineer, harass, threaten
bum *n.* derelict, loafer, hobo, tramp, vagrant, beggar
bump *n.* COLLISION: knock, jounce, jar, nudge; BULGE: swelling, projection, protuberance, knob, lump
bump *v.* COLLIDE: strike, crash, hit; SOUND: thud, whack, sock
bumper *n.* guard, absorber, cover, protector, fender
bun *n.* roll, muffin, scone, bread, roll, pastry

bunch n. cluster, clump, group, sheaf, tuft, shock, bundle, knot, collection

bungalow n. cottage, house, lodge

bungle v. botch, blunder, fumble, mishandle, fail

bungler n. muddler, numskull, dolt, dunce, clod

bunk n. BED: berth, cot, pallet; MEANINGLESS INFORMATION: rubbish, rot, hogwash, nonsense

burden v. hinder, encumber, hamper, strain, load, tax, try, trouble, oppress

burglar n. thief, housebreaker, robber, criminal

burglary n. crime, stealing, robbery, theft

burial n. interment, funeral

burlesque v. imitate, mock, satirize

burly adj. strong, muscular

burn v. ignite, kindle, incinerate, blaze, scorch

burnish v. polish, shine, smooth

burnt adj. scorched, singed, charred, burned

burrow n. hole, shelter

burrow v. dig, hide

burst v. EXPLODE: erupt, rupture, disintegrate; BREAK: crack, split, fracture, destroy

bury v. INTER: entomb, enshrine, embalm; HIDE: cover, conceal, secrete; DEFEAT: overcome, conquer

bush n. bramble, thicket, hedge, shrubbery, plant

bushy adj. fuzzy, shaggy, tufted, woolly, bristly

bushed adj. tired, fatigued

busy adj. active, occupied, diligent, employed, working

butcher v. MASSACRE: slaughter, slay, kill; RUIN: mutilate, spoil, botch, destroy

button n. knob, catch, disk, fastener

buy v. obtain, purchase, get, procure, gain, shop

buzz v. hum, drone, whir

cabaret *n.* bar, café, nightclub
cabin *n.* house, cottage, hut, home, shelter
cabinet *n.* advisors, council, bureau, ministry
cable *n.* rope, cord, chain, wire
cacophony *n.* dissonance, noise
cadaver *n.* body, corpse, remains
cadaverous *adj.* pale, gaunt
cadence *n.* rhythm, meter, flow, beat, measure
cadge *v.* beg, freeload
café *n.* coffeehouse, restaurant, cafeteria, lunchroom
cage *n.* coop, jail, crate, enclosure, pen
cagey *adj.* cunning, shrewd, clever
cajole *v.* appeal, wheedle
calamity *n.* tragedy, cataclysm, catastrophe, disaster
calculate *v.* count, measure, reckon, enumerate, determine, forecast, weigh, gauge, compute, cipher
calculating *adj.* scheming, shrewd, crafty
calendar *n.* schedule, journal, diary, daybook, chro-
nology, logbook, register, almanac, agenda, docket
calisthenics *n.* exercise, workout, gymnastics
calling *n.* profession, vocation, occupation, job, trade
callous *adj.* heartless, indifferent, unfeeling, hardened, insensitive
callow *adj.* inexperienced, immature
calm *adj.* tranquil, reserved, cool, composed, collected, impassive, aloof, serene, placid
calm *v.* tranquilize, soothe, pacify, quiet
calumniate *v.* defame, slander, sully, vilify
camouflage *v.* conceal, cover, veil, disguise, hide
campaign *v.* crusade, electioneer, run, contend, contest, lobby, barnstorm, stump
canal *n.* waterway, trench, ditch, channel, duct

cancel

cancel *v.* invalidate, rescind, repeal, retract, void
cancerous *adj.* carcinogenic, virulent, mortal, harmful
candid *adj.* sincere, open, frank, honest
candidate *n.* nominee, aspirant, office–seeker
candor *n.* frankness, honesty
canny *adj.* cautious, watchful, shrewd
canon *n.* law, principle, standard, decree, rule
cantankerous *adj.* quarrelsome, disagreeable
canteen *n.* container, jug, flask, bottle
canvas *n.* **SAILCLOTH:** tarpaulin tenting, awning, duck, tarp; **PAINTING:** portrait, oil, art
canyon *n.* gorge, gulch, gully, ravine, valley
capability *n.* capacity, skill, aptitude, ability
capable *adj.* proficient, competent, able, intelligent
capacity *n.* limit, size, volume, scope, dimensions
cape *n.* **CLOAK:** mantilla, mantle, shawl, wrap, poncho; **HEADLAND:** peninsula, point, promontory, jetty
caper *n.* **FROLIC:** play, romp; **PRANK:** trick, escapade
capital *n.* assets, cash, estate, property, wealth
capitalist *n.* entrepreneur, investor, financier
capitulate *v.* submit, surrender, yield
capsize *v.* upend, overturn, invert, tip over, upset
caption *n.* heading, title, inscription, subtitle
captious *adj.* critical, fault–finding
captivate *v.* attract, charm, fascinate, bewitch
captive *adj.* restrained, incarcerated, jailed, bound
captive *n.* prisoner, hostage, convict
capture *v.* take, hold, seize, apprehend, arrest
cardinal *adj.* primary, foremost
care *n.* **CONCERN:** worry, anxiety, distress; **CAUTION:** concern, regard, precaution, wariness, vigilance; **CUSTODY:** keeping, watch

44

careen *v.* lean, swerve

career *n.* work, occupation, vocation, job, profession

careful *adj.* thorough, deliberate, meticulous, finicky, exacting, wary, vigilant, painstaking, conscientious, cautious, guarded, discreet, thrifty

careless *adj.* loose, lax, incautious, reckless, indiscreet, imprudent, heedless, negligent, casual, rash

carelessness *n.* unconcern, nonchalance, neglect, negligence, disregard, imprudence, indifference

caress *v.* touch, love, embrace, cuddle, pat

cargo *n.* freight, shipload, baggage, lading, load

caricature *v.* mimic, ridicule, satirize

carnage *n.* bloodbath, massacre, slaughter

carnal *adj.* fleshly, worldly, sensuous, lewd

carnival *n.* merrymaking, festival, fair, entertainment

carol *n.* song, hymn, ballad

carouse *v.* drink, imbibe, party, revel

carriage *n.* BEARING: presence, look, demeanor, poise, air; VEHICLE: buggy, surrey, gig, sulky, hansom

carry *v.* TRANSPORT: convey, transfer, cart, take, bring, haul, tote; TRANSMIT: transfer, relay; SUPPORT bear, sustain, shoulder

cartel *n.* alliance, coalition, federation

carve *v.* fashion, shape, form, chisel, sculpture, cut

cascade *v.* cataract, flow, rapids

casket *n.* box, chest, coffin

cast *n.* REPRODUCTION: facsimile, replica, copy; ACTORS: players, company, troupe; APPEARANCE: aspect, complexion; TINGE: hue, shade, tint, color

cast *v.* THROW: pitch, fling, hurl; MOLD: shape, form

caste *n.* position, status, birth

casual *adj.* CHANCE: unplanned, spontaneous;

BLASÉ: apathetic, unconcerned, indifferent

catalog *n.* register, directory, index, classification

catalog *v.* list, organize

catastrophe *n.* disaster, calamity, misadventure, misery, affliction, devastation, tragedy, upheaval

categorize *v.* classify, type, arrange

caucus *n.* conference, faction

cause *n.* **AGENT:** condition, circumstances; **PURPOSE:** goal, motive, foundation, basis, reason; **BELIEF:** principles, conviction, creed, faith

cause *v.* originate, provoke, generate, occasion, begin

caution *n.* discretion, care, heed, prudence, warning

cautious *adj.* circumspect, watchful, wary, careful

cavil *v.* criticize, object

cavity *n.* pit, depression, basin, hole, hollow

cavort *v.* frolic, prance

cease *v.* stop, desist, terminate, discontinue, halt

cede *v.* relinquish, surrender, yield

celebrate *v.* **COMMEMORATE:** observe, consecrate, honor; **INDULGE:** feast, carouse, rejoice, revel

celebrity *n.* notable, dignitary, personage, luminary

celibate *adj.* unmarried, abstaining

cement *n.* adhesive, glue, tar, gum, mortar, paste

cement *v.* join, unite, mortar, plaster, connect, fasten

cemetery *n.* churchyard, necropolis, catacomb, tomb, vault, crypt, sepulcher, graveyard, mortuary

censor *n.* restrict, suppress, withhold, expurgate

censor *v.* review; ban

censorship *n.* restriction, restraint

censure *v.* **BLAME:** criticize, judge, disapprove; **SCOLD:** rebuke, reprove, attack

census *n.* count, enumeration, tabulation, tally

center *n.* **MIDDLE:** nucleus, core, heart; **HUB:** metropolis, plaza, mart; **ESSENCE:** gist, kernel, character
center *v.* focus, concentrate, centralize, converge
central *adj.* middle, midway, equidistant, focal
cerebral *adj.* brainy, intelligent
ceremonial *adj.* ritualistic, stately, solemn, formal
ceremonious *adj.* formal, ritualistic
ceremony *n.* function, commemoration, celebration, rite, observance, ritual, formality, custom, tradition
certain *adj.* **CONFIDENT:** assured, positive, untroubled, confident; **BEYOND DOUBT:** conclusive, incontrovertible, irrefutable, true, unmistakable; **FIXED:** settled, concluded, definite, determined; **SPECIFIC:** definite, particular, singular, precise, express
certainly *adv.* positively, absolutely, unquestionably
certificate *n.* document, warrant, credentials, certification, document, warranty, guarantee
certify *v.* swear, attest, state, declare, testify
cessation *n.* ending, stopping
chagrin *n.* embarrassment, setback
chain *n.* **LINKS:** series, string, cable, manacle; **SEQUENCE:** succession, progression, continuity
chain *v.* connect, secure, fasten hold, bind, restrain
challenge *v.* **COMPETE:** defy, denounce, invite, dare, threaten; **QUESTION:** dispute, inquire, ask, doubt
challenging *adj.* difficult, intriguing
champion *n.* conqueror, victor, hero
chance *adj.* accidental, unplanned, unintentional, aimless, incidental, fortuitous
chance *v.* risk, venture, stake, hazard, wager, jeopardize, speculate
change *v.* **MAKE DIFFERENT:** vary, alter, transform,

changeable

turn; **BECOME DIFFERENT:** evolve, transform, adapt, moderate, adjust; **EXCHANGE:** displace, supplant, transpose; **DRESS:** undress, disrobe

changeable *adj.* **FICKLE:** flighty, unreliable, unstable; **VARIABLE:** unsteady, unsettled, uncertain

channel *n.* conduit, duct, gutter, trough, artery

chant *n.* recitation, chorus, incantation

chaos *n.* confusion, disorder, turmoil, discord

character *n.* **SYMBOL:** mark, sign, figure, emblem; **QUALITY:** temperament, nature, attribute, characteristic; **ECCENTRIC:** crank, nut, oddball, weirdo

characteristic *n.* attribute, quality, faculty, peculiarity, aspect, distinction, nature, essence, component

charge *v.* **PRICE:** cost; **ACCUSE:** indict, censure, blame; **ATTACK:** assail, assault, invade

charitable *adj.* generous, philanthropic, forgiving

charlatan *n.* cheat, fake, fraud

charming *adj.* alluring, appealing, captivating, diverting, enchanting, fascinating, lovable, provocative

chart *n.* outline, diagram, plan, map, graph

chary *adj.* cautious, timid, wary

chase *v.* pursue, trail, track, seek, hunt

chasten *n.* correct, punish

chastise *v.* scold, discipline, spank, punish

cheap *adj.* **INEXPENSIVE:** competitive, reasonable, economical; **INFERIOR:** shoddy, poor

cheapen *v.* depreciate, degrade, spoil, demean

cheat *n.* rogue, charlatan, fraud, swindler, chiseler, deceiver, trickster, crook, shill

cheat *v.* defraud, swindle, beguile, deceive

check *v.* **CONTROL:** bridle, repress, inhibit, neutralize, restrain; **EXAMINE:** review, monitor, investigate

cheer *v.* **HEARTEN:** console, brighten, comfort, encourage, help; **APPLAUD:**, shout, salute, support, yell

cheerful *adj.* **HAPPY:** gay, merry, joyful; **BRIGHT:** sunny, sparkling, pleasant

cherish *v.* treasure, value, adore, love, protect

chest *n.* **BREAST:** thorax, bosom, peritoneum, ribs; **BOX:** case, coffer, cabinet, strongbox, crate

chew *v.* munch, masticate, nibble, gnaw, eat

chide *v.* scold, reprimand

chief *adj.* leading, first, foremost, main, principal

chilly *adj.* brisk, fresh, crisp, cold, cool

chivalrous *adj.* courteous, valiant, brave, noble, polite

choice *n.* selection, preference, election, favorite, pick

choke *v.* asphyxiate, strangle; gag, gasp

choose *v.* pick, prefer, appoint, favor, decide

chop *v.* cut, mince, fell, whack

chore *n.* task, routine, errand, job

chronic *adj.* deep–seated, persistent, lingering, protracted, prolonged, recurrent

chronologic, chronological *adj.* arranged, ordered, classified, sequential, consecutive, sequenced

chunk *n.* lump, piece, mass, part

churlish *adj.* crude, vulgar, grouchy, surly

churn *v.* stir, beat, mix, agitate

circle *n.* disk, ring, loop, orbit, hoop, periphery

circle *v.* circumscribe, enclose, circulate, surround

circuitous *adj.* roundabout, devious

circular *adj.* spherical, cyclical, globular, round

circulate *v.* send, report, distribute

circulation *n.* rotation, current, flow

circumference *n.* perimeter, periphery, boundary

circumspect *adj.* cautious, prudent

circumstance

circumstance *n.* situation, condition, contingency, status, occurrence, episode
circumstantial *adj.* inconclusive, presumptive
circumvent *v.* avoid, bypass, dodge, elude, evade
civic *adj.* civil, urban, municipal, public
civil *adj.* formal, polite, courteous, refined
claim *v.* DEMAND: request, own; STATE: assert, insist
clamber *v.* climb, scramble
clamor *n.* outcry, din, discord, noise, uproar
clamp *n.* snap, clasp, catch, fastener, lock
clan *n.* family, tribe, group, organization, race
clandestine *adj.* covert, furtive, secret, sly
clarify *v.* interpret, define, elucidate, explain
clash *v.* conflict, mismatch, contrast, differ
clasp *n.* fastener, buckle, pin, clamp
classic *n.* masterwork, masterpiece
classical *adj.* distinguished, superior, well–known
classify *v.* arrange, order, pigeonhole, organize, categorize, label, catalogue, tag, sort, index
clatter *n.* noise, racket, hubbub
clause *n.* provision, condition, codicil, requirement
clean *adj., adv.* PURE: unadulterated, undefiled, spotless, cleansed; DISTINCT: clear–cut, sharp, readable; THOROUGH: complete, entire, total, absolute
clean *v.* cleanse, wash, scrub, disinfect, polish, sterilize, scour
clean–cut *adj.* clear, precise; pleasing
clear *adj., adv.* OBVIOUS: explicit, plain, manifest; TRANSPARENT: limpid, translucent; UNCLOUDED: sunny, bright, fair; INNOCENT: exonerated, absolved
clearly *adv.* OBVIOUSLY: plainly, unmistakably, apparently, evidently; ACUTELY: sharply, audibly

clemency *n.* leniency, mercy
clench *v.* hold, grip, grasp, double up
clever *adj.* **SKILLFUL:** apt, expert, adroit, able; **IN-TELLIGENT:** smart, bright, shrewd
cliché *n.* platitude, slogan, banality, triviality, motto
client *n.* customer, patient, patron, buyer
climax *n.* crisis, peak, culmination, zenith, summit,
climb *v.* scale, ascend, surmount, mount
cling *v.* hold, adhere, attach, clasp, stick
clip *v.* shorten, snip, crop; strike; cheat; fasten
cloak *v.* cover, conceal, camouflage
clog *v.* obstruct, impede, seal, close, hinder
cloister *v.* seclude, protect
close *adj.* nearby; like; confining; restrictive, limited,
close *n.* ending, conclusion
close *v.* **END:** conclude, finish, terminate; **SEAL:** shut, clog, block, bar, dam, cork; **COME TOGETHER:** connect, meet, unite, agree, join; **SHUT:** slam, fasten, bolt, clench, bar, shutter, lock
closely *adv.* approximately, similarly, nearly, intimately, jointly, almost
clot *v.* thicken, coagulate, set, lump
cloth *n.* fabric, material, stuff, goods
clothe *v.* cover, attire, dress, costume
clothes, clothing *n.* apparel, raiment, garments, garb, vestments, attire, outfit, toggery, togs, duds
clown *n.* fool, buffoon, joker, harlequin
clumsy *adj.* ungainly, gawky, inexpert, awkward
cluster *n.* group, gathering, batch, clump, bunch
clutch *v.* grasp, grab, grip, hold, seize
clutter *n.* disarray, jumble, disorder, confusion
coach *v.* teach, train drill, instruct

coagulate *v.* clot, curdle, congeal, thicken
coalition *n.* union, group, association, faction
coarse *adj.* ROUGH: unrefined, crude; VULGAR: low, common, base, obscene, rude
coast *n.* shore, shoreline, beach, seaboard
coast *v.* glide, float, drift, ride
coax *v.* cajole, wheedle, inveigle, influence, urge
cocky *adj.* overconfident, flamboyant
codicil *n.* addendum, addition, appendix, rider
coerce *v.* force, compel, impel, constrain
cogent *adj.* forceful, compelling
cogitate *v.* consider, ponder, reflect
cognizance *n.* knowledge, awareness
coherent *adj.* comprehensible, intelligible, logical
coincide *v.* correspond, match, agree
coincidence *n.* chance, happening, accident
cold *adj.* WINTRY: crisp, cool, freezing, frosty, frigid, nippy, brisk, numbing, raw; UNFEELING: unfriendly, indifferent, reserved
collaborate *v.* cooperate, conspire
collapse *v.* drop, deflate, fall, fail
collateral *n.* security, guarantee, pledge, insurance
colleague *n.* associate, partner, collaborator
collect *v.* CONSOLIDATE: amass, accumulate, concentrate; CONGREGATE: assemble, flock, gather
collection *n.* assortment, accumulation, assemblage, concentration, mess, lot, heap, bunch
collector *n.* hobbyist, fancier, curator, hoarder
collide *v.* hit, strike, crash; clash, disagree, oppose
collision *n.* impact, contact, encounter, crash
collusion *n.* conspiracy, plot
colorful *adj.* bright, vivid; picturesque, quaint

colossal *adj.* large, huge, enormous, immense
column *n.* **SUPPORT:** pillar, shaft, pylon, post; **COMMENTARY:** article, editorial
coma *n.* unconsciousness, trance, stupor, sleep
combat *n.* conflict, battle, struggle, warfare, fight
combine *v.* link, join, fuse, merge, blend, mix, unite
comedian *n.* comic, jester, entertainer, actor, clown
comedy *n.* farce, satire, burlesque, slapstick
comely *adj.* attractive, pleasing
comfort *n.* contentment, relaxation, repose, ease
comfort *v.* soothe, encourage, reassure, console
comfortable *adj.* **CONTENTED:** relaxed, untroubled, soothed, satisfied; **SATISFACTORY:** snug, cozy, luxurious, rich, restful, pleasant
comic, comical *adj.* funny, silly, humorous, ironic
command *v.* **ORDER:** charge, tell, demand; **CONTROL:** rule, dominate, master
commemorate *v.* honor, solemnize, memorialize
commence *v.* begin, start, originate
commend *v.* praise, laud, support, acclaim, approve
commensurate *adj.* equivalent, comparable
comment *v.* remark, criticize, mention, interject, say
commentary *n.* criticism, analysis, interpretation
commerce *n.* trading, marketing, business
commission *n.* **AUTHORITY:** license, permission; **COMMITTEE:** representatives, board; **PAYMENT:** royalty, fee
commission *v.* delegate, appoint, authorize, charge
commit *v.* **PERPETRATE:** complete, perform; **ENTRUST:** delegate, promise, charge, employ, dispatch
commitment *n.* responsibility, duty, promise
commodious *adj.* comfortable, large, spacious

commodity *n.* goods, merchandise, wares
commotion *n.* disturbance, tumult, uproar
communal *adj.* shared, cooperative, mutual, public
communicate *v.* impart, inform, tell, confer, talk, converse, chat, write
communication *n.* utterance, writing, broadcasting, speaking, interchange
community *n.* public, people; village, colony, hamlet
compact *adj.* small, light, dense
compact *n.* covenant, understanding
compact *v.* pack, compress
companion *n.* comrade, escort, chaperon, bodyguard
companionship *n.* brotherhood, fellowship, friendship
company *n.* **ASSEMBLY:** throng, band, gathering; **BUSINESS:** firm, corporation; **GUEST:** visitor, caller
comparable *adj.* **SIMILAR:** akin, relative, alike, like; **EQUAL:** equivalent, tantamount
compare *v.* **LIKEN:** relate, associate, link, correlate; **EXAMINE:** contrast, weigh, analyze
compassion *n.* concern, sympathy, pity
compatible *adj.* agreeable, congruous, harmonious
compel *v.* force, enforce, constrain, coerce
compelling *adj.* forceful, impressive
compensate *v.* offset, repay, recompense, remunerate
compete *v.* strive, struggle, oppose, clash, encounter
competent *adj.* qualified, suitable, fit, skilled, able
competition *n.* rivalry; contest, meet, game
compile *v.* gather, collect, assemble, accumulate, edit
complacent *adj.* self–satisfied, egotistic, happy, smug
complain *v.* grumble, remonstrate, fret, fuss, gripe
complaint *n.* **OBJECTION:** charge, criticism, reproach, accusation; **ILLNESS:** ailment, disease, infirmity

complete *v.* execute, consummate, perfect, accomplish, realize, perform, achieve, fulfill, conclude
complex *adj.* MULTIPLE: combined, compounded; CONVOLUTED: intricate, complicated, tortuous, knotty
complex *n.* phobia, mania, insanity
complexion *n.* coloration, tinge, cast, pigmentation
compliance *n.* agreement, assent, conformity
complicate *v.* snarl, confound, jumble, tangle
complicated *adj.* intricate, tangled, complex
complicity *n.* collusion, conspiracy, involvement
compliment *v.* congratulate, honor, cheer, salute, hail, toast, applaud, commend, acclaim, glorify
complimentary *adj.* flattering, laudatory, approving
composure *n.* self-control, calmness, poise, aplomb
compound *v.* combine, mix
comprehend *v.* understand, grasp, discern, perceive
comprehensive *adj.* broad, extensive, sweeping
comprise *v.* include, contain, embrace, embody
compromise *v.* settle, agree, conciliate, negotiate
compulsive *adj.* driven, passionate
compulsory *adj.* obligatory, requisite, necessary
compunction *n.* apprehension, qualm, uneasiness,
conceal *v.* cover, screen, secrete, hide
concede *v.* acknowledge, grant, yield, admit, allow
conceit *n.* arrogance, narcissism, vanity
conceivable *adj.* believable, understandable, likely
concept *n.* theory, idea, notion, thought
conceptual *adj.* theoretical, ideal
concern *v.* PERTAIN: relate, influence; BOTHER: worry
conciliate *v.* appease, placate
concise *adj.* succinct, brief, condensed, short
conclave *n.* gathering, meeting, parley

conclude *v.* **CLOSE:** terminate, finish, complete, achieve; **DEDUCE:** presume, reason, gather, assume
concoct *v.* make, devise
concur *v.* correspond, coincide, agree, equal
concurrent *adj.* parallel, coexisting, simultaneous
condemn *v.* doom, sentence, damn, convict, punish
condescending *adj.* patronizing, disdainful, smug
condiment *n.* seasoning, relish
condition *n.* **REQUIREMENT:** stipulation, provision; **FITNESS:** tone, shape; **CIRCUMSTANCE:** situation, position, status; **MODIFIER:** limitation, restriction, qualification, restraint; **ILLNESS:** ailment, infirmity
condone *v.* forgive, disregard, excuse, overlook
conduct *n.* behavior, deportment, demeanor, manner
conduct *v.* **LEAD:** guide, escort, attend, accompany; **MANAGE:** administer, handle
confederacy *n.* alliance, coalition, federation
confer *v.* converse, deliberate, parley, discuss
conference *n.* meeting, discussion, gathering
confess *v.* acknowledge, own, concede, admit
confession *n.* disclosure, acknowledgment
confidant *n.* friend, adherent, companion
confident *adj.* assured, fearless, dauntless, bold
confidential *adj.* secret, classified, intimate, private
confine *v.* restrain, restrict; imprison, incarcerate
confirm *v.* **RATIFY:** affirm, settle, approve, endorse; **PROVE:** validate, verify, authenticate, explain
confiscate *v.* seize, appropriate, impound, usurp
conflict *v.* clash, contrast, contend, fight, oppose
conform *v.* adapt, accommodate, reconcile, agree
conformity *n.* **SIMILARITY:** correspondence, resemblance; **OBEDIENCE:** submission, compliance

confound *v.* confuse, bewilder, puzzle, perplex
confront *v.* brave, defy, repel, dare, face
confrontation *n.* meeting, battle, strife, dispute
confuse *v.* bewilder, befuddle, puzzle, perplex, confound, fluster, embarrass, disconcert, baffle, mystify
congeal *v.* thicken, solidify
congenial *adj.* friendly, compatible, harmonious
congregate *v.* gather, assemble, convene, meet
congruous *adj.* appropriate, suitable, fitting
conjecture *n.* guess, opinion, speculation
connect *v.* join, link, attach, associate, relate
connoisseur *n.* critic, expert, judge
connotation *n.* implication, meaning, insinuation,
conquer *v.* overcome, subdue, crush, defeat
conqueror *n.* vanquisher, champion, hero, winner
conquest *n.* triumph, success, conquering, victory
conscience *n.* duty, morals, shame
conscientious *adj.* thorough, fastidious, meticulous, complete, careful, reliable
conscious *adj.* awake, aware, sentient, cognizant, discerning, knowing, mindful, understanding
consecutive *adj.* ordered, chronological, sequential
consensus *n.* agreement, consent, unison, accord
consent *v.* accede, acquiesce, agree, allow, approve
consequence *n.* EFFECT: outgrowth, end, outcome, result; IMPORTANCE: moment, value, weight
conservative *adj.* cautious, reserved, conventional
consider *v.* contemplate, regard, think, believe
considerable *adj.* IMPORTANT: noteworthy, significant; SUBSTANTIAL: abundant, lavish, bountiful, plentiful
considerate *adj.* kind, solicitous, polite, thoughtful
consideration *n.* THOUGHTFULNESS: attentiveness,

consistent

kindness; **PAYMENT:** remuneration, salary, wage
consistent *adj.* constant, rational, regular
consolation *n.* sympathy, compassion, pity
console *v.* comfort, cheer, gladden, encourage
consolidate *v.* combine, mix, unify, compress, pack
consortium *n.* alliance, union
conspicuous *adj.* obvious, striking, prominent, flagrant, noticeable
conspiracy *n.* plan, intrigue, collusion, connivance
conspirator *n.* betrayer, schemer, cabalist, traitor
constant *adj.* unchanging, steadfast, steady, uniform, unvarying, unbroken, regular
consternation *n.* confusion, distress
constituent *adj.* component, element, ingredient, part
constitute *v.* **FOUND:** develop, create, establish; **MAKE UP:** frame, compound, compose
constraint *n.* **FORCE:** coercion, compulsion, pressure; **SHYNESS:** bashfulness, restraint, humility, reserve; **CONFINEMENT:** captivity, detention, restriction, arrest
constrict *v.* squeeze, contract, cramp, tighten
construct *v.* build, erect, make, fabricate, create
constructive *adj.* helpful, useful, instructive, valuable, effective
consult *v.* confer, parley, conspire, counsel, ask
consume *v.* **USE:** spend, deplete; **EAT:** absorb, devour
consumer *n.* user, customer, shopper, buyer
consummate *v.* complete, perfect
consumption *n.* spending, expense, use, waste,
contact *v.* touch, reach, communicate, talk
contagious *adj.* communicable, infectious, spreading, epidemic, deadly, endemic, catching
contain *v.* hold, keep, limit, stop, restrain

contaminate *v.* pollute, infect, defile, corrupt, dirty
contemplate *v.* study, ponder, consider, muse, think
contemporary *adj.* current, fashionable, modern
contempt *n.* disdain, disrespect, scorn, derision
contend *v.* compete, contest, battle, dispute, fight, argue, claim
content, contented *adj.* satisfied, appeased, gratified
contention *n.* ARGUMENT: quarrel, struggle, competition, dispute; ASSERTION: charge, declaration
contest *n.* competition, trial, match, challenge, game
contest *v.* dispute, challenge, compete, oppose,
contiguous *adj.* touching, adjacent
contingency *n.* possibility, likelihood, chance
continual *adj.* uninterrupted, unbroken, regular
continuation *n.* extension, supplement, addition
continue *v.* PERSIST: endure, persevere, progress; RESUME: renew, return, reinstate, reestablish
contort *v.* twist, deform, misshape, distort
contraband *n.* plunder, booty
contract *v.* AGREE: pledge, bargain, stipulate, obligate; REDUCE: diminish, shrink, recede, condense, compress, decrease; ACQUIRE: catch, get, incur
contradiction *n.* incongruity, inconsistency, opposition, difference, opposite
contrary *adj.* OPPOSED: antagonistic, hostile, counter; DISAGREEABLE: contradictory, unpropitious; OBSTINATE: willful, headstrong, stubborn
contrast *v.* compare, differentiate, deviate, differ, vary
contribute *v.* give, endow, bestow, present, confer, bequest, grant, donate, bequeath, subsidize
contrive *v.* create, devise, scheme, improvise, invent
control *v.* CHECK: constrain, repress, restrain; DIRECT:

controversial

lead, dominate, supervise, head, manage, govern
controversial *adj.* disputable, debatable, uncertain
controversy *n.* contention, debate, quarrel, difference
convene *v.* assemble, congregate, collect, gather
convenient *adj.* accessible, available, handy, close
convention *n.* **GATHERING:** assembly, convocation, meeting; **CUSTOM:** practice, habit, fashion
conventional *adj.* accepted, customary, typical, commonplace, traditional, formal
conversant *adj.* familiar, knowledgeable, experienced
conversation *n.* talk, discussion, discourse, speech
converse *v.* speak, talk, visit
converse *n.* antithesis, reverse, opposite
conversion *n.* change, turn, regeneration
convert *v.* alter, transform, change, reform
convey *v.* transport, transfer, communicate, send
convict *n.* captive, felon, criminal, prisoner
convict *v.* condemn, sentence, doom
conviction *n.* persuasion, confidence, belief, faith
convince *v.* persuade, establish, satisfy, teach
convincing *adj.* reasonable, plausible, likely
convivial *adj.* congenial, gregarious
cooperate *v.* conspire, participate, agree
copious *adj.* abundant, abounding
copy *v.* **IMITATE:** mimic, ape; **REPRODUCE:** duplicate, counterfeit, forge, depict, portray
cordial *adj.* friendly, genial, hearty, warm–hearted
core *n.* essence, gist, kernel, heart, center, hub
corporation *n.* enterprise, company, business
corporeal *adj.* material, tangible
corpse *n.* body, carcass, remains, cadaver
corral *v.* surround, capture

correct *adj.* ACCURATE: true, right; PROPER: suitable
correct *v.* adjust, remedy, rectify, amend, repair
correctness *n.* ACCURACY: precision, exactness; PROPRIETY: decency, decorum, fitness
correlation *n.* interdependence, equivalence
correspond *v.* BE SIMILAR: compare, match, resemble, conform; COMMUNICATE: write, reply, answer
correspondence *n.* LIKENESS: conformity, equivalence, similarity; COMMUNICATION: message, letter
corroborate *v.* confirm, prove, support, strengthen
corrupt *adj.* immoral, underhanded, fraudulent, crooked, nefarious, unscrupulous, shady, dishonest
corrupt *v.* debase, pervert, adulterate, taint, spoil
cost *n.* price, value, expense, payment, charge
costly *adj.* expensive, splendid, high–priced, precious
costume *n.* dress, clothing, attire, apparel, garb
couch *n.* sofa, lounge, davenport, chair
council *n.* group, cabinet, directorate, committee
counsel *n.* ADVICE: guidance, instruction, suggestion; ADVISER: lawyer, attorney, barrister
countenance *n.* appearance, aspect
countenance *v.* approve, endorse
counter *v.* react, respond
counter *n.* board, shelf, ledge, bench, table
counteract *v.* mitigate, check, invalidate, hinder
counterfeit *adj.* forged, fraudulent, fictitious, false
countermand *v.* cancel, reverse
countersign *n.* authentication, confirmation, sign
countless *adj.* innumerable, incalculable, infinite
coup *n.* feat, achievement
couple *n.* pair, two, set, brace,
couple *v.* join, unite, link, copulate

courage *n.* valor, boldness, spirit, audacity, mettle, stoutheartedness, gallantry, daring, spunk, strength
course *n.* route, passage, pathway, road
court *n.* **SQUARE:** patio, yard; **ARENA:** rink, ring, field
courteous *adj.* well–mannered, courtly, affable, polite
courtesy *n.* affability, politeness, refinement
covenant *n.* agreement, contract
cover *v.* **WRAP:** envelop, enshroud, encase; **PROTECT:** shield, screen, house, shelter; **HIDE:** screen, mask, disguise; **INCLUDE:** embrace, comprise, incorporate; **TRAVEL:** traverse, cross; **FLOOD:** drench, engulf; **REPORT:** recount, narrate, relate, broadcast, record
covert *adj.* hidden, disguised
cower *v.* cringe, shrink, quake, tremble, shake, snivel, flinch, quail, grovel
coy *adj.* shy, demur, evasive, bashful, humble
cozy *adj.* comfortable, secure, sheltered, snug, safe
crabby *adj.* grouchy, ill–humored
crack *n.* **OPENING:** crevice, cleft, fissure, rift; **BLOW:** hit, thwack, stroke; **COMMENT:** retort, jest, joke, remark
crack *v.* **BREAK:** cleave, burst, split, sever; **DAMAGE:** injure, hurt, impair; **SOLVE:** answer, decode
craft *n.* **TRADE:** occupation, career, work, job; **SKILL:** proficiency, competence, aptitude, ability
craftsman *n.* artisan, journeyman, machinist, artist
craggy *adj.* rough, steep, irregular
cramp *n.* spasm, crick, pang, pain
cramped *adj.* confined, restraining, restricted
crank *n.* **DEVICE:** bracket, bend, arm, handle; **PERSON:** eccentric, character, complainer, grouch
cranky *adj.* irritable, ill–tempered, disagreeable
crash *v.* **FALL:** plunge, tumble, drop; **COLLIDE:** jostle,

bump, jolt, hit; **MAKE NOISE:** clatter, bang, smash; **BREAK:** shatter, splinter, smash; **GO UNINVITED:** invade, intrude, interrupt, meddle

crate *n.* box, carton, cage, container, package

crater *n.* depression, hollow, opening, abyss, hole

craving *n.* need, longing, yearning, desire

crawl *v.* creep, wriggle, squirm, slither, writhe, grovel

crazy *adj.* crazed, demented, mad, insane, foolish

cream *n.* lotion, cosmetic, jelly, salve, emulsion

creamy *adj.* smooth, buttery, rich, soft

create *v.* originate, build, fashion, shape, fabricate

creative *adj.* imaginative, inventive, artistic, original

creature *n.* being, creation, beast, animal

credibility *n.* likelihood, probability, chance

credible *adj.* plausible, believable, reliable

creditor *n.* lender, mortgagor, banker

creed *n.* belief, doctrine, dogma, faith

creep *v.* slither, writhe, crawl

creepy *adj.* apprehensive, uneasy

crestfallen *adj.* saddened, shamed, disheartened

crevice *n.* crack, chasm, cleft, slit, gap

crew *n.* company, troupe, squad, organization, team

crime *n.* transgression, wrongdoing, offense, violation

criminal *adj.* illegal, felonious, bad

criminal *n.* lawbreaker, felon, crook, gangster, thief

cringe *v.* cower, shrink, flinch, quail, wince, crawl

crisis *n.* straits, plight, predicament, trauma, pickle

crisp *adj.* **INVIGORATING:** brisk, fresh, bracing, stimulating; **FRESH:** green, plump, ripe

criterion *n.* basis, foundation, standard, principle

critic *n.* **REVIEWER:** commentator, analyst, examiner; **FAULTFINDER:** detractor, complainer, mud–slinger

critical *adj.* **DISAPPROVING:** condemning, censuring, disparaging, sarcastic; **ANALYTICAL:** perceptive, discerning, observant; **CRUCIAL:** decisive, significant

criticize *v.* **EVALUATE:** study, analyze, examine; **FIND FAULT:** chastise, reprove, reprimand, blame

crook *n.* **CRIMINAL:** swindler, thief, rogue; **BEND:** notch, fork, angle, bend

crooked *adj.* **CURVED:** bowed, twisted, bent; **DISHONEST:** iniquitous, devious, corrupt, nefarious

crop *v.* trim, cut, clip

cross *adj.* angry, cranky, pettish, critical, irritable

cross *v.* **INTERSECT:** divide, traverse, span; **INTERBREED:** mingle, cross–pollinate, mix

crucial *adj.* **CRITICAL:** decisive, climatic, deciding; **SEVERE:** trying, taxing, hard, difficult

crude *adj.* unrefined, rough, unpolished, coarse

cruel *adj.* heartless, malevolent, vicious, savage

cruise *v.* travel, voyage, navigate, coast, sail

crumb *n.* piece, fragment, particle, scrap, pinch, bit

crumble *v.* decay, disintegrate, collapse

crumple *v.* collapse, rumple, crush, crease, wrinkle

crush *v.* **SUBDUE:** defeat, overwhelm, annihilate; **BREAK:** smash, pulverize, powder, grind

crust *n.* hull, rind, piecrust, shell, edge, border

cry *v.* weep, sob, wail, sorrow, grieve

cuddle *v.* embrace, snuggle, huddle, nestle

cuddly *adj.* affectionate, lovable

cue *n.* signal, hint, prompt

cuff *n.* slap, blow, punch, hit

culminate *v.* finish, close, end

cultivate *v.* nurture, educate, refine, improve, teach

cultivation *n.* horticulture, agriculture, gardening

cultural *adj.* educational, enlightening, enriching

culture *n.* FOLKWAYS: convention, custom, mores; REFINEMENT: breeding, gentility, manners, polish

cunning *adj.* sly, crafty, clever, skillful, ingenious

cure *v.* restore, heal, remedy

curious *adj.* INQUISITIVE: interested, inquiring, questioning; UNUSUAL: strange, odd, rare, queer, unique

current *adj.* prevailing, contemporary, fashionable

current *n.* drift, flow, tide

curt *adj.* brusque, brief, concise, terse, short

curtain *n.* hanging, screen, drape, drapery, shutter

curve *n.* arc, bow, arch

curve *v.* deviate, vow, crook, twist, bend

custodian *n.* caretaker, attendant, gatekeeper

custody *n.* care, protection, guardianship

custom *n.* tradition, practice, convention, ritual

customary *adj.* usual, habitual, conventional

cut *v.* REDUCE: shorten, curtail, lessen, decrease; SEVER: separate, cleave; CROSS: intersect, pass

cutback *v.* reduce, curtail, shorten, decrease

cycle *n.* sequence, series, succession, period

cynic *n.* skeptic, mocker, scoffer, detractor, critic

cynical *adj.* sardonic, unbelieving, sneering, sarcastic

dabble *v.* dally, trifle, putter

daffy *adj.* silly, ridiculous

dainty *adj.* delicate, fragile, petite, airy, lacy, cute

dally *v.* dawdle, trifle with, putter, dabble

dam *v.* obstruct, check, restrict, restrain

damage *v.* injure, scratch, mar, deface, break

damages *n.* compensation, reparations, costs, reimbursement, expense

damp *adj.* moist, humid, sodden, soggy, wet

danger *n.* risk, peril, jeopardy, threat, menace

dangerous *adj.* perilous, serious, vital, hazardous, risky, deadly, precarious, treacherous, unsafe

dangle *v.* hang, droop, sway, suspend

dank *adj.* damp, clammy

dare *n.* dare, challenge, defy

dare *v.* **VENTURE:** undertake, endeavor, hazard, risk, try; **DEFY:** confront, oppose, brave, challenge, face

daring *adj.* bold, courageous, fearless, brave

dark *adj.* **SINISTER:** evil, bad, gloomy, dismal, immoral, corrupt; **UNLIT:** dim, shadowy, somber, indistinct, dusky, murky, gloomy, obscure, shady, hazy

darken *v.* cloud, shade, shadow, blacken, shade

darkness *n.* **GLOOM:** murkiness, dimness, nightfall, night; **EVIL:** wickedness, sin, corruption; **SECRECY:** concealment, isolation, obscurity, seclusion, privacy

dart *n.* missile, barb, arrow, weapon

dart *v.* shoot, speed, plunge, thrust, hurtle, fling, heave, pitch, dash, spurt, skim, fly, scoot

dash *n.* little, sprinkle, scattering, grain, trace

dash *v.* **RUSH:** race, sprint, speed, hurry, run; **DISCOURAGE:** smash, dampen, dismay, dispirit

dashing *adj.* adventurous, dapper

data *n.* information, details, facts, statistics, figures

date *n.* **APPOINTMENT:** rendezvous, engagement, call, visit; **COMPANION:** partner, friend, lover

date *v.* **ACCOMPANY:** court, escort, accompany

dawn *n.* start, sunrise, daybreak, morning, beginning

daze *n.* stupor, bewilderment, distraction, confusion

daze *v.* stun, bewilder

dazzle *v.* blind, amaze,

dead *adj.* **LIFELESS:** deceased, perished, inanimate,

defunct, still; **NUMB:** insensible, anesthetized;
EXHAUSTED: wearied, worn, spent, tired

deaden v. anesthetize, dull, chloroform, numb

deafening adj. thunderous, overpowering, loud

deal n. agreement, pledge, pact, contract

deal v. trade, barter, bargain, buy, sell, distribute

dealer n. vendor, businessman, merchant

debar v. exclude, prohibit, restrict

debatable adj. disputable, unsettled, controversial, questionable

debate v. discuss, contend, contest, dispute, argue

debris n. remains, rubble, rubbish, wreckage, trash

debt n. obligation, liability, mortgage, note

debtor n. purchaser, borrower, mortgagor, buyer

decadent adj. immoral, wicked, degenerate, bad

deceit n. misrepresentation, trickery, fraud, duplicity, deception, dishonesty

deceitful adj. tricky, cunning, insincere, dishonest

deceive v. mislead, swindle, delude, defraud, victimize, betray, hoodwink, dupe, fleece, bilk

deceiver n. conniver, swindler, impostor, cheat

decent adj. seemly, respectable, nice, proper, ethical, virtuous, trustworthy, upright, good

deception n. trickery, craftiness, treachery, betrayal, pretense, deceit, duplicity, dishonesty

deceptive adj. misleading, misrepresenting

decide v. settle, determine, judge, select, pick

decipher v. interpret, decode, translate, explain, solve

decision n. judgment, resolution, result, opinion

decisive adj. conclusive, resolved, final, definitive, absolute, definite, determined

declaration n. statement, assertion, affirmation,

declare

proclamation, affidavit, testimony, announcement
declare *v.* state, assert, tell, affirm, maintain, testify, certify, contend, allege, profess, swear
decline *v.* DETERIORATE: decrease, degenerate, backslide; REFUSE: desist
decorate *v.* adorn, beautify, renovate, brighten, enhance, embellish, elaborate
decoration *n.* EMBELLISHMENT: adornment, ornamentation, design; CITATION: medal, ribbon, emblem
decorative *adj.* ornamental, aesthetic, embellishing, beautifying, florid, ornate
decrease *v.* lessen, diminish, decline, subside, shrink, reduce, check, curb, restrain, blunt, curtail
decree *n.* proclamation, edict, pronouncement, declaration, judgment
decrepit *adj.* worn, aged
dedicate *v.* devote, apportion, assign
dedication *n.* sanctification, devotion, celebration
deduce *v.* conclude, infer
deduction *n.* SUBTRACTION: reduction, abatement, decrease, discount; REASONING: inference, thought; CONCLUSION: answer, judgment, opinion
deed *n.* ACTION: act, commission, accomplishment; DOCUMENT: release, agreement, charter, title
deep *adj.* IMMERSED: subterranean, underground; COMPREHENSIVE: penetrating, acute, profound
default *n.* failure, neglect, shortcoming, insufficiency
defeat *v.* conquer, overcome, vanquish, subdue, best, overthrow, crush, overwhelm, repulse, decimate
defect *n.* imperfection, fault, deficiency, flaw
defect *v.* abandon, forsake, desert, leave
defective *adj.* imperfect, inadequate, faulty, poor

defend *v.* PROTECT: shield, shelter, screen; JUSTIFY: plead, alibi, endorse, recommend, support

defender *n.* champion, patron, guardian, protector

defense *n.* RESISTANCE: protection, security, backing; PLEA: denial, alibi, explanation, justification, proof

defer *v.* postpone, shelve, delay, suspend

deference *n.* regard, veneration, homage, reverence

deferent, deferential *adj.* respectful, obedient

defiance *n.* insubordination, rebellion, insurgence, disobedience

defiant *adj.* resistant, obstinate, rebellious

deficient *adj.* lacking, defective, insufficient, skimpy, meager, inadequate,

deficit *n.* shortage, paucity, deficiency, lack

defile *v.* corrupt, debase, ravish, violate, molest

define *v.* LIMIT: bound, confine, circumscribe, edge; DESCRIBE: designate, characterize, represent, exemplify, explain, name

definite *adj.* EXACT: fixed, precise, positive, decisive, specific, categorical; CLEAR: sharp, distinct, unmistakable, obvious, plain; POSITIVE: sure, certain

definition *n.* meaning, terminology, signification, translation, explanation, description

definitive *adj.* conclusive, precise, final, absolute

deform *v.* damage, disfigure, deface, injure

deformity *n.* malformation, ugliness, unsightliness

defraud *v.* hoax, dupe, cheat, deceive

deft *adj.* skillful, dexterous

defy *v.* resist, oppose, insult, face, dare

degenerate *adj.* corrupted, depraved, immoral, bad

degradation *n.* depravity, corruption, degeneration, evil

degrade *v.* disgrace, debase, demote, discredit, diminish, humble

degraded *adj.* disgraced, debased, depraved, bad

degree *n.* **MEASURE:** gradation, size, dimension, gauge; **RANGE:** extent, quality, potency, proportion, intensity, scope; **DIPLOMA:** baccalaureate, doctorate, sheepskin,

dehydrate *v.* dry, desiccate, parch, drain

deify *v.* exalt, idealize, worship

deity *n.* god, divinity

dejected *adj.* dispirited, depressed, sad

delay *v.* postpone, defer, deter, impede, detain, check, curb, procrastinate, suspend, interrupt

delectable *adj.* delicious, pleasing, tasty

delegate *n.* legate, emissary, proxy, deputy, consul, minister, ambassador, agent, representative

delegate *v.* authorize, appoint, commission, name, nominate, select, choose, assign, deputize

deliberate *adj.* intentional, conscious, studied, planned, willful, considered, calculated, intended, purposeful, premeditated, designed, unhurried

deliberate *v.* confer, consider, ponder

delicacy *n.* **FINENESS:** daintiness, flimsiness, softness, lightness; **FOOD:** tidbit, morsel, delight, import

delicate *adj.* **FINE:** dainty, fragile, frail, subtle, tactful; **SICKLY:** susceptible, feeble, weak

delicious *adj.* tasty, savory, appetizing, delectable

delight *n.* enjoyment, joy, pleasure, happiness

delight *v.* fascinate, amuse, please, entertain

delightful *adj.* charming, amusing, clever, pleasant

delineate *v.* depict, describe

delinquent *adj.* **LAX:** tardy, negligent, derelict, remiss, careless; **OVERDUE:** owed, due, unpaid

delirious *adj.* demented, crazy, irrational, insane

delirium *n.* hallucinations, confusion

deliver *v.* **BRING FORTH:** produce, provide; **FREE:** liberate, save; **TRANSFER:** pass, remit, give; **SPEAK:** present, address; **DISTRIBUTE:** allot, dispense

delude *v.* mislead, deceive

deluge *v.* flood, overwhelm

delusion *n.* phantasm, hallucination, fancy, illusion

demand *v.* request, charge, direct, command, ask

demanding *adj.* challenging, difficult, fussy, imperious, exacting, critical

demean *v.* debase, humble

demented *adj.* crazy, bemused, unbalanced, insane

demolish *v.* destroy, wreck, devastate, obliterate

demolition *n.* extermination, annihilation, wrecking, destruction, explosion

demonstrate *v.* **PROVE:** show, confirm; **ILLUSTRATE:** exhibit, manifest, parade, display

demonstration *n.* **EXHIBITION:** showing, presentation, display; **RALLY:** march, sit–in, protest

demoralize *v.* dishearten, confuse, weaken, unman, enfeeble, discourage

demure *adj.* modest, reserved

denial *n.* refusal, repudiation, rejection, refutation

denounce *v.* condemn, accuse, charge, blame, revile, reproach, rebuke, scold, reprimand

dense *adj.* **COMPACT:** thick, opaque, solid, impenetrable; **SLOW–WITTED:** stupid, dull, ignorant

deny *v.* contradict, disagree, disavow, disclaim, repudiate, controvert, renounce

depart *v.* leave, go, quit, withdraw

departure *n.* embarkation, evacuation, exodus, exit
dependable *adj.* trustworthy, steady, sure, reliable
dependent *adj.* **HELPLESS:** poor, immature, clinging, weak; **CONTINGENT:** conditional
depict *v.* represent, picture,
depletion *n.* exhaustion, consumption, deficiency
deplorable *adj.* tragic, distressing
deport *v.* exile, expel, banish
deposit *v.* **PLACE:** drop, put, install, leave; **PRESENT FOR SAFEKEEPING:** invest, store, bank, entrust
depreciate *v.* deteriorate, lessen, worsen, decrease
depreciation *n.* harm, reduction, shrinkage, loss
depress *v.* **PRESS DOWN:** squash, flatten; **DISMAY:** dampen, sadden, deject, oppress, discourage
depressed *adj.* discouraged, disheartened, sad
deprive *v.* strip, despoil, divest, seize
deputy *n.* assistant, lieutenant, aide, delegate
deranged *adj.*; disturbed, demented, crazy, insane
derelict *adj.* abandoned, negligent, delinquent
deride *v.* mock, ridicule, scorn, jeer
derivation *n.* root, source, beginning, origin
derive *v.* obtain, determine, conclude, assume
derivative *adj.* borrowed, learned
derogatory *adj.* disparaging, belittling, faultfinding, detracting, critical, sarcastic
descend *v.* plunge, sink, dip, plummet, tumble
descendants *n.* offspring, kin, children, family
descent *n.* **MOTION:** drop, sinking, reduction, tumble, decline, fall; **INCLINE:** declivity, slide, hill, inclination; **RELATIONSHIP:** extraction, origin, lineage, family
describe *v.* recount, portray, depict, picture, specify, illustrate, name, define, explain

description *n.* story, portrayal, account, characterization, brief, summary, depiction
descriptive *adj.* lifelike, vivid, picturesque, eloquent
desert *n.* waste, wastelands, wilderness
desert *v.* abandon, defect, leave
deserter *n.* runaway, fugitive, defector, traitor
deserve *v.* merit, earn, rate
deserved *adj.* justified, merited, rightful, fitting, just
deserving *adj.* needy; rightful, fitting, worthy
design *n.* plan, schematic, rendering, pattern, layout, diagram, drawing, sketch, blueprint, plan
design *v.* invent, devise, outline, sketch, plan
designate *v.* specify, appoint, indicate, name, choose
designation *n.* classification, appellation, class, name
designer *n.* planner, draftsman, modeler, architect, artist, sculptor
desire *n.* aspiration, longing, craving, lust, wish, mania, hunger, yearning, hankering, itch, yen, passion
desire *v.* want, wish, covet, crave, need
desist *v.* cease, abstain
desolate *adj.* forsaken, dreary, deserted, uninhabited, abandoned, isolated, disconsolate, forlorn,
desolation *n.* barrenness, devastation
despair *n.* hopelessness, depression, discouragement, desperation, gloom
despairing *adj.* despondent, miserable, sad
desperate *adj.* HOPELESS: despairing, downcast; RECKLESS: foolhardy, incautious, wild, careless, rash
despicable *adj.* detestable, contemptible, abject, base
despise *v.* disdain, scorn, condemn, hate
despondent *adj.* dejected, discouraged, depressed
destiny *n.* fate, future, fortune, doom

destitute

destitute *adj.* lacking, impoverished, poverty–stricken, penniless, poor

destroy *v.* ruin, demolish, raze, eradicate, annihilate, obliterate, extinguish, finish

destruction *n.* **DEMOLITION:** ruin, annihilation, eradication, liquidation, extermination, elimination; **REMAINS:** ashes, wreck, remnant, ruins

destructive *adj.* **HARMFUL:** hurtful, injurious, troublesome; **DEADLY:** fatal, ruinous, devastating, vicious

detach *v.* disconnect, remove, separate, divide

detached *adj.* **ALOOF:** impartial, disinterested, apathetic, uninvolved, unconcerned, indifferent; **CUT OFF:** separated, loosened, divided, disjoined

detail *n.* particular, trait, feature, aspect, minutia

detail *v.* itemize, catalogue, analyze, describe

detain *v.* delay, hold, keep, inhibit, restrain

detect *v.* distinguish, recognize, identify, discover

detection *n.* exposure, disclosure, discovery

detention *n.* custody, quarantine, arrest, confinement, restraint

deter *v.* discourage, caution, dissuade, prevent, warn

deteriorate *v.* worsen, depreciate, lessen, degenerate

determination *n.* resolution, persistence, obstinacy, resolve, conviction, firmness, purpose

determine *v.* **DEFINE:** circumscribe, delimit, restrict; **ASCERTAIN:** learn, discover; **RESOLVE:** settle, conclude, decide

detest *v.* dislike, loathe, abhor, despise, hate

detestable *adj.* disgusting, abhorrent, despicable

detract *v.* diminish, lessen, depreciate, discredit

detriment *n.* damage, loss

devastate *v.* ravage, sack, pillage, destroy

74

devastation *n.* destruction, defoliation, waste

develop *v.* **IMPROVE:** enlarge, expand, extend, promote, cultivate, intensify; **GROW:** mature, evolve; **REVEAL:** unfold, disclose, unravel, uncover, explain

deviate *v.* deflect, digress, wander, stray, differ

deviation *n.* change, alteration, difference, variation

device *n.* **APPARATUS:** instrument, contrivance, mechanism, appliance, contraption, implement, utensil, gadget; **METHOD:** artifice, scheme, design, dodge, trick, ruse, plan, technique

devious *adj.* deceptive, crafty, indirect, foxy, insidious, shrewd, dishonest

devoid *adj.* lacking, empty

devote *v.* assign, apply, consecrate, bless, dedicate

devotion *n.* affection, allegiance, consecration, faithfulness, fidelity, loyalty, worship

devour *v.* eat, gulp, swallow, gorge, absorb

devout *adj.* religious, sincere, devoted, pious, reverent, faithful, holy

diabolical *adj.* fiendish, wicked

diagnosis *n.* analysis, determination, investigation, summary

diagram *n.* sketch, drawing, layout, picture, description, design, plan

dialect *n.* idiom, jargon, cant, vernacular, patois

dialogue *n.* conversation, talk, exchange, remarks

diaphanous *adj.* fine, transparent, thin, airy

diary *n.* journal, chronicle, log, record

diatribe *n.* tirade, denunciation

dicker *v.* barter, bargain, trade, argue

dictator *n.* ruler, autocrat, despot, tyrant, oppressor

diction *n.* enunciation, articulation, vocabulary

die

die *v.* **EXPIRE:** perish, succumb, croak; **DECLINE:** fade, ebb, wither, decay, weaken, vanish

die–hard *n.* zealot, reactionary, extremist

diet *v.* reduce, fast, starve, abstain

differ *v.* vary, diverge, contrast, conflict, contrast

difference *n.* **VARIANCE:** deviation, departure, exception; **DISAGREEMENT:** divergence, opposition, dissimilarity, diversity, departure, differentiation, contrast

different *adj.* **UNLIKE:** diverse, separate, miscellaneous, assorted, various; **UNUSUAL:** unconventional, strange, startling

difficult *adj.* **LABORIOUS:** strenuous, exacting, arduous, labored, demanding, onerous, challenging, exacting, formidable; **INTRICATE:** involved, perplexing, puzzling, mystifying, bewildering, profound, complicated, deep, ambiguous, obscure

difficulty *n.* **OBSTACLE:** obstruction, impediment, misfortune, distress, barricade, hindrance, barrier; **DISTURBANCE:** trouble, distress, anxiety, frustration

diffident *adj.* shy, insecure

diffuse *v.* spread, disperse

digest *v.* **CONDENSE:** summarize, recap; **EAT:** absorb, consume; **UNDERSTAND:** learn, study

digit *n.* finger, toe, unit, symbol, numeral, number

dignify *v.* honor, exalt, elevate, praise

dignity *n.* poise, bearing, air, stateliness, splendor, majesty, class, pride

digress *v.* stray, deviate

dilemma *n.* predicament, quandary, difficulty

dilettante *n.* dabbler, trifler

diligence *n.* earnestness, perseverance, industry, vigor, carefulness, intensity, attention, care

diligent *adj.* industrious, painstaking
dilute *v.* thin, weaken, add, mix, reduce
diminish *v.* reduce, lessen, depreciate, decrease
dingy *adj.* drab, dirty, grimy, muddy, soiled
diplomacy *n.* finesse, tact, artfulness, skill, discretion
diplomat *n.* ambassador, consul, minister, legate, emissary, envoy, agent, representative, statesman
diplomatic *adj.* tactful, gracious, calculating, conciliatory, conniving, subtle, discreet, politic, polite
dire *adj.* serious, desperate, dreadful, terrible, horrible, frightful
direct *adj.* IMMEDIATE: prompt, succeeding, resultant; SINCERE: frank, straightforward, outspoken, candid; STRAIGHT: undeviating, unswerving
direct *v.* POINT OUT: guide, conduct, show, lead; COMMAND: instruct, order, govern, manage, charge; AIM: sight, train, level
direction *n.* TENDENCY: bias, bent, proclivity, inclination; SUPERVISION: management, superintendence, control, administration; POSITION: objective, bearing
directly *adv.* instantly, at once, quickly, immediately
directory *n.* reference, list, register, record, roster
disability *n.* feebleness, incapacity, injury, weakness
disable *v.* incapacitate, cripple, impair, damage
disadvantage *n.* obstacle, restraint, handicap, inconvenience, drawback, weakness
disagree *v.* DIFFER: dissent, object, oppose, quarrel; EFFECT: nauseate, bother
disagreeable *adj.* obnoxious, offensive, irritable, rude, bothersome, upsetting, disturbing, offensive
disagreement *n.* DISCORD: contention, strife, conflict, controversy, opposition, hostility, clash, quarrel;

INCONSISTENCY: discrepancy, dissimilarity, disparity

disappear *v.* fade, die, escape, evaporate, vanish

disappearance *n.* departure, desertion, escape, exodus, disintegration, evaporation

disappoint *v.* dissatisfy, disillusion, frustrate, miscarry, thwart, foil, baffle

disapprove *v.* condemn, chastise, reprove, denounce

disarray *n.* confusion, disorder

disaster *n.* calamity, mishap, debacle, misadventure, defeat, failure, tragedy, cataclysm, catastrophe

disastrous *adj.* calamitous, ruinous, harmful

disburse *v.* pay, expend, use, contribute, spend

discard *v.* reject, expel, dispossess, relinquish

discerning *adj.* discriminating, perceptive, penetrating, discreet

discharge *v.* **UNLOAD:** remove, unpack, empty; **RELEASE:** liberate, free, fire

discipline *v.* **TRAIN:** control; **PUNISH:** chastise, correct

disclose *v.* reveal, confess, publish

disclosure *n.* exposé. confession, admission

discomfort *n.* annoyance, uneasiness, trouble, displeasure, embarrassment

disconcert *v.* confuse, embarrass

disconnect *v.* detach, separate, disengage, cut, divide

disconsolate *adj.* dejected, gloomy, inconsolable,

discontinue *v.* stop, end, finish, close, cease

discord *n.* conflict, strife, contention, disagreement

discount *v.* **REBATE:** allow, deduct, lower, reduce; **MINIMIZE:** reject, diminish, discredit, decrease

discourage *v.* dissuade, repress, scare, dampen, daunt, demoralize, depress, frighten

discourse *v.* converse, write, speak

discourteous *adj.* impolite, rude, boorish, crude
discourtesy *n.* impudence, vulgarity, rudeness
discover *v.* invent, ascertain, detect, recognize, determine, observe, uncover, find, learn
discovery *n.* detection, disclosure, determination
discredit *v.* question, disbelieve, distrust, doubt
discreet *adj.* prudent, cautious, discerning, reserved, wary, watchful, circumspect, politic, diplomatic
discrepancy *n.* variance, inconsistency
discrete *adj.* unconnected, distinctive
discretion *n.* caution, wariness, prudence, tact
discriminate *v.* differentiate, separate, distinguish
discrimination *n.* PERCEPTION: acuteness, judgment; PARTIALITY: unfairness, bias, bigotry, prejudice
discuss *v.* talk, argue, debate, dispute, confer, reason
discussion *n.* conversation, exchange, contention, dialogue, dispute
disease *n.* sickness, malady, ailment, illness, infirmity
disfavor *n.* disapproval, displeasure, disappointment
disfigure *v.* deface, mar, mutilate, damage, hurt
disgrace *v.* dishonor, debase, shame, degrade, discredit, humble, stigmatize
disgraceful *adj.* dishonorable, disreputable, shocking, offensive, shameful
disguise *n.* mask, costume, masquerade, façade
disguise *v.* alter, conceal, cloak, cover, obscure
disgust *v.* offend, repel, revolt, nauseate, sicken, shock, upset, disturb
disgusting *adj.* repugnant, revolting, sickening, offensive
disheveled *adj.* untidy, rumpled
dishonest *adj.* deceitful, backbiting, treacherous,

sneaky, deceptive, underhanded, unscrupulous, disreputable, mean, low, contemptible, false

dishonor *n.* shame, ignominy, abasement, disgrace

disillusion *v.* disenchant, disappoint

disinclined *adj.* hesitant, reluctant

disinfect *v.* sanitize, sterilize, purify, fumigate, clean

disintegrate *v.* separate, disperse, crumble, dissolve

disinterested *adj.* impartial, indifferent, unconcerned

disjointed *adj.* disconnected, unattached, separated; incoherent, rambling

dislike *v.* detest, deplore, abhor, hate, abominate, loathe, despise, scorn

dislodge *v.* eject, evict, uproot, oust, remove

disloyalty *n.* treason, betrayal, dishonesty

dismal *adj.* dreary, bleak, gloomy, melancholy, desolate, morbid, ghastly, gruesome, cheerless, dusky, dingy, murky, bleak, somber, creepy, spooky

dismantle *v.* disassemble, undo, demolish, level, ruin, raze, fell, destroy

dismay *n.* terror, dread, anxiety, fear

dismiss *v.* reject, repudiate, disperse, expel, abolish, dispossess, exile, expatriate, banish, deport

dismissal *n.* expulsion, removal

disobedience *n.* insubordination, defiance, insurgence, mutiny, revolt, noncompliance, rebellion

disobedient *adj.* insubordinate, refractory, defiant, rebellious, unruly

disobey *v.* balk, decline, refuse, disregard, defy

disorder *n.* confusion, disarray, turmoil, chaos, anarchy, rebellion, trouble

disorder *v.* disarrange, clutter, scatter, disorganize

disorderly *adj.* CONFUSED: jumbled, scattered, messy,

untidy, cluttered, unkempt, disorganized; **UNRULY:** intemperate, drunk, rowdy

disorganize *v.* disperse, scatter, litter, disrupt

disorient, disorientate *v.* confuse, bewilder

disown *v.* disinherit, repudiate, deny

disparage *v.* discredit, belittle

disparate *adj.* dissimilar, diversified

dispatch *v.* **SEND:** transmit, express, forward; **END:** finish, conclude, kill

dispel *v.* disperse, dissipate, distribute, scatter

dispensable *adj.* unnecessary, trivial, useless

dispense *v.* distribute, apportion, assign, allocate

disperse *v.* scatter, separate, disband

displace *v.* **REMOVE:** transpose, dislodge; **MISLAY:** misplace, disarrange, lose

display *n.* exhibition, exhibit, presentation, demonstration, performance, parade, pageant

display *v.* show, exhibit, uncover, present, unveil

displease *v.* dissatisfy, annoy, vex, provoke, anger

displeasure *n.* disapproval, annoyance, resentment, anger

disposed *adj.* prone, inclined, apt, likely

disposition *n.* **ARRANGEMENT:** distribution, organization, plan; **TEMPERAMENT:** character, temper, mood

disproportionate *adj.* uneven, irregular

disprove *v.* refute, invalidate, deny

disputable *adj.* doubtful, dubious, questionable

dispute *n.* conflict, squabble, disturbance, feud

dispute *v.* argue, debate, contradict, quarrel, discuss

disqualify *v.* preclude, disentitle, disbar

disregard *v.* ignore, neglect

disreputable *adj.* offensive, shameful

disrespect

disrespect *n.* discourtesy, insolence, irreverence
disrespectful *adj.* discourteous, impolite, rude
disrupt *v.* intrude, obstruct, break, interrupt
disruption *n.* disturbance, agitation, confusion
dissatisfaction *n.* displeasure, disapproval, objection
disseminate *v.* scatter, spread, sow, propagate, broadcast, distribute
dissension *n.* disagreement, difference, dispute
dissent *v.* disagree, refuse, contradict, differ, oppose
disservice *n.* wrong, injury, injustice, insult
dissident *adj.* hostile, opposed
dissipated *adj.* scattered, dispersed, strewn, disseminated, wasted, squandered, spent, depleted
dissolution *n.* dissolving, termination
dissolve *v.* liquefy, evaporate, disintegrate: disappear
distant *adj.* **RESERVED:** aloof; **AFAR:** abroad, removed
distasteful *adj.* unpleasant, disagreeable, repugnant
distend *v.* inflate, stretch, enlarge, widen, distort
distinct *adj.* **PERCEPTIBLE:** clear, sharp, enunciated, audible lucid, plain, obvious, clear, definite; **DISCRETE:** separate, disunited
distinction *n.* **DEFINITION:** separation, difference; **ACHIEVEMENT:** repute, renown, prominence, fame
distinctive *adj.* unique, peculiar, distinguishing, characteristic
distinguish *v.* **DISCERN:** detect, notice, discover; **HONOR:** celebrate, acknowledge, admire, praise
distinguished *n.* **MARKED:** characterized, labeled, identified, unique, conspicuous, separated; **NOTABLE:** celebrated, eminent, illustrious, venerable, renowned, prominent, reputable, famous
distort *v.* alter, pervert, misinterpret, misconstrue

distortion *n.* **DEFORMITY:** twist, malformation, mutilation, contortion, **MISREPRESENTATION:** perversion, lie
distract *v.* detract, amuse, entertain, mislead
distracted *adj.* distraught, frenzied, troubled
distraction *n.* **CONFUSION:** perplexity, abstraction, complication, confusion; **DIVERSION:** amusement, pastime, preoccupation, entertainment, game
distraught *adj.* troubled, distressed
distress *n.* pain, anxiety, worry, sorrow, wretchedness, suffering, ordeal, anguish, grief, trouble
distress *v.* irritate, disturb, upset, bother
distribute *v.* disburse, dispense, issue, allocate
distributor *n.* wholesaler, jobber, merchant
district *n.* area, neighborhood, community, vicinity
distrust *v.* mistrust, suspect, disbelieve, doubt
distrustful *adj.* doubting, fearful, suspicious
disturb *v.* trouble, worry, perplex, startle, alarm, arouse, depress, distress, provoke, irritate, harass
diverge *v.* radiate, veer, swerve, deviate
divers *adj.* several, varied
diverse *adj.* dissimilar, assorted, different, distinct
diversify *v.* vary, expand, alter, change, increase
diversion *n.* entertainment, amusement, recreation, play, sport
divert *v.* deflect, redirect, avert, turn; distract, disturb
dividend *n.* bonus, profit, share
divine *adj.* godlike, sacred, hallowed, consecrated, anointed, sanctified, ordained, revered, venerated
division *n.* **PARTITION:** section, compartment, parcel, branch; **RIFT:** disagreement, difficulty, dispute
divulge *v.* reveal, disclose, impart, confess, expose
do *v.* **EXECUTE:** complete, fulfill, obey, perform, act,

work, labor, produce, create, accomplish, succeed, perform; **SUFFICE:** serve, satisfy

docile *adj.* submissive, meek, mild, tractable, pliant, willing, obliging, manageable, tame, obedient

doctor *n.* physician, surgeon, intern, veterinarian, chiropractor, homeopath, osteopath, healer, shaman, quack, anesthetist, dentist, pediatrician, gynecologist, oculist, obstetrician, psychiatrist, psychoanalyst, orthopedist, neurologist, cardiologist, pathologist, dermatologist, endocrinologist, opthamologist, urologist, hematologist

doctor *v.* treat, attend, administer

doctrine *n.* policy, conviction, tradition, canon

document *n.* record, paper, diary, report

documentary *n.* book, movie, report

dogmatic *adj.* authoritarian, dictatorial, stubborn, intolerant, opinionated, domineering, tyrannical

dolt *n.* simpleton, nitwit, blockhead, fool

domain *n.* territory, dominion, field, specialty, area

domestic *adj.* indigenous, native, homemade

domesticate *v.* control, adapt, tame, breed, housebreak, teach, train

domicile *n.* residence, home

dominant *adj.* commanding, authoritative, assertive, aggressive, powerful

dominate *v.* control, rule, manage, subjugate, govern

domineering *adj.* assertive, overbearing, despotic, imperious, oppressive

dominion *n.* sovereignty, region, district, state, nation

donate *v.* contribute, grant, bestow, bequeath, distribute, give, provide

donation *n.* contribution, offering, present, gift

donor *n.* benefactor, contributor, patron, philanthropist, giver

dote *v.* adore, pet, admire, love

doubt *n.* uncertainty, skepticism, mistrust, suspicion, misgiving, apprehension

doubt *v.* wonder, question

doubtful *adj.* UNCERTAIN: dubious, questioning, unsure, wavering, hesitating, unresolved, suspicious; IMPROBABLE: questionable, unconvincing

doubtless *adj.* positively, certainly, unquestionably, surely

douse *v.* immerse, wet, submerge, drench, soak

dowdy *adj.* shabby, untidy, slovenly, plain

doze *v.* sleep, nap, drowse, slumber

drab *adj.* dismal, dingy, colorless, dreary, dull

draft *n.* SKETCH: layout, plans, blueprint, design; CURRENT: breeze, gust, puff, wind; SELECTION: conscription, induction

drag *n.* IMPEDANCE: restraint, hindrance, burden, impediment, barrier; TIRESOME: bother, annoyance, hang–up, nuisance

drag *v.* PULL: haul, move, transport, draw; LAG: straggle, dawdle, loiter, pause; SLOW: crawl, delay

drain *n.* duct, channel, sewer, conduit, pipe

drain *v.* EXHAUST: weary, tire, spend, weaken; EMPTY: exude, trickle, ooze, dry, flow

drama *n.* play, production, dramatization, show, melodrama, tragicomedy, opera, operetta, mystery

dramatic *adj.* tense, climactic, moving, exciting

dramatist *n.* playwright, author, writer

dramatize *v.* enact, perform, exaggerate

drastic *adj.* extreme, extravagant, exorbitant, radical

draw *v.* **PULL:** drag, attract, lug, tow, haul; **PORTRAY:** sketch, outline, trace, depict

drawback *n.* disadvantage, shortcoming, hindrance

dread *n.* awe, horror, terror, fear

dreadful *adj.* unpleasant, hideous, fearful, shameful, frightful

dreary *adj.* bleak, dismal, dull. damp, raw, cold

dribble *v.* trickle, spout, squirt, drop

drift *n.* tendency, bent, trend, inclination, impulse, bias, leaning, disposition

drift *v.* wander, stray, gravitate, flow

drink *v.* swallow, gulp, sip, guzzle, imbibe

drive *n.* **RIDE:** trip, outing, airing, tour, excursion, jaunt, spin, journey; **PATH:** driveway, approach, avenue, boulevard, road; **FORCE:** energy, effort, enthusiasm, vigor, impulse

drive *v.* urge, impel, propel, compel, coerce, induce, force, press, stimulate, provoke, push

drop *n.* **SMALL AMOUNT:** speck, dash, dab, bit; **DECLINE:** fall, tumble, reduction, decrease, slump, lowering

drowsy *adj.* sleepy, sluggish, languid, indolent, lazy

drug *n.* pills, medicine, sedative, potion, essence, salts, powder, tonic, opiate, downers,

drug *v.* anesthetize, desensitize, dope, deaden

drunk *adj.* intoxicated, inebriated, befuddled, tipsy, smashed, tanked, soused, pickled, stewed, tight

dry *adj.* **ARID:** parched, desiccated, barren, dehydrated, drained; **BORING:** uninteresting, tedious, dull; **HUMOROUS:** sarcastic, cynical, biting, funny

dry *v.* evaporate, dehydrate, blot, sponge, scorch

dubious *adj.* **DOUBTFUL:** indecisive, perplexed, hesitant, uncertain, questionable; **VAGUE:** ambiguous,

indefinite, unclear, obscure
due *adj.* SCHEDULED: expected; FITTING: deserved; COLLECTABLE: unsatisfied, outstanding, unpaid
dull *adj.* COLORLESS: gloomy, somber, drab, dismal, dark, dingy, dusky, plain, gray, flat; UNINTELLIGENT: slow, retarded, witless, stupid; UNINTERESTING: prosaic, hackneyed, monotonous, humdrum, tedious, dreary, dismal, insipid, boring, ordinary, uninspiring, tame, routine, repetitious
duly *adv.* properly, rightfully, decorously, justly
dumb *adj.* simple–minded, dull, stupid
dumfound *v.* astonish, shock
dungeon *n.* cell, vault
duplicity *n.* deception
durability *n.* stamina, persistence, endurance
durable *adj.* strong, form, enduring, permanent
duration *n.* interval, span, term
duress *n.* threat, coercion, compulsion, control, pressure, restraint
dusk *n.* gloom, twilight, dawn, night
dutiful *adj.* obedient, devoted, respectful, conscientious, faithful
duty *n.* obligation, liability, burden, responsibility
dwell *v.* reside, live, inhabit, stay, lodge, settle, remain, continue, occupy
dweller *n.* inhabitant, tenant, occupant, resident
dwelling *n.* house, establishment, lodging, home
dynamic *adj.* forceful, intense, energetic, compelling, vigorous, magnetic, electric, effective, influential, charismatic, active, powerful
dynasty *n.* succession, sovereignty
eager *adj.* impatient, anxious, keen, fervent, zealous

early

early *adj.*, *adv.* primitive; premature, preceding, un-expected, punctual

earn *v.* DESERVE: win, merit, gain; PAYMENT: obtain, attain, get, procure, realize, acquire, secure

earnest *adj.* serious, intense, important, ardent, zeal-ous, warm, enthusiastic

earthly *adj.* human, mortal, global, mundane

earthy *adj.* coarse, dull, crude, unrefined, natural

ease *n.* COMFORT: rest, peace, prosperity, leisure, calm, tranquillity; WITHOUT DIFFICULTY: snap, breeze, cinch, pushover

ease *v.* relieve, alleviate, allay, comfort, soothe, un-burden, release, soften, calm, pacify

easily *adv.* readily, effortlessly, smoothly

easy *adj.* UNTROUBLED: secure, prosperous, leisurely, calm, peaceful, tranquil, contented, carefree, un-hurried, relaxing; MANAGEABLE: simple, smooth, simple, pushover; LAX: lenient, indulgent, kind

eat *v.* DEVOUR: chew, swallow, feast, dine, gorge, feed; REDUCE: erode, corrode, waste, rust, spill

ebb *v.* decline, recede, subside, decrease

ebullient *adj.* exuberant enthusiastic

eccentric *adj.* unconventional, odd, queer, strange, unusual

eccentricity *n.* peculiarity, abnormality, idiosyncrasy

eclipse *v.* darken, diminish, obscure

economic *adj.* business, financial, commercial

economical *adj.* CAREFUL: thrifty, prudent, frugal, miserly, watchful, tight; INEXPENSIVE: cheap, reason-able, fair, moderate; EFFICIENT: practical, methodical

economist *n.* statistician, analyst, expert

economize *v.* husband, manage, stint, conserve,

scrimp, skimp

ecstasy *n.* joy, rapture, delight, happiness

ecumenical *adj.* general, universal,

edible *adj.* palatable, good, delicious, satisfying, savory, tasty, nutritious, digestible

edict *n.* decree, order

educate *v.* teach, train, inform, refine, tutor, instruct

education *n.* **LEARNING:** schooling, study, instruction, guidance, apprenticeship, tutelage, reading, indoctrination; **KNOWLEDGE:** learning, wisdom, scholarship

educational *adj.* enlightening, instructive, enriching, cultural

educator *n.* pedagogue, instructor, tutor, teacher

effect *n.* conclusion, consequence, outcome, result

effect *v.* produce, cause, make, begin

effective *adj.* efficient, serviceable, useful, adequate, productive, competent, practical

effectual *adj.* adequate, efficient, qualified, effective

effervescent *adj.* bubbly, lively, vivacious

efficiency *n.* productivity, capability, ability

efficient *adj.* competent, fitted, able, capable, qualified, skilled, adept, experienced, practical, productive, economical, effective, expedient, streamlined

effort *n.* attempt, undertaking, struggle, try, venture

effortless *adj.* simple, offhand, smooth, easy

effrontery *n.* boldness, insolence

egotism *n.* conceit, vanity, pride, self–love, arrogance, overconfidence, haughtiness

egotistical *adj.* conceited, vain, boastful, pompous, arrogant, insolent, affected, self–centered, blustering, proud, pretentious, overbearing

egregious *adj.* bad, outrageous

eject *v.* discard, reject, oust, evict

elaborate *adj.* **ORNAMENTED:** gaudy, decorated, showy, fussy, dressy, flowery, flashy, ornate; **DETAILED:** intricate, complicated, involved, complex

elect *v.* choose, name, select

elective *adj.* optional, voluntary, selective

elegance *n.* taste, cultivation, polish, splendor, beauty, gracefulness, magnificence, courtliness, charm, sophistication, style

elegant *adj.* ornate, polished, perfected, elaborate, adorned, embellished, artistic, rich

element *n.* substance, component, portion, particle, detail, part

elementary *adj.* primary, introductory, rudimentary, easy, fundamental, essential, basic

elevate *v.* **RAISE:** lift, hoist, heave, tilt; **PROMOTE:** advance, appoint, further

elevated *adj.* towering, tall, high, raised

eligibility *n.* fitness, acceptability, capability, ability

eligible *adj.* qualified, suitable, fit, usable

eliminate *v.* remove, reject, exclude, disqualify, oust, discard, dismiss, drop

elongate *v.* prolong, lengthen, extend, stretch

eloquence *n.* fluency, wit, wittiness, expressiveness, diction, articulation, delivery, poise

eloquent *adj.* vocal, articulate, outspoken, fluent

else *adj.* different, other, more

elude *v.* evade, escape, dodge, shun, avoid

elusive *adj.* fleeting, fugitive, temporary

embargo *n.* restriction, prohibition, impediment, restraint

embarrass *v.* distress, disconcert, chagrin, confound,

trouble, disturb, fluster, shame

embarrassment *n.* chagrin, mortification, discomfiture, humiliation, awkwardness

embezzle *v.* thieve, forge, pilfer, steal

embezzlement *n.* fraud, misappropriation, theft

embezzler *n.* thief, robber, defaulter, criminal

embrace *v.* hug, enfold, squeeze, grip

emerge *v.* rise, arrive, appear, form, evolve

emergency *n.* crisis, predicament, difficulty

emigrant *n.* exile, expatriate, colonist, migrant, pilgrim, refugee

emigrate *v.* migrate, immigrate, quit, leave

emigration *n.* departure, leaving, displacement, exodus, movement, migration, settling

eminence *n.* standing, prominence, distinction, fame

eminent *adj.* renowned, exalted, celebrated, prominent, dignified, distinguished

emissary *n.* intermediary, ambassador, consul, agent

emotion *n.* excitement, sentiment, passion

emotional *adj.* hysterical, demonstrative, ardent, enthusiastic, passionate, excitable, impulsive, impetuous, temperamental, irrational, sentimental, affectionate, neurotic, high–strung

emphatic *adj.* definite, assured, strong, determined, forceful, earnest, positive, dynamic

employ *v.* USE: operate, manipulate, apply; ENGAGE: contract, procure, hire

employer *n.* owner, manager, proprietor, director, executive, superintendent, supervisor, businessman

employment *n.* job, profession, vocation, business, trade, work

emulate *v.* imitate, equal, compete, follow

91

encompass *v.* include, encircle, gird, surround

encounter *n.* **MEETING:** interview, rendezvous, appointment; **VIOLENCE:** conflict, clash, collision, fight

encourage *v.* support, inspire, cheer, praise, fortify, help, aid, reassure, reinforce, back, strengthen

encouraging *adj.* bright, good, promising, hopeful

endeavor *n.* effort, undertaking

endeavor *v.* attempt, aim, try

endorse *v.* **SIGN:** countersign, underwrite, subscribe, notarize; **SUPPORT:** approve, sanction, acknowledge

endorsement *n.* support, sanction, permission

endurable *adj.* tolerable, supportable, bearable

endurance *n.* sufferance, fortitude, tolerance, perseverance, stamina

endure *v.* **CONTINUE:** sustain, prevail, stay, persist; **BEAR UP:** suffer, tolerate, allow, permit, withstand

engross *v.* absorb, busy, fill, occupy

enhance *v.* embellish, magnify, amplify, increase

enigma *n.* problem, riddle, parable, puzzle

enjoy *v.* relish, luxuriate, delight, like

enjoyable *adj.* agreeable, welcome, genial, pleasant

enjoyment *n.* satisfaction, gratification, diversion, entertainment, indulgence

enlighten *v.* inform, divulge, acquaint, teach, tell

enormous *adj.* monstrous, immense, huge, large

enterprise *n.* undertaking, endeavor, affair, business

entertain *v.* **AMUSE:** cheer, delight, beguile, charm, captivate, stimulate, satisfy, distract, indulge; **HOST:** receive, invite, welcome

entertainer *n.* performer, player, artist, actor

entertaining *adj.* diverting, amusing, engaging, enchanting, witty, clever, interesting, captivating, stimulating, absorbing

entertainment *n.* amusement, enjoyment, diversion

enthusiasm *n.* excitement, interest, fervor, ardor, eagerness, zeal

enthusiast *n.* ZEALOT: fanatic, fan, believer; FOLLOWER: partisan, supporter, participant

enthusiastic *adj.* interested, excited, exhilarated, eager, ardent, spirited, zestful, fervent

entrance *n.* access, entry, passage, approach, admittance, introduction, debut, enrollment

entrance *v.* delight, enchant

envelop *v.* encompass, contain, hide, surround, wrap

envelope *n.* pouch, pocket, container, wrapper

enviable *adj.* good, superior, excellent

envious *adj.* covetous, resentful, desiring, wishful, greedy, jealous

envy *v.* begrudge, covet, crave

episode *n.* event, happening, occurrence, event

equilibrium *n.* balance, stability

equip *v.* outfit, train, furnish, implement, provide

equipment *n.* tools, implements, utensils, apparatus, devices, tackle, machinery, fittings

equitable *adj.* fair, impartial, just, moral

equity *n.* FAIRNESS: impartiality; ASSETS: investment, money, property

equivalent *adj.* equal, corresponding, commensurate, comparable, similar

eradicate *v.* destroy, eliminate, exterminate

erase *v.* remove, delete, obliterate, cut, eradicate

erect *adj.* vertical, upright, perpendicular, straight

erect *v.* construct, fabricate, build

erection *n.* building, construction

erratic *adj.* **WANDERING:** rambling, roving; **STRANGE:** eccentric, queer, unusual; **VARIABLE:** deviating, inconsistent, unpredictable, irregular

erroneous *adj.* inaccurate, incorrect, untrue, false

erudite *adj.* scholarly, learned

erupt *v.* eruct, eject, emit, explode

eruption *n.* burst, outburst, flow, explosion

escape *n.* flight, retreat, evasion, avoidance

escape *v.* elude, avoid, flee, evade, disappear, vanish

escort *n.* guide, attendant, guard, companion

escort *v.* accompany, attend, date

espouse *v.* marry, advocate, adopt, uphold, support

essay *n.* dissertation, treatise, tract, writing

essence *n.* pith, core, kernel, gist, nature, basis, substance, nucleus, germ

essential *adj.* **BASIC:** fundamental, primary; **NECESSARY:** imperative, required, indispensable

establish *v.* **FOUND:** institute, organize, erect, build; **PROVE:** verify, authenticate, confirm; **SECURE:** fix, stabilize, fasten

establishment *n.* business, organization, company, corporation, enterprise

ethical *adj.* moral, humane, respectable, decent, honest, noble

ethics *n.* morality, mores, decency, integrity, honor

etiquette *n.* conduct, manners, behavior

euphoria *n.* relaxation, health, well–being, happiness

evade *v.* avoid, dodge, shun, elude, baffle, shift, conceal, deceive, veil, hide

evasion *n.* subterfuge, equivocation, lie, trick

evasive *adj.* vague, fugitive, shifty, sly

event *n.* occasion, incident, occurrence, happening,

affair, function, experience, situation

eventful *adj.* momentous, memorable, important

eventual *adj.* inevitable, ultimate, consequent

eventually *adv.* ultimately, finally

evolve *v.* unfold, emerge, develop, grow

exact *adj.* ACCURATE: precise, correct, perfect, definite; CLEAR: sharp, distinct

exacting *adj.* precise, careful, critical, difficult

exactness *n.* precision, scrupulousness, accuracy

exaggerate *v.* overstate, misrepresent, falsify, magnify, amplify, heighten, intensify, distort, stretch, overdo, elaborate, color, fabricate

exaggerated *adj.* overwrought, extravagant, melodramatic, distorted, pronounced

exaggeration *n.* misrepresentation, elaboration

examination *n.* SCRUTINY: inspection, analysis, study; TEST: review, questionnaire, quiz, exam, midterm

examine *v.* INSPECT: analyze, scrutinize, explore, probe; TEST: question, interrogate

exasperate *v.* annoy, irritate

exceed *v.* excel, outdo

exceedingly *adv.* greatly, remarkable, very

excel *v.* surpass, transcend, exceed

excellence *n.* superiority, distinction, perfection

excellent *adj.* outstanding, exceptional, first-class, choice, select, exquisite, high-grade

excess *n.* ABUNDANCE: profusion, surplus; OVERINDULGENCE: prodigality, dissipation, intemperance, greed, waste

excessive *adj.* immoderate, extravagant, exorbitant, extreme

excitable *adj.* sensitive, high-strung, nervous

excite *v.* provoke, stimulate, inflame, arouse, stir, provoke, incite

excitement *n.* disturbance, tumult, turmoil, stir, agitation, stimulation, commotion, fuss

exclaim *v.* shout, call, yell

exclamation *n.* yell, clamor, cry

exclude *v.* except, reject, ban, bar

exclusion *n.* prohibition, repudiation, separation, eviction, expulsion

execute *v.* perform, act, do, effect

exemplify *v.* illustrate, represent

exempt *adj.* privileged, excused, unrestricted

exemption *n.* exception, immunity, privilege

exhaust *v.* debilitate, tire, weaken, weary; deplete, use

exhaustion *n.* weariness, fatigue, depletion

exhilaration *n.* elation, excitement

exhort *v.* entreat, beg

exist *v.* live, survive, be, endure

existence *n.* being, actuality, reality, presence

exorbitant *adj.* excessive, extravagant, wasteful

exotic *adj.* FOREIGN: imported, extrinsic; PECULIAR: strange, different, fascinating, unusual

expand *v.* extend, augment, dilate, grow

expanse *n.* extent, reach, area, space, span, spread, scope, range

expansion *n.* enlargement, augmentation, extension, increase

expect *v.* ANTICIPATE: await, hope; REQUIRE: demand, exact; ASSUME: presume, suppose, suspect

expectancy *n.* hope, prospect, likelihood, anticipation

expectant *adj.* hopeful, awaiting, anticipating, eager

expedient *adj.* convenient, profitable, useful, practical

expedite *v.* speed, quicken

expel *v.* **EJECT:** dislodge, evict; **DISMISS:** suspend, discharge, oust

expenditure *n.* outgo, payment, expense

experience *n.* background, skill, knowledge, practice, maturity, judgment, know-how

experience *v.* undergo, feel, endure

expert *adj.* skillful, practiced, proficient, able

expert *n.* graduate, master, specialist

explain *v.* interpret, elucidate, illustrate, clarify, illuminate, expound, teach, demonstrate, define

explainable *adj.* explicable, accountable, intelligible, understandable

explanation *n.* account, justification, analysis, commentary, brief, breakdown, proof

expletive *n.* exclamation

explicit *adj.* clear, express, sure, plain, definite, understandable

exploit *n.* deed, venture, escapade, achievement

exploit *v.* utilize, employ, use

exploration *n.* investigation, research, search

explore *v.* examine, search, hunt, seek

explorer *n.* adventurer, traveler, pioneer, voyager, seafarer, mountaineer, scientist, navigator

explosion *n.* detonation, blast, burst, discharge

explosive *adj.* stormy, fiery, forceful, raging, violent, uncontrollable, frenzied, savage

expose *v.* **UNCOVER:** disclose, reveal, unmask, unfold; **ENDANGER:** imperil

exposition *n.* **MAKING CLEAR:** elucidation, delineation, explication, explanation; **EXHIBITION:** exhibit, showing, performance, display

exposure *n.* disclosure, betrayal, display, publication, unveiling

express *v.* declare, tell, signify, utter

expression *n.* appearance, cast, character, looks, grimace, smile, smirk, mug, sneer, pout, grin

expressive *adj.* eloquent, demonstrative, dramatic, stirring, articulate, spirited, lively, stimulating

expulsion *n.* ejection, suspension, purge, removal

exquisite *adj.* fine, scrupulous, precise, dainty

extemporaneous *adj.* spontaneous, impromptu

extend *v.* enlarge, lengthen, increase, reach, continue, spread

extension *n.* section, branch, addition

extensive *adj.* wide, broad, great

extent *n.* SIZE: span, space, area, expanse, bulk; DEGREE: scope, reach, range, magnitude, intensity

exterior *adj.* outer, outlying, outermost, outside

exterminate *v.* annihilate, eradicate, abolish, destroy

extinction *n.* extermination, destruction

extinguish *v.* smother, choke, quench, douse, stifle

extort *v.* extract, wrench, force, steal

extortion *n.* fraud, blackmail, theft

extra *adj.* additional, other, spare, reserve, supplemental, auxiliary, added, more

extract *v.* evoke, derive, secure, obtain

extract *n.* distillation, infusion, concentration, essence

extraneous *adj.* foreign; incidental

extraordinary *adj.* unusual, remarkable, curious, amazing

extravagance *n.* excess, lavishness, improvidence, waste

extravagant *adj.* lavish, prodigal, immoderate, wasteful

extreme *adj.* outermost, utmost, immoderate, excessive, outrageous, preposterous, exaggerated

extremist *n.* zealot, fanatic, die–hard, radical

exuberance *n.* fervor, eagerness, exhilaration, zeal

exuberant *adj.* ardent, vivacious, passionate, zealous

eye *n.* APPRECIATION: perception, taste, discrimination; CENTER: focus, core, heart, kernel, nub

eyesore *n.* distortion, deformity, ugliness

eyewitness *n.* onlooker, passer–by, observer

fable *n.* story, allegory, tale, parable

fabric *n.* cloth, textile, stuff, material, goods

fabricate *v.* PRODUCE: construct, erect, make, form, build, manufacture, devise; LIE: misrepresent, contrive, prevaricate

fabulous *adj.* fictitious, remarkable, amazing, immense, unusual

façade *n.* face, appearance, look, front

face *n.* VISAGE:, countenance, appearance, features, silhouette, profile; SURFACE: front, finish; PRESTIGE: status, standing, reputation

face *v.* CONFRONT: defy, meet, challenge, encounter, endure, suffer, bear; REFINISH: front, redecorate, cover, paint

facet *n.* surface, aspect, face, side, plane

facetious *adj.* humorous, whimsical, ridiculous, funny

facile *adj.* easy, simple, obvious, apparent, fluent

facilitate *v.* promote, aid, simplify, help

facility *n.* EQUIPMENT: material, tools, plant, buildings; AGENCY: department, bureau, company, office

facsimile *n.* copy, duplicate, reproduction, mirror

fact *n.* **CERTAINTY:** truth, actuality, reality, evidence, **EVENT:** action, deed, happening, occurrence, manifestation, experience, act, episode, incident

faction *n.* party, clique, gang, crew, wing, block, lobby, sect, cell

factious *adj.* turbulent, contentious

factor *n.* agent, cause, part, portion, constituent, determinant

factory *n.* manufactory, plant, shop, industry, mill, foundry, forge

factual *adj.* exact, specific, descriptive, accurate

faculty *n.* **ABILITY:** aptitude, peculiarity, strength, forte; **TEACHERS:** instructors, mentors, professors, tutors, lecturers, advisers, scholars, fellows

fad *n.* fancy, style, craze, fashion, eccentricity, innovation, vogue, fashion

fade *v.* **PALE:** bleach, blanch, dim, vanish; **DIMINISH:** hush, quiet, sink, decrease

fail *v.* miss, falter, flounder, fizzle, flop, lessen, worsen, sink, decrease

failure *n.* **DEFAULT:** fiasco, bankruptcy, miscarriage, breakdown, stoppage, collapse, downfall, flop, washout; **UNSUCCESSFUL PERSON:** incompetent, underachiever, dropout, dud

faint *adj.* **FALTERING:** shaky, dizzy, weak, **VAGUE:** thin, hazy, indistinct, dull; **SUBDUED:** low, soft, quiet, muffled, hushed

faint *v.* swoon, drop, collapse, succumb

fair *adj.* **JUST:** forthright, impartial, scrupulous, honest, decent, honorable, righteous, reasonable, even-handed, principled, trustworthy; **AVERAGE:** ordinary, mediocre, commonplace; **PLEASANT:** clear, sunny, bright, calm, placid, tranquil, favorable, balmy, mild

fair *n.* exposition, carnival, bazaar, festival, market

fairly *adv.* **HONESTLY:** reasonably, honorably, justly; **SOMEWHAT:** moderately, reasonably, adequately

fairy *n.* spirit, sprite, elf, nymph, pixy

faith *n.* **TRUST:** confidence, credence, assurance, acceptance, conviction, sureness, reliance; **FORMAL BELIEF:** creed, doctrine, dogma, tenet, revelation, credo, gospel, canon, theology

faithful *adj.* reliable, dependable, incorruptible, honest, honorable, scrupulous, firm, sure, unswerving, conscientious, steadfast

fake *adj.* pretended, fraudulent, bogus, false

fake *n.* counterfeit, copy, imitation, fraud, fabrication, forgery; cheat, charlatan

fake *v.* feign, simulate, disguise, pretend

fall *v.* **DROP:** decline, sink, topple, settle, droop, stumble, trip, plunge, descend, totter, recede, ebb, diminish, flop; **SUBMIT:** yield, surrender, succumb, resign, capitulate

fallacy *n.* inconsistency, mistake, ambiguity, paradox, miscalculation, quirk, flaw, heresy, error

fallibility *n.* imperfection, misjudgment, frailty, uncertainty

fallible *adj.* frail, imperfect, erring, unreliable, questionable, wrong

fallow *adj.* unplowed, unplanted, unproductive

false *adj.* **UNFAITHFUL:** treacherous, disloyal, underhanded, deceitful, unscrupulous, untrustworthy; **SPURIOUS:** fanciful, untruthful, deceptive, fallacious, misleading, erroneous, inaccurate, fraudulent;

falsehood

COUNTERFEIT: fabricated, bogus, forged, faked, contrived, phony

falsehood *n.* deception, prevarication, story, lie

falsify *v.* misrepresent, adulterate, counterfeit, deceive, lie, forge

falter *v.* waver, fluctuate, be undecided, hesitate

fame *n.* renown, glory, distinction, eminence, esteem, name, note, greatness, rank, position, standing, pre-eminence, regard, popularity

familiar *adj.* everyday, customary, accustomed, common, ordinary, informal, commonplace

familiarity *n.* friendliness, acquaintanceship, fellowship, friendship; comprehension, awareness, experience

familiarize *v.* acquaint, accustom

family *n.* household, relatives, clan, relations, tribe, dynasty, descendants, forbears, heirs, genealogy, descent, parentage, extraction, kinship, lineage

famine *n.* starvation, want, misery, hunger

famished *a.* starving, hungering, starved, hungry

famous *adj.* known, renowned, eminent, foremost, famed, celebrated, noted, prominent, reputable, renowned, notable, notorious

fan *n.* supporter, follower, amateur, devotee

fanatical *adj.* enthusiastic, obsessed, passionate, devoted, zealous

fanciful *adj.* unreal, incredible, whimsical, fantastic

fancy *adj.* elaborate, ornamental, intricate, elegant, embellished, rich, adorned, ostentatious, gaudy, showy, baroque, lavish, ornate

fancy *n.* **WHIMSY:** imagination, caprice, levity, humor; **WHIM:** notion, impulse, idea; **INCLINATION:** wishes, will, preference, desire

fantastic *adj.* fanciful, whimsical, capricious, strange, odd, queer, quaint, peculiar, outlandish, wonderful, exotic, ludicrous, ridiculous, preposterous, grotesque, absurd

fantasy *n.* illusion, flight, figment, fiction

far *adj.* distant, faraway, remote

farce *n.* satire, travesty, burlesque

fare *n.* FOOD: menu, rations, meals; FEE: charge, passage, passage, tariff, expense

fare *v.* experience, prosper, happen

farewell *n.* good–bye, valediction, parting, departure

farfetched *adj.* strained, unbelievable, fantastic

farm *v.* cultivate, till, garden, ranch, homestead

farmer *n.* planter, grower, stockman, agriculturist, rancher, homesteader, peasant, peon, herdsman, plowman, sharecropper, gardener, horticulturist

farsighted *adj.* aware, perceptive, sagacious

farthest *adj.* remotest, ultimate, last, furthest

fascinate *v.* charm, captivate, entrance, enchant, bewitch, enrapture, delight, please, attract, lure, seduce, entice, intoxicate, tantalize

fascination *n.* charm, enchantment, attraction

fashion *n.* manner, custom, convention, vogue, mode, usage, observance, style, craze

fashion *v.* make, model, shape, form, create, mold, adapt

fashionable *adj.* smart, stylish, chic

fast *adj.* RAPID: swift, fleet, quick, speedy, brisk, accelerated, hasty, nimble; FIXED: attached, immovable, firm

fasten *v.* lock, fix, tie, lace, close, bind, tighten,

attach, secure, anchor, grip, clasp, clamp, pin, nail, tack, bolt, rivet, set, weld, cement, glue

fat *adj.* portly, stout, obese, corpulent, fleshy, plump, bulky, heavy

fatal *adj.* mortal, lethal, deadly

fatality *n.* casualty, death

fate *n.* destiny, fortune, luck, doom

fated *adj.* lost, destined, elected, doomed

fateful *adj.* MOMENTOUS: portentous, critical, decisive, crucial; FATAL: destructive, ruinous, lethal, deadly

father *n.* PARENT: sire, progenitor, procreator, forebear, ancestor; ORIGINATOR: founder, inventor, promoter, author; PRIEST: pastor, ecclesiastic, parson

fatigue *n.* weariness, exhaustion, lassitude

fatten *v.* feed, stuff, plump, cram, fill

fault *n.* DELINQUENCY: wrongdoing, transgression, crime, impropriety, misconduct, malpractice, failing; ERROR: defect, blunder, mistake, misdeed; RESPONSIBILITY: liability, accountability, blame

favor *v.* indulge, prefer, pick, choose, value, prize, esteem

favorable *adj.* well–disposed, kind, well–intentioned, propitious, beneficial

favorite *adj.* beloved, favored, preferred, adored

favorite *n.* darling, pet

favoritism *n.* bias, partiality, inequity, inclination

faze *v.* discourage, bother, intimidate, worry, disturb

fear *n.* dread, fright, dismay, awe, anxiety, foreboding, concern, alarm

fearful *adj.* timid, shy, apprehensive, cowardly

fearless *adj.* bold, daring, courageous, dashing, brave

feasible *adj.* expedient, worthwhile, convenient,

practicable, possible, attainable

feast *n.* banquet, entertainment, festival, fiesta, barbecue, picnic, dinner

feast *v.* eat, entertain

feat *n.* deed, act, effort, achievement

feature *n.* **ATTRACTION:** highlight, specialty; **ARTICLE:** editorial, story; **CHARACTERISTIC:** quality, peculiarity

federation *n.* confederacy, alliance

fee *n.* price, remuneration, salary, charge, pay

feeble *adj.* weak, faint, fragile, puny, strengthless

feeble–minded *adj.* foolish, retarded, senile, dull

feed *n.* fodder, provisions, supplies, pasture, forage

feed *v.* feast, nourish, dine, fatten, cater, serve

feel *v.* **TOUCH:** caress, fondle, paw, grasp; **EXPERIENCE:** sense, perceive; **BELIEVE:** consider, hold, think

feeling *n.* **SENSATION:** sensibility, sensitiveness, perception, receptivity, responsiveness, awareness, enjoyment, sensuality, pain, pleasure, reflex; **REACTION:** opinion, thought, outlook, attitude; **SENSITIVITY:** taste, tenderness, discrimination, discernment, refinement, culture, faculty, judgment

feign *v.* pretend, dissemble, imagine, fabricate

fellow *n.* **YOUTH:** chap, lad, boy, stripling, apprentice, adolescent, juvenile, youngster, kid; **ASSOCIATE:** member, peer, colleague, friend

fellowship *n.* **COMRADESHIP:** conviviality, sociability, intimacy, friendliness, affability, camaraderie; **PAYMENT:** stipend, scholarship, honorarium, subsidy

felon *n.* criminal, outlaw, delinquent, convict

felony *n.* crime, misconduct, offense, transgression

feminine *adj.* soft, delicate, gentle, ladylike, matronly, maidenly, tender, womanly

fence n. hedge, divider, barrier, backstop, railing, barricade, barrier

ferment v. effervesce, foam, froth, bubble, seethe, fizz, work, ripen, rise

ferocious adj. savage, fierce, wild

ferocity n. fierceness brutality barbarity cruelty

ferry n. ferryboat passage boat barge packet boat

ferry v. carry, convey

fertile adj. productive, inventive, fruitful, rich, productive, fat, teeming, yielding, arable, flowering

fertility n. fruitfulness, virility, productiveness

fertilization n. **IMPREGNATION:** pollination, breeding, propagation, procreation

fervent adj. zealous, eager, ardent, enthusiastic

fervor n. ardor, enthusiasm, zeal

festival n. celebration, festivity, feast

festive adj. gay, merry, joyful, happy

festivity n. revelry, amusement, entertainment

fetch v. get, retrieve, carry

fetish n. fixation, craze, mania, obsession

fetter n. shackle, restraint

fetus n. embryo, organism, child

feud n. quarrel, strife, bickering, fight

feverish adj. burning, hot

few adj. sparse, scanty, scattering, inconsiderable

fib n. prevarication, fabrication, misrepresentation, lie

fiber n. thread, filament, cord, string, strand

fibrous adj. veined, hairy, coarse, stringy

fickle adj. inconstant, capricious, whimsical, mercurial, changing

fiction n. novel, tale, romance, story

fictitious adj. imaginary, made–up, untrue, false

fidelity *n.* faithfulness, fealty, loyalty, devotion

fidget *v.* stir, twitch, worry, wiggle

field *n.* pasture, meadow, acreage, plot, patch, garden, grasslend, tract

fiend *n.* MONSTER: barbarian, brute, beast, devil; ADDICT: fan, aficionado, monomaniac

fierce *n.* ferocious, savage, wild, untamed, brutal, monstrous, vicious, dangerous, violent, threatening

fiery *adj.* impetuous, hotheaded

fight *n.* CONFLICT: struggle, battle, strife, contention, feud, quarrel, dispute, confrontation, brawl, fracas, altercation, bickering, wrangling, argument, debate, conflict, clash, scuffle, engagement; METTLE: hardihood, boldness, courage

fight *v.* conflict, battle, oppose, grapple

figurative *adj.* metaphorical, allegorical, illustrative

figure *n.* FORM: design, statue, shape, structure; TORSO: body, frame, development, build, posture, attitude, pose, carriage; SUM: total, number; PRICE: value, worth

figure *v.* COMPUTE: calculate, reckon, number, count; CONCLUDE: suppose, think, opine, decide

file *v.* SMOOTH: abrade, rasp, scrape, finish; ARRANGE: classify, index, categorize, catalogue, register, list

fill *v.* pack, stuff, charge, inflate

filter *v.* strain, purify, sieve, refine, clarify, separate

filth *n.* dirt, contamination, pollution, muck, slop, squalor, grime, garbage, sludge

filthy *adj.* dirty, foul, squalid, nasty, corrupt

final *adj.* last, terminal, concluding, ultimate, decisive

finance *n.* business, commerce, economics

finances *n.* resources, money, capital, funds, wealth

financial *adj.* economic, business, monetary, commercial

financier *n.* capitalist, banker, merchant, executive

find *v.* discover, detect, notice, perceive, discern, uncover, expose

finding *n.* verdict, decision, sentence, judgment

fine *adj.* **EXACT:** precise, accurate, definite; **SMALL:** thin, subtle; **LIGHT:** powdery, granular

fine *n.* punishment, penalty, damage, forfeit

fine *v.* penalize, exact, tax, levy, punish

finish *v.* **END:** perfect, achieve; **POLISH:** wax, stain, cover, paint; **COMPLETE:** cease, close, end, stop

fire *n.* burning, flame, blaze, embers, sparks, glow, warmth, combustion, conflagration

fire *v.* **INFLAME:** kindle, enkindle, ignite, light, burn, rekindle, relight, animate; **DISCHARGE:** shoot, set, off, hurl; **DISMISS:** discharge, eject

firm *adj.* **FIXED:** stable, solid, rooted, immovable, fastened, motionless, secured; **HARD:** solid, dense, compact, impenetrable, impervious, rigid, hardened, inflexible, unyielding; **SETTLED:** determined, steadfast, resolute, constant

firmament *n.* sky, heavens

first *adj.* beginning, original, primary, prime, initial, earliest, introductory

first–rate *adj.* prime, very, good, choice, excellent

fishy *adj.* improbable, dubious, implausible, unlikely

fit *adj.* **APPROPRIATE:** suitable, proper, practicable, advantageous, beneficial, desirable; **HEALTHY:** trim, competent, robust

fit *n.* **ADJUSTMENT:** adaptation; **CONVULSION:** attack, rage, spasm, seizure, stroke, paroxysm; **TANTRUM:**

burst, rush, outburst, huff, rage, spell

fit *v.* ADAPT: arrange, alter, adjust; QUALIFY: belong, conform, relate, match, correspond

fitting *n.* connection, component, constituent

fixture *n.* equipment, convenience, appliance, machine, device, equipment

fizzle *n.* disappointment, fiasco, defeat, failure

flabby *adj.* soft, yielding, limp, tender, fat

flag *n.* banner, standard, colors, emblem

flagrant *adj.* obvious, notorious, disgraceful, infamous, outrageous

flair *n.* talent, aptitude, gift, ability

flamboyant *adj.* bombastic, ostentatious, ornate

flame *n.* blaze, flare, flash, fire

flame *v.* burn, blaze, oxidize

flange *n.* edge, rim

flap *n.* fold, tab, cover, appendage, tag

flap *v.* flutter, flash, swing, wave

flare *v.* blaze, glow, burn, flash

flash *v.* gleam, glimmer, sparkle, glitter, glisten, glare, shine, glow, twinkle, reflect, radiate, flicker

flashy *adj.* gaudy, showy, ostentatious, ornate

flask *n.* bottle, decanter, jug, canteen

flat *adj.* LEVEL: even, smooth, extended, prostrate, horizontal, prone; TASTELESS: unseasoned, insipid, flavorless

flatter *v.* adulate, glorify, praise

flattery *adj.* adulation, compliments, praise, tribute, fawning, blarney

flaunt *v.* display, vaunt, brandish, boast

flavor *n.* taste, tang, relish

flavor *v.* season, salt, pepper, spice,

flavoring *n.* essence, extract, seasoning, additive
flaw *n.* defect, imperfection, stain, blemish
flaw *v.* mar, crack
fleck *n.* spot, mite, dot, bit
flee *v.* run, desert, escape, retreat
fleet *adj.* swift, transient
flexibility *n.* pliancy, suppleness, elasticity, litheness
flexible *adj.* limber, lithe, supple, elastic, malleable, pliable, tractable
flicker *v.* sparkle, twinkle, glitter, flash, shine
flight *n.* **ESCAPE:** fleeing, retreat; **STEPS:** stairs, staircase, ascent; **SOARING:** flying, aviation, aeronautics, gliding
flighty *adj.* capricious, fickle, whimsical, changing
flimsy *adj.* thin; weak; slight, infirm, frail, insubstantial, fragile, decrepit
flinch *v.* wince, start, blench
fling *n.* escapade, indulgence, party, celebration
fling *v.* hurl, toss, sling, dump, throw
flippant *adj.* pert, frivolous, impudent, saucy, rude
flirt *n.* coquette, tease, siren
flirt *v.* trifle, tease, seduce
float *v.* waft, drift
flock *n.* congregation, group, pack, litter, herd
flock *v.* gather, throng, congregate, crowd
flog *v.* beat, lash
flood *v.* inundate, swamp, overflow, deluge, submerge, immerse
floor *n.* **DECK:** tiles, planking, carpet, rug, linoleum; **LEVEL:** story, landing, basement, mezzanine, downstairs, upstairs, loft, attic, garret, penthouse
flop *v.* **FALL:** tumble, slump, drop; **FAIL:** miscarry,

founder, bomb

flounder *v.* struggle, wallow, blunder

flourish *v.* THRIVE: increase, wax, succeed, adorn; BRANDISH: wave

flout *v.* sneer, disregard

flow *n.* current, tide, movement, progress

flow *v.* stream, course, move, run, rush, whirl, surge, spurt, squirt, gush, trickle, spew

flower *n.* spray, cluster, shoot, posy, herb, vine, annual, perennial, plant

flower *v.* bloom, open, blossom, blow

flowery *adj.* elaborate, ornamented, rococo, ornate

fluctuate *v.* waver, vacillate, falter, hesitate

fluctuation, *n.* variation, inconstancy, change

fluent *adj.* eloquent, glib, smooth, verbose, chatty, articulate, persuasive, silver–tongued

fluid *adj.* flowing, liquid, watery, molten, liquefied

fluid *n.* liquid, liquor, solution

flunk *v.* fail, miss, drop

fluster *v.* disconcert, confuse

flutter *v.* flap, ripple, wiggle, wave

flutter *n.* agitation, motion

fly *v.* FLEE: escape, retreat, withdraw; SOAR: float, glide, hover, swoop, drift, circle; RUSH: dart, speed

foam *n.* froth, fluff, bubbles, lather

focus *v.* ATTRACT: converge, convene, center; CLEAR: adjust, detail, sharpen

foe *n.* enemy, opponent, antagonist, adversary

fog *n.* mist, haze, cloud, film, steam, wisp, smoke, soup, smog

foggy *adj.* dull, misty, gray, hazy

foible *n.* failing, weakness

fold *v.* DOUBLE: crease, crimp, ruffle, pucker, gather, lap, overlap, overlay; FAIL: bankrupt, close

folder *n.* circular, pamphlet, paper, bulletin, advertisement, brochure, throwaway

foliage *n.* leaves, greenery

folk *n.* people, race, nation, community, tribe, society, population, settlement, clan, confederation

folklore *n.* customs, superstitions, traditions, tales, lore, legends, folkways, myth

folks *n.* family, kin, relatives, relations

follow *v.* COME AFTER: ensue, postdate, succeed; IMITATE: conform, copy, mirror, reflect, mimic; OBSERVE: heed, regard, watch, comply; UNDERSTAND: comprehend, catch, realize; RESULT: happen, ensue

follower *n.* attendant, companion, lackey, helper, partisan, disciple, pupil, protégé, supporter, backer, devotee, believer, member, admirer

following *adj.* subsequent, succeeding, next, ensuing

following *n.* clientele, audience, adherents, supporters, patrons

foment *v.* encourage, incite

fond *adj.* loving, enamored, attached, affectionate

food *n.* victuals, foodstuffs, nutriment, refreshment, edibles, comestibles, provisions, stores, sustenance, rations, board, cuisine, nourishment, fare

fool *n.* nitwit, simpleton, dunce, oaf, ninny, nincompoop, dolt, buffoon, blockhead, clown

fool *v.* deceive, trick, dupe, mislead

foolish *adj.* silly, simple, half–witted, stupid

foothold *n.* ledge, footing, niche, step

forbear *v.* abstain, stop

forbearance *n.* patience, clemency

forbid *v.* prohibit, debar, restrain, inhibit, preclude, oppose, obstruct, bar, prevent, outlaw, disallow, ban

forbidding *adj.* unpleasant, offensive, repulsive, grim

force *n.* STRENGTH: energy, power, might; DOMINANCE: forcefulness, competency, energy, persistence, willpower, drive, determination, authority; ORGANIZATION: group, band, unit

force *v.* compel, coerce, press, drive, make, impel, oblige, require, demand, command, impose, exact

forceful *adj.* commanding, dominant, powerful

forebode *v.* apprehend, foretell

foreboding *n.* premonition, dread, presentiment, anticipation, apprehension

forecast *n.* prognosis, divination, foresight, prophecy

forecast *v.* predict, predetermine, foretell

forefather *n.* ancestor, progenitor, forebear, father, parent, sire, forerunner, predecessor, originator, precursor, procreator, patriarch, founder, kinsman

foregoing *n.* prior, former, previous, preceding

foreign *adj.* alien, remote, exotic, strange, distant, different, alien, imported, borrowed, abroad

foreigner *n.* stranger, immigrant, newcomer, alien

foreman *n.* overseer, manager, supervisor, superintendent, head, boss

foremost *adj.* original, primary, first

forerunner *n.* herald, harbinger, precursor, sign

foresee *v.* prophesy, understand, predict, foretell

foresight *n.* carefulness, husbandry, prudence

forestall *v.* thwart, prevent, preclude, hinder

foretell *v.* prophesy, predict, divine, foresee, forebode, augur, portend, foreshadow

forethought *n.* provision, planning, foresight

forever *adv.* always, everlastingly, perpetually, eternally, endlessly, forevermore

forewarn *v.* admonish, alarm, warm

forfeit *v.* lose, sacrifice, relinquish, abandon

forge *v.* counterfeit, falsify, fabricate, feign, imitate, copy, duplicate, reproduce

forgery *n.* imitation, copy, counterfeit, fake

forget *v.* neglect, overlook, ignore, slight, disregard, skip, exclude

forgetful *adj.* inattentive, neglectful, heedless, careless, distracted

forgive *v.* pardon, overlook, excuse, exonerate

forgiveness *n.* absolution, pardon, acquittal, exoneration, dispensation, reprieve, amnesty, respite

forgo *v.* quit, relinquish, waive, abandon

fork *v.* branch, divide

form *n.* SHAPE: figure, appearance, arrangement, configuration, formation, structure, contour, profile, silhouette; CEREMONY: manner, mode, custom, method; PATTERN: model, die, mold; DOCUMENT: chart, questionnaire, application

form *v.* SHAPE: mold, model, make, fashion, construct, devise, design, produce, build, create; INSTRUCT: rear, breed, teach; DEVELOP: accumulate, harden, set, rise, appear, grow, mature, materialize

formal *adj.* REGULAR: orderly, precise, set; POLITE: reserved, distant, stiff, conventional

formality *n.* decorum, etiquette, correctness, behavior

format *n.* arrangement, construction, form

formation *n.* form, structure, arrangement, composition, development, fabrication, generation, creation, genesis, constitution

former *adj.* earlier, previous, foregoing, preceding
formerly *adj.* before, once, previously, earlier
formula *n.* equation, recipe, directions, method
formulate *v.* systematize, express, form
forsake *v.* desert, abandon, leave, quit
fort *n.* fortress, stronghold, citadel, acropolis
fortification *n.* stronghold, fort, fortress, defense, barricade, battlement, stockade, bastion, bulwark
fortify *v.* strengthen, barricade, entrench, buttress
fortitude *n.* strength, firmness, valor, fearlessness, determination
fortress *n.* stronghold, fort
fortune *n.* CHANCE: luck, fate, uncertainty; WEALTH: riches, possessions, inheritance, estate
fortunate *adj.* lucky, favorable
forward *adj.* bold, presumptuous, impertinent, fresh
fossil *n.* remains, specimen, skeleton, relic
foster *v.* nurse, raise, cherish, nourish, encourage
foul *adj.* FILTHY: impure, disgusting, nasty, vulgar, coarse, offensive; UNFAIR: inequitable, unjust
found *v.* institute, establish, endow
foundation *n.* BASIS: reason, justification, authority; BASE: footing, pier, groundwork, bed, substructure, underpinning; INSTITUTION: organization, endowment, institute, society, charity
founder *n.* originator, patron
foxy *adj.* sly, crafty
fraction *n.* fragment, section, portion, part, division
fractious *adj.* cross, irritable
fracture *n.* rupture, shattering, breach, dislocation, shearing, separating
fracture *v.* break, crack

fragile *adj.* frail, brittle, delicate, dainty, weak
fragment *n.* piece, scrap, remnant, bit
fragrance *n.* perfume, aroma, smell
fragrant *adj.* aromatic, sweet, perfumed
frail *adj.* fragile, feeble, breakable, tender, dainty
frame *n.* SKELETON: framework, scaffolding, support; BORDER: margin, fringe, hem, trim, outline
frame *v.* MAKE: construct, erect, raise, build; SURROUND: encircle, confine, enclose
franchise *n.* right, privilege
frank *adj.* candid, open, sincere, direct, ingenuous, forthright, outspoken, straightforward, blunt
frantic *adj.* excited, distracted, frenetic, frenzied
fraternity *n.* society, brotherhood, fellowship
fraud *n.* DECEIT: trickery, duplicity, guile, deception; TRICKSTER: impostor, pretender, charlatan, cheat
fraudulent *adj.* deceitful, tricky, dishonest
freak *n.* monstrosity, rarity, malformation, oddity, aberration, curiosity
free *adj.* SOVEREIGN: independent, autonomous, liberated, democratic; UNIMPEDED: unobstructed, unconstrained, unhampered, loose; GRATIS: gratuitous, complimentary
free *v.* release, discharge, rescue, extricate, undo, acquit, dismiss, pardon, redeem, disentangle
freedom *n.* LIBERTY: independence, sovereignty, autonomy; EXEMPTION: privilege, immunity, license, indulgence, latitude
freeway *n.* turnpike, superhighway, road
freeze *v.* SOLIDIFY: congeal, harden; CONTROL: seal, terminate, immobilize
freight *n.* CARGO: load, encumbrance, consignment,

goods, tonnage

frenzy *n.* excitement, rage, craze, furor, insanity

frequency *n.* repetition, recurrence, reiteration, regularity

frequent *adj.* OFTEN: habitual, customary, intermittent, periodic, commonplace; REGULAR: repeated, recurrent, incessant, continual

frequent *v.* visit, attend

fresh *adj.* NEW: green, recent, current, late, untried; NOT PRESERVED: unsalted, uncured, unsmoked; UNSPOILED: uncontaminated, preserved; COLORFUL: vivid, bright; POTABLE: drinkable, cool, clear, pure, clean, sweet, safe; REFRESHED: rested, restored, relaxed, reinvigorated, revived; INEXPERIENCED: untrained, untried, unskilled

fret *v.* worry, irritate, agitate, vex, bother

friction *n.* RUBBING: attrition, abrasion, erosion, grinding; ANTAGONISM: trouble, animosity, quarrel, discontent, hatred

friend *n.* schoolmate, playmate, roommate, companion, intimate, confidant, comrade, fellow, pal, chum, crony, buddy, side–kick

friendly *adj.* kindly, amiable, neighborly, sociable, civil, affectionate, attentive, agreeable, accommodating, pleasant, cordial, congenial

fright *n.* fear, panic, terror, dread, horror, shock

frighten *v.* terrify, scare, intimidate, threaten, badger, petrify, terrorize

frightful *adj.* FEARFUL: awful, dreadful, terrible; UNPLEASANT: calamitous, shocking, offensive

frill *n.* ruffle, frivolity, ornamentation

frisky *adj.* spirited, dashing, playful, active

frivolous *adj.* unimportant, slight, trifling, superficial, petty, trivial

frock *n.* dress, garment

frontier *n.* boundary, wilderness, hinterland

frosting *n.* covering, coating, icing

frosty *adj.* frigid, freezing, chilly, cold

froth *n.* foam, bubbles, fizz, effervescence, lather

frown *v.* scowl, grimace, pout, glare, sulk, glower

frugal *adj.* thrifty, economical, sparing, saving, parsimonious, careful

fruitful *adj.* prolific, productive, fecund, fertile

fruitless *adj.* vain, unprofitable, empty, futile

frustrate *v.* defeat, thwart, foil, balk, prevent

frustration *n.* disappointment, impediment, failure

fry *v.* sauté, sear, singe, brown, pan–fry

fudge *n.* candy, penuche, chocolate, divinity

fuel *n.* coal, gas, oil, charcoal, propane, peat, firewood, kindling, gasoline, kerosene

fugitive *adj.* fleeting, passing

fugitive *n.* outlaw, runaway, exile, outcast

fulfill *v.* complete, accomplish, effect, achieve

full *adj.* SATURATED: crammed, packed, stuffed, jammed, glutted, gorged, loaded; ABUNDANT: copious, ample, plentiful, sufficient, adequate, lavish, extravagant, profuse

fumble *v.* mishandle, bungle, mismanage, botch

fun *n.* amusement, relaxation, diversion, entertainment, pleasure, celebration, holiday, enjoyment

function *n.* duty, employment, capacity, use; action, event, party

function *v.* perform, run, work, operate

functional *adj.* utilitarian, practical

fund *n.* money, capital, endowment, gift
fundamental *adj.* basic, underlying, primary, rudimentary, elemental, structural, original
funds *n.* capital, wealth, cash, collateral, money, assets, currency, savings, revenue, wherewithal, stocks, bonds, property, means, affluence, belongings, resources, securities, profits
funeral *n.* interment, burial, entombment, requiem
funny *adj.* COMIC: laughable, comical, whimsical, amusing, entertaining, diverting, humorous, witty, jocular, droll; SUSPICIOUS: curious, unusual, odd
fur *n.* pelt, hide, hair, coat, brush
furbish *v.* polish, spruce, renovate
furious *adj.* raging, enraged, fierce, angry
furnace *n.* heater, boiler, kiln, stove, forge
furnish *v.* supply, equip, stock, provide
furor *n.* tumult, excitement, stir, disturbance
further *adj.* additional, more, distant
further *v.* promote, advance
fury *n.* rage, anger, wrath
fuse *v.* meld, blend
fuss *n.* quarrel, complaint, bother, disturbance, stir
fuss *v.* wrangle, whine, whimper, object, complain
fussy *adj.* fastidious, particular, meticulous, careful
futile *adj.* useless, vain, fruitless, hopeless, impractical, unsuccessful, purposeless, ineffective, ineffectual, unproductive, empty, hollow
future *adj.* impending, imminent, destined, fated, prospective, expected, approaching, ultimate
fuzz *n.* nap, fluff, fur, hair
gab *vi.* talk, chatter, gossip, jabber, babble
gabble *v.* jabber, cackle

gadget

gadget *n.* device, contrivance, object, contraption
gag *v.* RETCH: sicken, choke, vomit; MUZZLE: muffle, silence, stifle, throttle
gaiety *n.* merriment, jollity, mirth, exhilaration
gain *n.* profit, increase, accrual, accumulation
gain *v.* INCREASE: augment, expand, enlarge, grow; ADVANCE: progress, overtake; ACHIEVE: attain, realize, reach, succeed
gait *n.* walk, step, stride, pace, carriage, movement
gale *n.* wind, hurricane, blow, typhoon, storm
gallant *adj.* noble, brave, courteous, bold, courageous, intrepid
gallantry *n.* heroism, valor, bravery, courage
gallery *n.* ONLOOKERS: spectators, audience, public; MUSEUM: salon, studio, hall, showroom
gallop *v.* leap, run, spring, bound, hurdle, swing, stride, lope, amble, trot
gamble *v.* bet, wager, plunge, speculate, risk, chance
gambol *v.* leap, play
game *adj.* spirited, hardy, resolute, brave
game *n.* ENTERTAINMENT: sport, play, recreation; MEAT: fish, fowl, quarry, prey, wildlife
gang *n.* band, group, horde, troop, organization
gangster *n.* criminal, gunman, racketeer
gap *n.* BREACH: cleft, rift, hole; BREAK: hiatus, recess, lull, pause; PASS: chasm, hollow, ravine, gorge, canyon, gully, gulch
garbage *n.* refuse, trash, waste
garden *n.* patch, field, plot, bed, terrace, oasis
garish *adj.* showy, gaudy, ostentatious, ornate
garment *n.* dress, attire, apparel, clothes
garnish *v.* adorn, decorate, embellish, beautify, deck

gaseous *adj.* vaporous, effervescent, aeriform, light
gash *n.* wound, slash, slice, cut
gasp *v.* gulp, pant, puff, wheeze, blow, snort
gate *n.* entrance, ingress, passage, barrier, doorway
gather *v.* **COLLECT:** aggregate, amass, accumulate, assemble, garner; **INFER:** conclude, deduce, assume; **ASSEMBLE:** meet, congregate, flock, convene, collect, reunite, converge, concentrate
gathering *n.* assembly, meeting, conclave, caucus, parley, council, conference, congregation, rally, throng, collection, huddle, turnout, convention, reunion, meet
gaudy *a.* showy, flashy, tawdry, ornate
gauge *v.* measure, check, weigh, calibrate, calculate
gaunt *adj.* thin, lean, haggard, emaciated, scraggy
gauze *n.* fabric, veil, bandage, dressing
gawk *v.* stare, ogle, gaze, look
gay *adj.* lively, showy, merry, cheerful, vivacious
gaze *v.* stare, watch, gape, look
gazette *n.* journal, newspaper
gear *n.* **COG:** pinion, sprocket; **BELONGINGS:** equipment, material, tackle
gem *n.* stone, jewel, bauble, ornament
genealogy *n.* derivation, lineage, extraction, family
general *adj.* **COMPREHENSIVE:** broad, universal, extensive, ecumenical, ubiquitous; **COMMON:** usual, customary, prevailing; **NOT SPECIFIC:** indefinite, uncertain, imprecise, vague
generality *n.* abstraction, principle
generalize *v.* theorize, speculate, postulate
generally *adj.* commonly, ordinarily, regularly
generate *v.* produce, form, make, beget, create

generosity *n.* hospitality, benevolence, charity, philanthropy, altruism, unselfishness, kindness

generous *adj.* bountiful, lavish, profuse, prodigal, unstinting, magnanimous

genesis *n.* generation, creation

genial *adj.* cordial, kind, warmhearted, friendly

genius *n.* talent, intellect, intelligence, gift, aptitude, astuteness, acumen, capability

gentility *n.* decorum, propriety, refinement, behavior

gentle *adj.* **SOFT:** tender, smooth; **KIND:** tender, considerate, benign; **TAMED:** domesticated, trained;

genuine *adj.* **AUTHENTIC:** actual, original, authenticated; **SINCERE:** unaffected, reliable, staunch, trustworthy, certain, valid, positive, frank

germ *n.* microbe, bacterium, micro–organism, virus, parasite, bug

germinate *v.* sprout, begin, generate

gesture *n.* movement, indication, intimation, sign

get *v.* **OBTAIN:** procure, capture, take, grab, attain, gain, secure, collect, purchase, receive, possess, acquire; **BECOME:** grow, develop; **RECEIVE:** take, accept; **BEAT;** vanquish, overpower, defeat; **PREPARE:** make, arrange; **CONTRACT:** succumb, catch; **UNDERSTAND:** comprehend, perceive, know; **IRRITATE:** annoy, provoke, vex, bother

ghastly *adj.* terrifying, hideous, horrible, frightening, frightful, repulsive, disgusting, abhorrent, offensive

ghost *n.* spirit, apparition, vision, specter, phantom, spook, devil

giant *adj.* monstrous, colossal, enormous, large

giant *n.* colossus, behemoth, monster, leviathan

gibberish *n.* jargon, chatter, claptrap, nonsense

gibe *v.* sneer, mock, taunt

giddy, *adj.* high, towering, lofty, steep

gift *n.* **PRESENT:** donation, grant, endowment, bequest, legacy, reward, remembrance, bonus, subsidy, contribution; **TALENT:** aptitude, faculty, capacity, capability, ability

gigantic *adj.* massive, huge, immense, large

giggle *v.* laugh, titter, chuckle, snicker

gimmick *n.* device, stratagem, catch, method, trick

girdle *n.* belt, cinch, sash, underwear

girdle *v.* bind, enclose, encircle, clasp, surround

girl *n.* schoolgirl, lass, woman, coed, lassie, damsel, maid, maiden

girth *n.* circumference, size

gist *n.* substance, essence, significance, basis

give *v.* **BESTOW:** donate, grant, confer, impart, present, endow, bequeath, award, contribute, convey; **YIELD:** retreat, collapse, fall, contract, shrink, recede

glacial *adj.* icy, frozen, polar, cold

glad *adj.* exhilarated, animated, jovial, happy

glamour *n.* allurement, charm, attraction, beauty

glance *v.* **LOOK:** see, peep, glimpse; **RICOCHET:** skip, rebound, bounce

glare *v.* **SHINE:** light, beam, glow, radiate; **STARE:** pierce, glower, scowl, frown

glaring *adj.* **SHINING:** blinding, dazzling, blazing, bright; **OBVIOUS:** evident, conspicuous, obtrusive

glass *n.* tumbler, goblet, beaker, chalice, cup

gleam *v.* glow, flash

glee *n.* joy, gaiety, joviality, merriment, mirth

glib *adj.* fluent, pat

glide *v.* float, drift, waft, skim, fly, flit, soar

glimmer *n.* gleam, flash, flicker, light
glimpse *n.* view, flash, impression, sight
glisten *v.* sparkle, glitter, shimmer, flicker, shine
glitter *n.* luster, brilliancy, sparkle, shimmer, gleam
glitter *v.* glare, shimmer, sparkle, shine
globule *n.* drop, particle
gloom *n.* **DARKNESS:** cloudiness; **SADNESS:** depression, dejection, melancholia, despondency, morbidity, pessimism, foreboding, misgiving, mourning
gloomy *adj.* dreary, depressing, discouraging, dismal
glorify *v.* laud, commend, acclaim, praise
glorious *adj.* splendid, excellent, exalted, grand, illustrious, celebrated, remarkable
glory *n.* **SPLENDOR:** grandeur, majesty, brilliance, richness, beauty, fineness; **HONOR:** renown, distinction, reputation, fame
glory *v.* triumph, exult, boast
gloss *n.* brightness, sheen
glossy, *adj.* shining, reflecting, lustrous, bright
glow *v.* shine, gleam, redden, radiate, burn
glower *v.* stare, scowl
glue *n.* adhesive, paste, gum, cement, repair
glue *v.* paste, join
glum *adj.* sullen, moody, morose, sad
glut *v.* **OVEREAT:** stuff, cram, gorge, feast, devour; **OVERSUPPLY:** overwhelm, overstock, fill, flood
gluttony *n.* voracity, edacity, intemperance, greed
gnarled *adj.* knotted, twisted, contorted, bent
gnaw *v.* tear, crunch, champ, masticate, bite, chew
go *v.* **LEAVE:** withdraw, depart, vacate, flee, fly, run, escape; **PROCEED:** advance, progress, move; **FUNCTION:** run, perform, operate; **SUIT:** conform,

accord, harmonize, agree, fit; **EXTEND:** stretch, cover, reach; **ELAPSE:** transpire, pass; **DIE:** depart, succumb

goad *v.* prod, urge, prompt, spur, drive, press, push, impel, force, stimulate, provoke, encourage

goal *n.* aim, ambition, object, intent, end, purpose

go–between *n.* middleman, referee, mediator, agent

god *n.* deity, divinity, spirit

godly *adj.* righteous, devout, pious, holy

gone *adj.* moved, withdrawn, retired, departed, dissolved, decayed, extinct

good *adj.* **MORAL:** upright, honest, respectable, noble, ethical, fair, pure, decent, honorable; **KIND:** considerate, tolerant, generous; **RELIABLE:** trustworthy, dependable, loyal; **SOUND:** safe, solid, stable, reliable; **PLEASANT:** agreeable, satisfying, enjoyable; **HEALTHY:** sound, normal, vigorous; **OBEDIENT:** dutiful, tractable, well–behaved; **GENUINE:** valid, real, sound; **DELICIOUS:** tasty, flavorful, tasteful

good–for–nothing *n.* loafer, vagabond, bum, vagrant

good–looking *adj.* clean–cut, attractive, impressive, beautiful, handsome

good–natured *adj.* cordial, kindly, amiable, friendly

goodness *n.* decency, morality, honesty, virtue

goof *v.* err, flub, fail

gorge *n.* chasm, abyss, crevasse, ravine

gorge *v.* glut, surfeit, stuff, eat, fill

gorgeous *adj.* beautiful, dazzling, superb, sumptuous, impressive, grand

gory *adj.* blood–soaked, bloodstained, offensive

gossip *n.* **RUMOR:** scandal, meddling, hearsay, slander, defamation; **TALEBEARER:** snoop, meddler, tattler, scandalmonger, muckraker, backbiter

gossip *v.* tattle, chat, report, blab, babble, repeat

govern *v.* rule, administer, oversee, supervise, dictate, tyrannize

governmental *adj.* political, administrative, executive, regulatory, bureaucratic, supervisory

gown *n.* dress, garment, garb, clothes, dress

grab *v.* seize, clutch, grasp, take

grace *n.* **CHARM:** nimbleness, agility, poise, dexterity, symmetry, balance, style, harmony; **MERCY:** forgiveness, love, charity

graceful *adj.* **SUPPLE:** agile, lithe, nimble, dexterous, sprightly, elegant; **WELL–PROPORTIONED:** elegant, neat, trim, dainty, comely, slender, exquisite, statuesque; **CULTURED:** seemly, becoming, polite

gracious *adj.* **GENIAL:** amiable, courteous, condescending, polite; **MERCIFUL:** tender, loving, charitable, kind

grade *n.* **RANK;** class, category, classification; **SLOPE:** incline, gradient, slant, inclination, pitch, ascent, descent, ramp, climb, elevation, height, hill; **EMBANKMENT:** fill, causeway, dike, dam

grade *v.* arrange, rate, assort, rank

gradual *adj.* creeping, regular, continuous, regulated

grand *adj.* splendid, stately, dignified, regal, noble, illustrious, august, majestic, overwhelming

grandeur *n.* splendor, magnificence, pomp, glory, luxury, stateliness, beauty, ceremony, majesty

grandstand, *n.* seats, spectators

grant *n.* gift, boon, reward, present, allowance, stipend, donation, endowment, bequest

grant *v.* **BESTOW:** impart, allow; **ADMIT:** concede, accede, acquiesce, acknowledge

graph *n.* diagram, chart, design, plan

graphic *adj.* **PICTORIAL:** illustrated, visual, sketched, pictured; **VIVID:** clear, picturesque, comprehensible, striking, expressive, eloquent, poetic

grasp *n.* grip, hold, clutch, cinch

grasp *v.* **SEIZE:** clutch, enclose, clasp, grip, hold; **UNDERSTAND:** comprehend, perceive, apprehend, follow

grassland *n.* plains, meadow, prairie, field

grate *v.* rub, rasp, grind, abrade

grateful *adj.* thankful, appreciative, pleased, obliged

gratify *v.* please, satisfy

gratitude *n.* appreciation, acknowledgment, thanks

gratuitous *adj.* free, voluntary

gratuity *n.* present, tip

grave *adj.* **WEIGHTY:** important, momentous, consequential, critical; **SOMBER:** solemn, serious, sober

grave *n.* vault, sepulcher, tomb, crypt, mausoleum, catacomb

gravity *n.* importance, seriousness, significance

gravy *n.* juices, sauce, dressing

graze *v.* **FEED:** browse, nibble, forage, eat, munch, ruminate; **PASS LIGHTLY:** brush, scrape, rub, touch

greasy *adj.* creamy, fatty, oily

great *adj.* **LARGE:** numerous, big, commanding, vast; **EXCELLENT:** exceptional, surpassing, transcendent; **EMINENT:** grand, majestic, exalted, famous, renowned, celebrated, distinguished, noted

greedy *adj.* avid, grasping, rapacious, selfish, miserly, intemperate, mercenary, covetous

green *adj.* **VERDANT:** growing, leafy, sprouting, grassy, flourishing, lush; **IMMATURE:** young, unripe, maturing, developing; **INEXPERIENCED:** youthful, callow

greet *v.* hail, welcome, address, recognize, embrace,

nod, acknowledge, bow

greeting *n.* salutation, welcome, regards

gregarious *adj.* companionable, friendly

grief *n.* sorrow, sadness, melancholy, mourning, misery, anguish, despondency, heartache, gloom

grievance *n.* hardship, injury, complaint, objection

grieve *v.* lament, bewail, regret, sorrow, mourn

grill *v.* broil, roast, sauté, barbecue, cook

grim *adj.* **SULLEN:** gloomy, sulky, morose, glum; **STERN:** austere, strict, harsh, severe; **RELENTLESS:** implacable, inexorable

grimace *n.* smirk, smile, sneer

grime *n.* dirt, soil, smudge, filth

grin *n.* smile, simper, smirk, wry

grin *v.* smirk, simper, beam, smile

grind *v.* crush, powder, mill, granulate, crumble

grip *n.* **GRASP:** hold, clutch, clasp, catch, clench, embrace, handshake; **SUITCASE:** valise, satchel, bag

grip *v.* grasp, clutch, clasp, seize

gripe *n.* complaint, grievance, beef, objection

gripe *v.* grumble, mutter, fuss, complain

grit *n.* pluck, courage; sand, dust

gritty *adj.* rough, abrasive, sandy, granular, scratchy

groan *n.* moan, sob, grunt, cry

groan *v.* moan, murmur, keen, cry

groceries *n.* food, edibles, comestibles, foodstuffs

groggy *adj.* sleepy, dizzy, reeling, tired

groom *v.* tend, rub, down, comb, brush

groove *n.* furrow, rut, channel, trench, depression, furrow, gutter, ditch

grope *v.* feel, search, fumble, touch, feel

gross *adj.* **WHOLE:** total, entire; **FAT:** corpulent, obese, huge; **OBSCENE:** indecent, lewd, coarse, shameful

grotesque *adj.* ludicrous, odd, bizarre, malformed, ugly, distorted, deformed

grotto *n.* cave, cavern, hollow

grouch *n.* complainer, grumbler, growler, bear, sourpuss, sorehead, crab, crank, bellyacher

grouch *v.* mutter, grumble, gripe, complain

grouchy *adv.* surly, ill–tempered, crusty, irritable

group *n.* **GATHERING:** assemblage, cluster, crowd; **COLLECTION:** accumulation, assortment, combination; **ORGANIZATION:** association, club, society

group *v.* assemble, file, assort, arrange, classify

grovel *v.* crawl, wallow, beg, kneel, crouch, kowtow, cower, snivel

grow *v.* **INCREASE:** expand, swell, wax, thrive, enlarge, multiply, flourish; **CHANGE:** become, develop, evolve, progress, age, ripen, blossom, mature; **CULTIVATE:** raise, tend, foster, produce, plant, breed

growl *v.* snarl, grumble, bark, grunt, cry

grown *adj.* aged, adult, mature

grub *v.* dig, root

grudge *n.* enmity, spite, rancor, animosity, hatred

grudge *v.* envy, begrudge, covet

gruel *n.* porridge, cereal

gruesome *adj.* horrible, ghastly, grim, grisly, frightful

gruff *adj.* bluff, churlish, harsh, grating, hoarse

grumble *v.* complain, growl, whine, protest, fuss

grumpy *adj.* sullen, grouchy, cantankerous, irritable

grunt *v.* snort, groan, mutter, grumble

guarantee *n.* surety, promise, bond

guarantee *v.* pledge, endorse, warrant, insure

guaranty *n.* warranty, contract, certificate

guard *n.* sentry, sentinel, watchman
guard *v.* protect, watch, patrol, picket, tend
guarded *adj.* **PROTECTED:** secured, defended, safe;
CAUTIOUS: circumspect, attentive, careful
guardian *n.* protector, overseer, trustee, custodian,
keeper, defender, supervisor, baby–sitter
guess *v.* estimate, presume, infer, speculate, imagine,
surmise, theorize, venture, suppose, presume
guest *n.* visitor, caller
guidance *n.* direction, leadership, supervision
guide *n.* leader, pilot, pathfinder, scout, escort, director, conductor, pioneer
guide *v.* lead, direct, conduct, escort
guilt *n.* responsibility, culpability, blame, error, fault,
liability, weakness, failing
guilty *adj.* condemned, censured, incriminated, in-
dicted, judged, damned, reproachable, chargeable
guise *n.* appearance, disguise
gulch *n.* ravine, gully, ditch, gorge
gulf *n.* **CHASM:** abyss, abysm, depth, ravine, **BAY:** inlet,
sound, cove
gull, *v.* deceive, trick, cheat
gullible *adj.* innocent, trustful, simple, naïve
gully *n.* channel, ditch, chasm, crevasse, ravine
gulp *v.* swallow, gasp, swig
gurgle *v.* babble, ripple, murmur
guru *n.* teacher, instructor, mentor
gush *v.* **FLOW:** pour, well, spew
gust *n.* blast, burst, blow, breeze, wind
gusto, *n.* enjoyment, zest, zeal, fervor, ardor
gutter *n.* channel, gully, sewer, drain, trough
guttural *adj.* throaty, gruff, deep, hoarse

guy n. MAN: chap, lad, fellow; GUIDE: rope, chain, cable

guzzle v. swill, quaff, swig, drink

gymnasium n. arena, coliseum, ring, rink, pit, gym

gymnast n. acrobat, tumbler, jumper, athlete

gypsy n. wanderer, tramp, vagrant, traveler

habiliments n. dress, garments

habit n. CUSTOM: mode, practice, fashion, manner; DRESS: costume; OBSESSION: addiction, fixation

habitat n. environment, territory, surroundings

habitual adj. customary, frequent, periodic, continual, routine, rooted, systematic, recurrent, repeated, accustomed, established, repetitious, stereotyped

hack adj. routine, trite

hack v. chop, whack, mangle, cut

hackneyed adj. commonplace, trite

hag n. crone, shrew, ogress, hellcat, fishwife, harridan, witch

haggard adj. gaunt, worn, tired

haggle v. bargain, wrangle, deal, argue, buy, sell

hail v. call, greet, salute, cheer, welcome, honor

halfhearted adj. indecisive, irresolute, indifferent

half–truth n. lie, deception

halfway adj. partial, midway, incomplete, partially, imperfectly, insufficiently, moderately, middling

halfway adv. half, partly

hall n. PUBLIC ROOM: chamber, assembly, arena, ballroom, church, clubhouse, salon, lounge, gymnasium, amphitheater, gallery; ENTRANCE: foyer, corridor, hallway

hallmark n. label, endorsement, seal, emblem

hallow v. bless, sanctify

hallucination n. delusion, vision

hallway *n.* foyer, entrance, way, corridor, entrance
halt *n.* stop, cessation
halt *v.* check, terminate, suspend, interrupt, block, stem, deter, stall, curb, restrict, arrest, suppress, intercept, obstruct, hinder, impede, squelch
halve *v.* divide, split, bisect
ham *n.* overacter, amateur, nonprofessional
hamlet *n.* town, village
hamper *v.* hinder, slow, thwart, embarrass
hand *n.* **WORKMAN:** helper, worker, laborer; **PENMANSHIP:** calligraphy, script; **APPLAUSE:** ovation, reception, handclapping; **CARDS:** deal, round, game
handbag *n.* pocketbook, bag, purse
handbook *n.* textbook, directory, guidebook
handcuff *v.* restrain, shackle
handicap *n.* disadvantage, obstacle, impediment, affliction, hindrance, disorder, injury
handicap *v.* encumber, hinder
handily *adv.* easily, skillfully, smoothly, cleverly
handkerchief *n.* napkin, hanky
handle *v.* **HOLD:** touch, finger, check, examine, feel; **MANAGE:** manipulate, operate, use, work; **DEAL:** retail, market, sell
handsome *adj.* attractive, impressive, stately, robust, well–dressed, slick, beautiful
hand–to–mouth *adj.* marginal, minimal, borderline
handwriting *n.* penmanship, hand, writing, script, scrawl, scribble, calligraphy, scratching
handy *adj.* **CONVENIENT:** near, nearby; **DEXTEROUS:** able; **USEFUL:** beneficial, advantageous, gainful, helpful, profitable, usable
hang *v.* **SUSPEND:** dangle, droop, drape; **WAVE:** flap,

swing; **KILL:** execute, lynch

hanging *adj.* **DANGLING:** swaying, swinging, overhanging, pendulous, drooping; **TENTATIVE:** uncertain

hang–out *n.* bar, joint, hole, headquarters, room

hang–up *n.* problem, predicament, difficulty

haphazard *adj.* accidental, random, offhand, casual, slipshod, reckless, irregular, unplanned, aimless

happen *v.* befall, occur, ensue, arise, transpire

happening *n.* incident, affair, accident, event

happily *adv.* joyously, gladly, cheerily, gaily, merrily, brightly, blissfully, cheerfully, gleefully

happiness *n.* mirth, merrymaking, cheer, merriment, delight, gladness, hilarity, gaiety, cheerfulness, rejoicing, exhilaration

happy *adj.* joyous, merry, mirthful, gay, laughing, contented, genial, satisfied, cheery, jolly, sparkling, blissful, exhilarated, pleased, gratified, ecstatic, overjoyed, radiant, smiling, elated

happy–go–lucky *adj.* easygoing, unconcerned, thoughtless, irresponsible

harangue *n.* speech, tirade

harass *v.* annoy, attack, tease, vex, irritate, bother

harbor *n.* refuge, port, pier, inlet, wharf, dock

harbor *v.* **PROTECT:** shelter, secure, defend, lodge; **CONSIDER:** entertain, cherish, regard

hard *adj.* **COMPACT:** unyielding, solid, impermeable, tough, dense, firm; **DIFFICULT:** arduous, tricky, trying, tedious, complex, abstract, puzzling, troublesome, laborious; **CRUEL:** perverse, unrelenting, vengeful; **SEVERE:** harsh, exacting, grim

hard–core *adj.* inflexible, dedicated, steadfast, unwavering, faithful

harden *v.* steel, temper, solidify, crystallize, clot, petrify, compact, concentrate, fossilize, toughen

hardheaded *adj.* willful, stubborn, headstrong

hardhearted *adj.* cold, unfeeling, heartless, cruel

hardly *adv.* scarcely, barely, imperceptibly, infrequently, somewhat, rarely, slightly, sparsely

hardship *n.* trial, sorrow, worry, difficulty, grief

hardware *n.* appliance, fixture, casting, metalware, implement, tool, fitting, utensil, equipment

hardy *adj.* tough, resistant, solid, staunch, seasoned, fit, acclimatized, rugged, robust, hearty, hale, vigorous, powerful, sturdy, solid, substantial, strong

hark, harden *v.* listen, heed

harm *n.* INJURY: infliction, impairment, damage; EVIL: wickedness, outrage, abuse

harm *v.* injure, wreck, cripple, hurt

harmful *adj.* injurious, detrimental, hurtful, noxious, evil, adverse, sinister, virulent, corroding, toxic, painful, crippling, malicious, malignant, unwholesome, corrupting, menacing, damaging, catastrophic, disastrous, destructive, unhealthy, mortal

harmless *adj.* pure, innocent, powerless, controllable, manageable, safe, trustworthy, sanitary

harmonious *adj.* HARMONIC: tuneful, musical, melodic; CONGRUOUS: agreeable, corresponding, suitable, adapted, similar, like, cooperative, friendly, conforming, balanced, symmetrical

harp *v.* carp, nag, repeat, pester, complain

harridan *n.* witch, hag, nag

harrow *v.* torment, distress

harry *v.* plunder, harass

harsh *adj.* rough, severe, discordant, jangling,

cacophonous, grating, dissonant, creaking, clashing, jarring, clamorous, hoarse, rasping, screeching, ear-splitting, tuneless, shrill

harvest *n.* crops, yield, fruit, grain, produce, vegetable

harvest *v.* glean, gather, accumulate, collect, garner, cut, pluck, pick, cull, hoard, mow

hasp *n.* fastener, latch

hassle *n.* dispute, squabble

haste *n.* speed, dispatch, precipitation, rashness, impetuousness, foolhardiness, recklessness, hastiness, carelessness, heedlessness

hasten *v.* HURRY: rush, fly, sprint; EXPEDITE: accelerate, quicken, push, urge, goad, press

hasty *adj.* HURRIED: quick, speedy, swift, fast; CARELESS: precipitate, foolhardy, careless, rash

hat *n.* headgear, headpiece, helmet, chapeau, bonnet, cap, derby, sombrero, topper, bowler, Panama, fedora, beret, turban, hood, cowl, beret

hatch *v.* produce, originate, bear

hatchway *n.* hatch, door, entrance

hate *n.* dislike, animosity, enmity, hatred

hate *v.* DETEST: abhor, abominate, loathe, despise, dislike, resent

hateful *adj.* odious, detestable, repugnant, offensive

hatred *n.* dislike, abhorrence, loathing, rancor, repugnance, repulsion, disgust, contempt, displeasure, bitterness, antagonism, animosity, pique, grudge, malice, malevolence, spleen, hostility, alienation

haughty *adj.* disdainful, arrogant, proud, egotistic

haul *n.* PULL: tug, lift, wrench; DISTANCE: voyage, trip; SPOILS: take, find, booty

haul *v.* drag, pull, bring, draw

haunt *v.* **FREQUENT:** habituate, visit; **OBSESS:** torment, possess, trouble, hound, terrify, plague, vex, harass, worry, frighten, annoy, bother, disturb

haunting *adj.* eerie, unforgettable, seductive, frightful

have *v.* **OWN:** keep, retain, use, maintain, control, treasure, hold, possess; **BEAR:** beget, produce

haven *n.* harbor, port, refuge, shelter

havoc *n.* destruction, confusion, devastation, plunder

hazard *n.* chance, risk, peril, jeopardy, danger

hazard *v.* chance, try, guess, gamble, risk

haze *n.* fog, mist, smog, cloudiness

hazy *adj.* vague, cloudy, foggy, murky, misty, unclear, overcast, filmy, gauzy, vaporous, smoky, dim, indistinct, dusky, obscure, veiled, blurred, faint

head *n.* **SKULL:** brainpan, scalp, crown, bean, noggin, noodle; **LEADER:** chief, commander, officer, ruler; **TOP:** summit, peak, crest; **BEGINNING:** front, start, source, origin; **INTELLIGENCE:** brains, foresight, ingenuity, judgment

head *v.* lead, direct, oversee, supervise, manage

headache *n.* **PAIN:** migraine, neuralgia; **PROBLEM:** vexation, mess, difficulty, trouble

headway *n.* progress, advance, increase, promotion

heal *v.* cure, restore, renew, regenerate, remedy, rejuvenate, medicate, revive, rehabilitate, resuscitate, salve, help, ameliorate, doctor

health *n.* vigor, wholeness, healthfulness, fitness, bloom, hardiness, stamina, energy, strength

healthy *adj.* sound, trim, robust, vigorous, well, hearty, athletic, able–bodied, virile, blooming, sturdy, firm, lively, flourishing, good, fit, rugged

heap *n.* pile, mass, stack, quantity

heap *v.* pile, add, lump, load, pack
hear *v.* LISTEN: attend, catch, apprehend, eavesdrop, perceive, overhear; TRY: judge, examine, referee
hearsay *n.* rumor, scandal, report, gossip
heart *n.* FEELING: response, sympathy, sensitivity, emotion; CENTER: core, middle, pith; SPIRIT: courage, fortitude, gallantry
heartache *n.* sorrow, pain, despair, anguish, grief
heartless *adj.* cruel, unkind, insensitive, ruthless
hearty *adj.* warm, zealous, sincere, cheery, cheerful, jovial, animated, ardent, genial, enthusiastic, genuine, passionate, intense, exuberant, devout, unfeigned, fervent, responsive, friendly
heat *n.* WARMTH: fever, sultriness; FERVOR: ardor, passion, excitement, desire
heat *v.* warm, inflame, kindle, thaw, boil, sear, singe, scorch, ignite
heated *adj.* WARMED: cooked, fried, baked FERVENT: fiery, ardent, avid, excited, passionate
heathen *adj.* infidel, atheist, barbarian
heave *v.* THROW: toss; MOVE: rock, bob, pitch, lurch, roll, reel, sway, throb, slosh
heavenly *adj.* DIVINE: celestial, supernal, angelic, holy; BLISSFUL: sweet, enjoyable, excellent, pleasant
heavy *adj.* WEIGHTY: ponderous, huge, stout, dense, substantial, hefty, large; BURDENSOME: troublesome, oppressive, vexatious, difficult, disturbing, onerous; DULL: listless, slow, apathetic, indifferent; GLOOMY: dejected, cloudy, overcast, dark, dismal, sad
heavy-handed *adj.* oppressive, harsh, cruel, severe
heckle *v.* torment, disturb, pester, bother, ridicule
hectic *adj.* frantic, unsettled, boisterous, restless,

confused, disordered

hector *v.* bully, annoy, tease, vex

heed *n.* notice, care

height *n.* altitude, elevation, prominence, loftiness, highness, tallness, stature, expanse, extent, length

heighten *v.* INCREASE: sharpen, redouble, emphasize, strengthen; RAISE: uplift, elevate, lift

heinous *adj.* hateful, atrocious, wicked

heir *n.* inheritor, successor, descendent, heiress, beneficiary, inheritor, prince

heirloom *n.* legacy, inheritance, bequest, gift, antique

heist *n.* robbery, burglary

heist *v.* rob, steal

helm *n.* leadership, control

help *n.* ASSISTANCE: advice, comfort, aid, support, gift, charity, encouragement, subsidy, service, relief, endowment, cooperation, guidance; EMPLOYEE: aid, representative, assistant, faculty, staff; RELIEF: maintenance, sustenance, nourishment, remedy

help *v.* assist, advise, encourage, cooperate, intercede, befriend, accommodate, sustain, benefit, bolster, promote, back, advocate, abet, stimulate, uphold, further, boost, support

helpful *adj.* USEFUL: valuable, significant, serviceable, profitable, advantageous, favorable, convenient, suitable, practical, operative, usable, applicable, desirable, convenient; CURATIVE: healthy, salutary, restorative, healthful; OBLIGING: accommodating, considerate, neighborly, kind

helping *n.* portion, serving, plateful, share

helpless *adj.* INCOMPETENT: incapable, unfit, inexpert; DEPENDENT: feeble, unable, weak, vulnerable

hem *n.* border, skirting, edging, edge, fringe, rim

henpeck *v.* nag, bully, suppress, intimidate, bother

herald *n.* proclaimer, forerunner

herd *n.* flock, group, drove, pack, brood, swarm, lot, bevy, covey, gaggle, nest, brood, flight, school, clan

herdsman *n.* shepherd, herder, rancher

hereditary *adj.* inherited, genetic, paternal

heredity *n.* ancestry, inheritance, genetic

heresy *n.* dissent, nonconformity, dissidence, sectarianism, schism, unorthodoxy, secularism

heretic *n.* schismatic, apostate, sectarian, cynic

heritage *n.* **INHERITANCE:** legacy, birthright, ancestry, dowry, share, endowment, status, heredity; **TRADITION:** culture, custom, fashion, system

hermit *n.* ascetic, recluse

hero *n.* champion, model, conqueror, god, martyr, warrior, saint, star, knight–errant

heroic *adj.* valiant, valorous, fearless, brave, noble

heroism *n.* fortitude, valor, bravery, courage, strength

hesitancy *n.* indecision, wavering, procrastination, delay, pause

hesitant *adj.* **DOUBTFUL:** skeptical, irresolute, uncertain; **SLOW:** delaying, wavering, dawdling, lazy

hesitate *v.* pause, stop, falter, vacillate, flounder, ponder, delay, weigh, consider, deliberate, linger

hesitation *n.* **DOUBT:** equivocation, skepticism, irresolution, uncertainty; **DELAY:** wavering, dawdling

hex *n.* spell, curse

hex *v.* curse, enchant

hiatus *n.* break, pause

hidden *adj.* secluded, private, covert, concealed, occult, masked, screened, veiled, clouded, obscured,

hide

disguised, unseen, camouflaged, shrouded, shadowy, clandestine, cloistered, surreptitious

hide *n.* skin, pelt, rawhide, fur, leather

hide *v.* conceal, shroud, curtain, veil, camouflage, cover, mask, cloak, screen, suppress, withhold, shield, secrete, hoard, closet, obscure, disguise

hideous *adj.* frightful, shocking, revolting, hateful, ghastly, grisly, ugly

hideout *n.* lair, den, refuge, retreat, shelter

hierarchy *n.* government, authority, ministry, regime

high *adj.* **TOWERING:** tall, gigantic, big, colossal, tremendous, great, giant, huge, formidable, immense, steep, elevated, lofty, soaring, raised; **EXALTED:** eminent, leading, powerful, distinguished, noble; **EXPENSIVE:** costly, precious, **EXTRAORDINARY:** great, special, unusual; **SHRILL:** piercing, sharp, penetrating; **DRUNK:** intoxicated, tipsy, inebriated

high-flown *adj.* lofty, exalted, pretentious

high-pressure *adj.* forceful, compelling, powerful

high-spirited *adj.* daring, dauntless, reckless, brave

high-strung *adj.* nervous, tense, impatient, restless

highway *n.* roadway, parkway, freeway, turnpike

hijack *v.* rob, steal, privateer, capture, seize

hike *n.* walk, tour, trek, trip, backpack, journey

hike *v.* **TRAMP:** tour, explore, travel, walk; **RAISE:** lift, advance, increase

hilarious *adj.* gay, merry, funny, amusing, lively, witty, entertaining

hill *n.* mound, knoll, butte, bluff, promontory, precipice, rising, headland, upland, inclination, slope, ascent, grade, incline, rise, foothill, dune, climb, elevation, hillside, hilltop

hinder *v.* stop, impede, obstruct, check, retard, fett- block, thwart, bar, clog, encumber, burden, inhib shackle, interrupt, arrest, curb, oppose, deter, ha per, frustrate, intercept, prohibit, stall, slow, dow smother, disappoint, spoil, gag, annul

hindrance *n.* obstacle, barrier, interference

hinge *n.* joint, pivot, juncture, articulation, link

hinge *v.* hang, turn, depend, connect, couple, join

hint *n.* allusion, mention, inkling, implication, refer- ence, observation, notice, tip, clue, omen, scent, no- tion, taste, suspicion, innuendo, sign, impression, indication, suggestion

hint *v.* intimate, inform, imply, infer, acquaint, re- mind, recall, cue, prompt, insinuate, indicate, wink, advise, suggest

hip *n.* **AWARE:** informed, enlightened, knowledgeable, cognizant; **FASHIONABLE:** modern, stylish

hire *v.* engage, secure, enlist, appoint, delegate, authorize, retain, commission, empower, select, pick, contract, procure

historic *adj.* factual, traditional, chronicled, old

history *n.* account, annals, records, archives, chroni- cle, writings, evidence, record

hit *adj.* struck, slugged, cuffed, smacked, clouted, banged, smashed, tapped, rapped, swatted, hurt

hit *n.* **STROKE:** blow, slap, rap, punch; **SUCCESS:** favor- ite, sellout, knockout

hit *v.* **STRIKE:** knock, sock, slap, bump, thump, col- lide, punch, hammer, whack, jab, tap, pelt, cuff, clout, club; **REACH:** find, win

hitch *n.* **KNOT:** loop, noose, tie; **DIFFICULTY:** obstacle, hindrance, block

hitch *v.* hook, unite, yoke, hook, fasten, join

hoard *n.* cache, treasure

hoard *v.* amass, acquire, keep, accumulate, save

hoary *adj.* white, old

hoax *n.* trick, fabrication, deceit, deception, lie

hobby *n.* pursuit, avocation, pastime, diversion, interest, activity, pursuit, sport, amusement, craft

hobo *n.* vagrant, vagabond, wanderer, beggar

hock *v.* sell, pledge, deposit, pawn

hod *n.* trough, scuttle

hodgepodge *n.* mixture, jumble, combination, mess

hoist *n.* lift, crane, derrick, elevator

hoist *v.* raise, lift

hokum *n.* nonsense, trickery, chicanery

hold *v.* **POSSESS:** keep, retain, have, accept; **SUPPORT:** sustain, brace, buttress, prop; **GRASP:** grip, clutch, embrace, squeeze, hug, seize; **CONFINE:** imprison, enclose, restrain; **RESIST:** persevere, continue, endure; **ADHERE:** cling, fasten, stick

holdout *n.* die–hard, objector, resister, resistance

holdover *n.* remnant, relic, surplus, remainder

holdup *n.* robbery, burglary, stick–up, crime, theft

hole *n.* **CAVITY:** perforation, puncture, slot, eyelet, split, tear, cleft, opening, fissure, gap, gash, rift, rupture, aperture, breach, eye, crater, gorge, hollow, chasm, crevasse, **BURROW:** den, lair; **DIFFICULTY:** impasse, tangle, mess, crisis, emergency

holiday *n.* festival, fiesta, carnival, jubilee, anniversary, celebration

holiness *n.* devoutness, humility, saintliness, devotion, worship

hollow *adj.* **CONCAVE:** sunken, depressed, excavated,

indented; **CAVERNOUS:** deep, resonant, booming, rumbling, reverberating, muffled, dull, resounding; **UNSOUND:** empty, pretentious

hollow *n.* cavity, dale, bowl, basin, valley

hollow *v.* scoop, excavate, indent, dig, shovel

holocaust *n.* loss, fire, destruction

holy *adj.* devout, pious, righteous, moral, just, good, angelic, godly, reverent, venerable, humble, saintly, innocent, godlike, saintlike, perfect, faultless, chaste, upright, virtuous, dedicated, devoted, spiritual, religious

homage *n.* loyalty, worship, respect, adoration, deference, devotion, reverence

home *n.* **DWELLING:** residence, habitation, abode, lodging, quarters, domicile, shelter; **ASYLUM:** orphanage, sanitarium, hospital

homecoming *n.* welcome, celebration, entry, arrival

homely *adj.* **UNPRETENTIOUS:** plain, snug, simple, cozy, modest; **PLAIN:** unattractive, uncomely

homespun *adj.* hand–crafted, domestic, homemade

homestead *n.* property, house, ranch, estate, home

homogenize *v.* blend, combine

homologous *adj.* equivalent, associated

honest *adj.* **TRUTHFUL:** trustworthy, unimpeachable, legitimate, straight; **FRANK:** candid, straightforward, aboveboard; **FAIR:** just, equitable, impartial

honesty *n.* fidelity, scrupulousness, candor, openness, morality, goodness, virtue

honk *v.* blare, trumpet, bellow, sound

honor *n.* distinction, recognition, attention, reputation, tribute, integrity

honor *v.* **RESPECT:** worship, sanctify, venerate, praise;

VALUE: admire, esteem, compliment; **ACCEPT:** clear, pass, acknowledge

honorable *adj.* reputable, creditable, distinguished, famous, noble

honorary *adj.* titular, nominal, complimentary

hood *n.* **COVERING:** cowl, shawl, bonnet, veil, capuchin, mantle; **CANOPY:** awning, cover; **HOODLUM:** criminal, gangster, crook

hoodlum *n.* rowdy, thug, gangster, crook, criminal

hook *n.* lock, catch, clasp, fastener

hook *v.* **BEND:** curve, angle, crook, arch; **CATCH:** pin, secure, fasten

hoot *n.* howl, whoop, boo, cry

hop *v.* leap, jump, skip, bounce

hope *n.* **FAITH:** expectation, anticipation; **DREAM:** desire, purpose, wish, goal

hope *v.* expect, desire, await, suppose, believe, anticipate, trust

hopeful *adj.* **OPTIMISTIC:** expectant, trustful, anticipating, trusting, confident; **ENCOURAGING:** promising, reassuring, favorable, cheering, propitious, auspicious, uplifting, heartening, inspiring

hopeless *adj.* unfortunate, bad, incurable, vain, irreversible, irreparable, disastrous, tragic, desperate

horde *n.* crowd, swarm, pack, throng, gathering

horizon *n.* range, border, limit, boundary, extent

horizontal *adj.* **LEVEL:** aligned, parallel, flat, straight; **EVEN:** flush, uniform, regular, smooth

horrible *adj.* repulsive, dreadful, disgusting, terrible, frightful, shameful, shocking, awful

horrid *adj.* shocking, hideous, disturbing, shameful, offensive, pitiful

horrify *v.* shock, terrify
horror *n.* fear, terror, awe, fright
hors d'oeuvre *n.* appetizer, canapé
horseman *n.* cavalryman, knight, dragoon, equestrian, jockey, cowboy, rider
horticulture *n.* cultivation, agriculture, farming
hospitable *adj.* kind, receptive, cordial, courteous, open, friendly
hospital *n.* clinic, infirmary, sanitarium, dispensary
hospitality *n.* companionship, fellowship, entertainment, welcome
hostile *adj.* unfriendly, antagonistic, hateful, opposed
hostility *n.* abhorrence, aversion, bitterness, hatred
hot *adj.* **BURNING:** fiery, flaming, blazing, baking, roasting, scorching, blistering, searing, sizzling, broiling, scalding, parching; **AROUSED:** furious, ill-tempered, indignant, angry
hotel *n.* motel, lodging, inn, hostel, resort, tavern
hotrod *n.* car, racer, dragster
hound *n.* dog, cur
hound *v.* bully, pester, badger, provoke, annoy
house *n.* **HOME:** habitation, dwelling, residence; **FAMILY:** line, tradition, ancestry; **LEGISLATURE:** congress, council, parliament
housekeeper *n.* caretaker, servant
hover *v.* remain, wait, float, linger
howl *v.* cry, wail, bawl, lament, yell
hub *n.* center, core, middle, focus, heart
hubbub *n.* uproar, bustle
huddle *v.* crowd, cluster, group, conference
hue *n.* color, tint, value, dye
huff *n.* anger, annoyance, pique

huff *v.* puff, blow, bluster, bully
huffy *adj.* offended, piqued, angry, insulted, irritable
hug *v.* embrace, hold, squeeze, clasp, press, cling, clutch, envelop, enfold, nestle, cuddle
huge *adj.* large, tremendous, enormous, immense
hulking *adj.* bulky, massive
humane *adj.* merciful, kind, benevolent, sympathetic, understanding, compassionate, kindhearted, tenderhearted, forgiving, charitable, tender, generous, lenient, tolerant, altruistic, philanthropic, magnanimous, unselfish, warmhearted
humanitarian *adj.* humane, kindly
humble *adj.* **MEEK:** submissive, gentle, diffident, retiring, bashful, shy, timid, reserved, deferential, mild, withdrawn, hesitant, fearful, tentative, obedient, passive, tame, restrained, subdued; **UNPRETENTIOUS:** unassuming, modest, seemly, becoming, homespun, natural, servile, shabby, beggarly, insignificant, plain, common, homely, simple
humble *v.* humiliate, shame, mortify, chasten, demean, demote, lower, crush, degrade, discredit, deflate, squelch, squash
humbug *n.* hoax, fraud, lie, deception, nonsense
humdrum *adj.* monotonous, common, uninteresting, dull
humid *adj.* moist, damp, stuffy, sticky, muggy, close
humiliate *v.* humble, shame, debase, chasten, mortify, degrade, dishonor, demean, conquer, vanquish, disgrace, embarrass
humiliation *n.* chagrin, mortification, disgrace, embarrassment, shame
humility *n.* meekness, timidity, submissiveness,

servility, subservience, resignation, shyness

humor *n.* COMEDY: entertainment, amusement, jesting, raillery; WITTICISM: pleasantry, banter, joke, mirth; DISPOSITION: wittiness, jolliness, gaiety, joyfulness, playfulness

humor *v.* indulge, pamper, gratify, please, appease, placate, comfort

humorous *adj.* amusing, funny, comical, entertaining

hunch *n.* intuition, notion, feeling, premonition, instinct, anticipation, clue, foreboding, portent, apprehension, misgiving, qualm, suspicion, inkling

hunger *n.* longing, yearning, lust, want

hunger *v.* crave, desire

hungry *adj.* starved, famished, ravenous, desirous, unsatisfied, unfilled, starving, voracious

hunk *n.* lump, chunk, mass, clod, slice, morsel

hunt *v.* PURSUE: follow, stalk, hound, trail, seek, track, chase; INVESTIGATE: search, probe, seek

hurdle *n.* obstacle, barricade, blockade, barrier

hurl *v.* throw, cast, fling, heave

hurrah *v.* applaud, cheer, approve

hurry *v.* HASTEN: scurry, scuttle, dash, sprint, rush, scoot, dart, spring, speed, fly, bustle, race; URGE: drive, push, spur, goad

hurt *adj.* injured, harmed, wounded, disfigured, suffering, distressed, tortured, unhappy

hurt *v.* INJURE: cut, bruise, slap, abuse, flog, whip, torture, stab, harm, wound, lacerate, bite, burn, punch, pinch, scourge, lash, cane, switch; HARM: maltreat, injure, spoil, damage, destroy; PAIN: ache, throb, sting

hurtful *adj.* aching, injurious, deadly, harmful

husband *v.* economize, conserve
hush *v.* calm, soothe, quiet, silence, gag, stifle
husky *adj.* **HOARSE:** rough, throaty, growling, gruff; **STRONG:** muscular, sinewy, strapping
hustle *v.* rush, push, hurry, race, run, speed
hut *n.* shanty, lean–to, shack, dugout, hovel
hygiene *n.* health, sanitation, cleanliness
hygienic *adj.* healthful, sanitary, clean, pure, sterile
hyperbole *n.* metaphor, exaggeration
hypnotic *adj.* narcotic, soporific, soothing
hypnotize *v.* mesmerize, fascinate, captivate, stupefy, soothe, anesthetize
hypocrisy *n.* pretense, affectation, bigotry, sanctimony, dishonesty, lie
hypocrite *n.* pretender, fraud, faker, deceiver, charlatan, trickster, rascal
hypothesis *n.* theory, supposition, assumption, guess, opinion
hypothetical *adj.* **SUPPOSED:** imagined, uncertain, vague, assumed, likely, **POSTULATED:** academic, philosophical, logical
hysteria, hysterics *n.* neurosis, emotionalism, delirium, agitation, confusion, excitement, nervousness
hysterical, *adj.* frantic, convulsed, raving, delirious, emotional, neurotic, distracted, distraught, unrestrained, convulsive, uncontrollable, agitated, frenzied, tempestuous, impassioned, overwrought
icon *n.* image, picture
iconoclast *n.* dissenter, rebel
idea *n.* **CONCEPT:** belief, theory, hypothesis, assumption, conjecture, notion, thought; **FANCY:** whimsy, whim, fantasy, imagination

ideal *adj.* **TYPICAL:** model, archetypal; **PERFECT:** best, theoretical, supreme, fitting, exemplary, excellent

ideal *n.* concept, paragon, goal, prototype, model

idealism *n.* principle, conscience, philosophy, ethics

identical *adj.* same, alike, twin, indistinguishable

identification *n.* **CLASSIFYING:** naming, cataloguing, description, classification; **CREDENTIALS:** passport, testimony, papers, badge

identify *v.* classify, catalog, analyze, describe, name

identity *n.* characteristics, identification, individuality, uniqueness, name

ideology *n.* philosophy, belief, doctrine, ethics

idiom *n.* expression, usage, jargon, argot

idiot *n.* simpleton, nincompoop, booby, fool

idiotic *adj.* thick–witted, dull, moronic, stupid

idle *adj.* unemployed, unoccupied, uncultivated, fallow, motionless, inert, resting

idle *v.* loiter, slack, shirk, loaf

idol *n.* image, icon, god, figurine, fetish, totem

idolatry *n.* worship, love, infatuation, fervor, zeal

idolize *v.* worship, glorify, adore, canonize

ignite *v.* fire, light, enkindle, burn

ignoble *adj.* mean, dishonorable

ignominy *n.* shame, disgrace

ignorance *n.* incomprehension, incapacity, inexperience, illiteracy, simplicity, shallowness

ignorant *adj.* **UNAWARE:** unconscious, shallow, superficial, inexperienced, unwitting, unintelligent, obtuse, dense, shallow, stupid; **UNTRAINED:** illiterate, uneducated, misguided, apprenticed, naïve

ignore *v.* disregard, reject, overlook, neglect

ilk *n.* type, kind

ill *adj.* **BAD:** harmful, evil, noxious, unfavorable; **SICK:** unwell, unhealthy, ailing

ill *n.* evil, depravity, misfortune, mischief, wrong

illegal *adj.* unlawful illicit banned outlawed unauthorized unlicensed, illegitimate, prohibited, forbidden, criminal

illegible *adj.* unreadable, faint, unintelligible, confused, obscure

illicit *adj.* unlawful, prohibited, unauthorized, illegal

illiteracy *n.* ignorance, stupidity, idiocy

illiterate *adj.* ignorant, uneducated, unenlightened

illness *n.* sickness, infirmity, disorder, attack, convalescence, complaint, collapse, breakdown, confinement, weakness, disease, ailment, malady

illogical *adj.* irrational, unreasonable, absurd, fallacious, incorrect, inconsistent, unscientific, contradictory, unsound, implausible

ill–tempered *adj.* cross, touchy, querulous, irritable

illuminate *v.* **BRIGHTEN:** lighten, illumine, decorate, light; **CLARIFY:** illustrate, explain, interpret, elucidate

illumination *n.* **LIGHT:** flame, brilliance, lighting; **CLARIFICATION:** instruction, teaching, education, information, knowledge

illusion *n.* deception, fancy, hallucination, mirage, apparition, delusion, trick, dream

illusory *adj.* deceiving, unreal

illustrate *v.* explain; picture, portray, depict

illustration *n.* explanation, picture, engraving, vignette, inset, newsphoto, chart, diagram

illustrative *adj.* symbolic, representative, pictorial, descriptive, explanatory, graphic

illustrious *adj.* distinguished, famous

image *n.* LIKENESS: idol, representation, effigy, form, drawing, portrait, photograph, replica, picture; CONCEPT: conception, perception, thought, idea

imagery *n.* metaphor, representation, comparison

imaginable *adj.* conceivable, comprehensible, sensible, possible, plausible, believable, reasonable, likely

imaginary *adj.* fancied, illusory, visionary, dreamy, hypothetical, theoretical, imagined, hallucinatory, whimsical, fabulous, nonexistent, mythological, legendary, fictitious, unreal

imagination *n.* inventiveness, conception, sensitivity, visualization, awareness, insight

imaginative *adj.* creative, inventive, artistic, original

imagine *v.* conceive, invent, picture, conjure, envision, invent, fabricate, formulate, devise, conceptualize, dream, perceive, create

imbalance *n.* unevenness, inequality, irregularity

imbecilic *adj.* foolish, silly

imbibe *v.* ingest, gorge, guzzle, drink, swallow

imbroglio *n.* commotion, entanglement, fracas

imbue *v.* permeate, invade, absorb

imitate *v.* MIMIC: impersonate, mirror, mime, ape, simulate, parody; COPY: duplicate, counterfeit, falsify, reproduce; RESEMBLE: simulate, parallel

imitation *n.* SIMULATION: duplication, mimicry, impersonation, copy; COUNTERFEIT: likeness, replica, substitution, forgery

imitative *adj.* deceptive, false, forged, sham

immaculate *adj.* pure, unsoiled, unsullied, spotless, stainless, bright, clean

immanent *adj.* deep–seated, inherent

immaterial *adj.* unimportant, insignificant

151

immature *adj.* childish, youthful, sophomoric, naïve
immediate *adj.* now, next, prompt, following
immense *adj.* large, gigantic, tremendous, enormous
immerse *v.* plunge, involve, submerge, douse, steep, soak, drench, dunk, souse
immigrant *n.* outsider, newcomer, alien
immigrate *v.* move, enter
immigration *n.* colonization, settlement, migration
imminent *adj.* impending, approaching, coming
immobility *n.* firm, fixed, motionless
immodest *adj.* brazen, shameless, bold, egotistic
immoral *adj.* sinful, corrupt, shameless, bad
immorality *n.* vice, depravity, dissoluteness, evil
immortal *adj.* **DEATHLESS:** undying, imperishable, endless, timeless, everlasting, indestructible, enduring, eternal; **ILLUSTRIOUS:** celebrated, eminent, glorious, famous
immovable *adj.* solid, stable, fixed, firm
immune *adj.* exempt, free, unsusceptible, privileged, excused, safe
immunity *n.* **EXEMPTION:** privilege, license, freedom; **IMMUNIZATION:** resistance, protection
immure *v.* confine, imprison
impact *n.* shock, impression, contact, collision
impair *v.* diminish, spoil, injure, hurt, break, damage
impart *v.* **GIVE:** bestow, grant, present, allow; **INFORM:** tell, announce, divulge, admit, reveal
impartial *adj.* unbiased, disinterested, equal, fair
impartiality *n.* objectivity, candor, equality, fairness
impasse *n.* deadlock, standstill, cessation, pause
impassioned *adj.* ardent, fervent, passionate
impassive *adj.* emotionless, unemotional, unmoved

impatience *n.* agitation, restlessness, anxiety, excitement, nervousness

impatient *adj.* anxious, eager, feverish, restless

impeach *v.* charge, arraign, denounce, indict, discredit, reprimand, blame, incriminate, try

impeccable *adj.* flawless, perfect

impede *v.* hinder, obstruct, slow

impediment *n.* obstruction, hindrance, obstacle, difficulty, barrier

impel *v.* drive, force, urge

impend *v.* approach, threaten

impenetrable *adj.* **DENSE:** impervious, hard, compact, firm, thick; **INCOMPREHENSIBLE:** unintelligible, inscrutable, unfathomable, obscure

impenitent *adj.* unrepentant, remorseless

imperative *adj.* **NECESSARY:** obligatory, mandatory; **AUTHORITATIVE:** masterful, commanding, dominant, aggressive, powerful

imperfect *adj.* flawed, incomplete, deficient, faulty

imperfection *n.* fault, flaw, stain, blemish

imperious *adj.* haughty, arrogant

impersonal *adj.* detached, disinterested, indifferent

impersonate *v.* portray, mimic, represent, imitate

impersonation *n.* role, enactment, performance

impertinent *adj.* impudent, saucy, insolent, rude

impervious *adj.* impassable, impermeable, impenetrable, watertight

impetuous *adj.* hasty, impulsive

impetus *n.* force, momentum, stimulus, incentive, purpose, reason

impinge *v.* encroach, infringe, strike, touch

impious *adj.* sinful, profane, blasphemous, bad

implement *n.* tool, instrument, appliance, utensil
implicate *v.* involve, connect, associate, link, relate
implication *n.* indication, inference, guess
implicit *adj.* **UNDERSTOOD:** implied; **DEFINITE:** certain, absolute, accurate, inevitable
imply *v.* indicate, intimate, suggest, hint, implicate, signify, mean, indicate
impolite *adj.* discourteous, churlish, rude, sullen
impolitic *adj.* imprudent, unwise
import *n.* meaning, signification
importance *n.* import, consequence, bearing, influence, emphasis, weight, relevance
important *adj.* **WEIGHTY:** significant, momentous, essential, critical, primary, foremost, marked, valuable, crucial, vital, serious, consequential; **EMINENT:** illustrious, well–known, influential, famous
importune *v.* urge, entreat
impose *v.* force, presume, burden, compel
imposing *adj.* stirring, overwhelming, impressive
imposition *n.* burden, pressure, encumbrance, demand, restraint
impossibility *n.* hopelessness, difficulty, futility
impossible *adj.* inconceivable, vain, unattainable, insurmountable, unworkable, futile, hopeless
impostor *n.* fraud, deceiver, pretender, charlatan
imposture *n.* ruse, deceit, hoax, sham
impotent *adj.* **WEAK:** powerless, inept, infirm, unable; **STERILE:** barren, frigid, unproductive
impound *v.* appropriate, take, usurp, seize
impoverish *v.* bankrupt, exhaust, destroy
impoverished *adj.* bankrupt, broke, poor, ruined
impractical *adj.* unrealistic, unworkable, improbable,

illogical, absurd, wild, impossible, idealistic

impregnable *adj.* invulnerable, unassailable

impregnate *v.* **PERMEATE:** fill, pervade, soak, infuse; **BEGET:** conceive, reproduce, fertilize

impress *v.* **MARK:** indent, emboss, imprint, dent, stamp; **FASCINATE:** affect, dazzle, stir, fascinate

impression *n.* **MARK:** imprint, dent, indentation, depression; **EFFECT:** response, reaction; **NOTION:** theory, conjecture, supposition, guess, opinion

impressionable *adj.* perceptive, receptive, affected

impressive *adj.* stirring, moving, inspiring, thrilling, intense, dramatic, absorbing, profound, remarkable, extraordinary, notable, momentous

imprint *n.* **IDENTIFICATION:** banner, trademark, emblem, signature; **IMPRESSION:** dent, indentation

imprint *v.* print, stamp, designate, mark

imprison *v.* jail, confine, incarcerate, detain, hold, intern, cage, enclose

improbable *adj.* doubtful, unlikely

improper *adj.* indecent, incongruous, inadvisable, untimely, inappropriate, unbefitting, unsuitable

improve *v.* update, refine, enrich, enhance, augment

improvement *n.* betterment, advancement, development, growth, enrichment, renovation, reorganization, amendment, revision, refinement, modernization, enhancement, remodeling, supplement

impudent *adj.* bold, insolent, forward, rude

impulse *n.* **THROB:** surge, pulsation, beat; **FANCY:** urge, stimulus, whim, caprice, spontaneity, notion, inclination, disposition

impulsive *adj.* impetuous, spontaneous

impure *adj.* adulterated, diluted, debased, tainted,

contaminated, polluted, corrupted, doctored
impute *v.* ascribe, assign, charge
inability *n.* incompetence, incapacity, shortcoming, failure, weakness, lack, frailty
inaccessible *adj.* distant, rare, remote, separated
inaccuracy *n.* mistake, exaggeration, deception, error
inaccurate *adj.* incorrect, inexact, fallacious, incorrect, mistaken, wrong
inactive *adj.* idle, lazy, dormant, still, motionless
inadequacy *n.* inferiority, weakness, defect, flaw, drawback, shortcoming, blemish, lack
inadequate *adj.* insufficient, lacking, scanty, meager, deficient, imperfect, defective, unsatisfactory
inane *adj.* senseless, pointless, foolish, silly
inanimate *adj.* lifeless, dull, inert, idle, motionless
inappropriate *adj.* improper, unsuitable
inapt *adj.* unfit, unsuitable
inarticulate *adj.* MUTE: reticent, speechless, wordless; INCOMPREHENSIBLE: obscure, unintelligible, vague
inattentive *adj.* preoccupied, indifferent, negligent, careless, diverted
inaugurate *v.* induct, begin, introduce, initiate, begin
incalculable *adj.* unpredictable, uncertain
incantation *n.* chant, charm, recitation, supplication
incapable *adj.* inadequate, incompetent, inexperienced, naïve, poor, unqualified, unsuited
incapacitate *v.* disable, disqualify, invalidate
incarcerate *v.* confine, imprison
incarnate *adj.* bodily, manifest, personified
incense *n.* scent, fragrance, essence, perfume
incense *v.* inflame, anger
incentive *n.* motive, spur, inducement, stimulus,

impetus, enticement, temptation, inspiration, encouragement, reason

incessant *adj.* continual, ceaseless, constant

inchoate *adj.* shapeless, formless

incidence *n.* range, occurrence, scope

incident *n.* occurrence, happening, episode, event

incidental *adj.* subsidiary, related, subordinate

incinerate *v.* burn, cremate

incise *v.* cut, engrave, dissect, chop, split, divide

incision *n.* cut, gash, slash, surgery

incisive *adj.* cutting, keen, sarcastic, trenchant

incite *v.* rouse, stir, stimulate, provoke, spur, goad, persuade, induce, urge, inspire

inclement *adj.* stormy, severe; cruel, merciless

inclination *n.* TENDENCY: bias, bent, propensity, predilection, penchant, leaning, disposition, preference, drift, trend; SLANT: pitch, slope, incline, angle, ramp, bank, lean, list, grade

incline *v.* LEAN: tilt, bow, nod; TEND: prefer, favor

inclined *adj.* leaning, sloping

include *v.* contain, embrace, involve, incorporate, constitute, interject, insert

inclusive *adj.* including, incorporating

incoherent *adj.* UNCONNECTED: disorganized; INDISTINCT: unintelligible, muddled, muttered, muffled

income *n.* revenue, earnings, salary, wages, profit, dividends, proceeds, receipts, commission

incommensurate *adj.* disproportionate, inadequate

incomparable *adj.* excellent, exceptional, matchless, perfect, superior, unequaled, unique, unusual

incompatible *adj.* irreconcilable, incongruous, contrary, clashing, contradictory, inconstant, discordant

incompetent

incompetent *adj.* incapable, unfit, unskilled, bungling, ineffectual, clumsy, awkward, inexperienced
incomplete *adj.* imperfect, rough, unfinished
inconceivable *adj.* unthinkable, unbelievable
incongruous *adj.* inconsistent, contradictory
inconsequential *adj.* irrelevant, trivial, unnecessary
inconsiderate *adj.* thoughtless, boorish, impolite, discourteous, rude
inconsistent *adj.* illogical, contradictory, incoherent
inconspicuous *adj.* concealed, hidden, obscure
inconstant *adj.* varying, fickle
inconvenience *n.* trouble, discomfort, bother
incorporation *n.* embodiment, addition
incorrect *adj.* false, mistaken, unreliable, wrong
incorrigible *adj.* bad, difficult
increase *n.* growth, addition, development, spread, enlargement, expansion, escalation
increase *v.* extend, enlarge, expand, dilate, broaden, widen, thicken, deepen, build, lengthen, augment, escalate, amplify, supplement
incredible *adj.* unbelievable, improbable, ridiculous
incredulous *adj.* disbelieving, skeptical
incriminate *v.* charge, involve, implicate, blame
incumbent *adj.* binding, obligatory
incurable *adj.* fatal, serious, hopeless, deadly
incursion *n.* inroad, invasion
indebted *adj.* obligated, grateful, appreciative
indecent *adj.* offensive, immoral, bad, lewd, shameful
indecency *n.* vulgarity, impropriety
indecision *n.* hesitation, doubt, uncertainty
indecisive *adj.* irresolute, unstable
indefinite *adj.* vague, uncertain, unsure, unsettled

indelible *adj.* ingrained, enduring, strong, permanent
indemnify *v.* compensate, protect
indentation *n.* imprint, recession, depression, dent
independence *n.* freedom, sovereignty, license
indestructible *adj.* durable, immortal, permanent
index *v.* list, catalog, alphabetize, arrange, tabulate
indicate *v.* SIGNIFY: symbolize, betoken, intimate, mean; DESIGNATE: show, name, point
indication *n.* symptom, evidence, sign, hint
indicator *n.* dial, pointer
indictment *n.* accusation, detention, incrimination
indifferent *adj.* unconcerned, cool, unemotional, unsympathetic, heartless, unresponsive, unfeeling, nonchalant, impassive, detached, callous, stony, remote, reserved, distant, arrogant, unmoved
indigent *adj.* destitute, impoverished, poor
indignant *adj.* angry, upset, displeased, piqued
indignity *n.* affront, humiliation, injury, insult
indirect *adj.* devious, roundabout, tortuous, twisting, devious, sinister, rambling, oblique
indiscreet *adj.* imprudent, misguided, rash, tactless
indiscriminate *adj.* random, chaotic, aimless
indispensable *adj.* necessary, required, essential
indisposed *adj.* DISINCLINED: reluctant, unwilling; ILL: ailing, sickly, weak
indisputable *adj.* incontrovertible, undeniable, undoubted, unquestionable, certain
indistinct *adj.* vague, confused, indefinite, obscure
individual *adj.* personal, particular, solitary, distinctive, personalized, sole, private
indoctrinate *v.* instruct, implant, influence, teach
indomitable *adj.* invincible, unconquerable

induce

induce *v.* begin, cause, effect, persuade, produce
inducement *n.* incentive, influence, motive
induct *v.* admit, recruit, enroll, conscript, draft
induction *n.* **REASONING:** rationalization, conjecture, reason; **INITIATION:** ordination, consecration
indulge *v.* humor, coddle, entertain, gratify
indulgence *n.* **HUMORING:** coddling, pampering, spoiling, placating, gratifying; **REVELRY:** intemperance, greed, waste
industrious *adj.* diligent, intent, involved, active, busy
industry *n.* activity, persistence, application, perseverance, enterprise, zeal, inventiveness, attention
inebriate *v.* exhilarate, intoxicate, stupefy
ineffective *adj.* inadequate, incompetent, weak
inefficient *adj.* prodigal, improvident, wasteful
ineligible *adj.* unqualified, unsuitable, unfit
inept *adj.* bungling, clumsy, incompetent, awkward
inert *adj.* inactive, sluggish, still, dormant, idle
inevitable *adj.* unavoidable, irresistible, fated, sure, inescapable, destined, unalterable, ordained
inexorable *adj.* rigid, stubborn, inflexible
inexperienced *adj.* unskilled, untried, youthful, new, immature, tender, raw, green
infallible *adj.* perfect, accurate, certain
infamous *adj.* notorious, wicked, heinous, offensive
infant *n.* baby, minor, child, tot
infantile *adj.* childlike, juvenile, childish, naïve
infect *v.* taint, defile, spoil
infer *v.* deduce, conclude, gather, assume
inferior *adj.* subordinate, mediocre, common, poor
inferiority *n.* deficiency, inadequacy, weakness
infernal *adj.* fiendish , devilish

infest *v.* **CONTAMINATE:** pollute, infect, corrupt; **INVADE:** crowd, jam, teem, flood, flock, overwhelm

infidelity *n.* unfaithfulness, adultery

infiltrate *v.* permeate, pervade, penetrate, join

infinite *adj.* endless, limitless, countless, incalculable, boundless, immense, endless

infinitesimal *adj.* tiny, small

infirm *adj.* sickly, weak

infirmary *n.* clinic, sickroom, hospital

infirmity *n.* disease, weakness, frailty, debility

inflame *v.* **AROUSE:** incense, disturb, excite; **HURT:** redden, swell; **BURN:** kindle, scorch, ignite

inflate *v.* **DISTEND:** expand, swell, bloat, balloon, widen; **EXAGGERATE:** magnify, overestimate, raise

inflection *n.* tone, enunciation, intonation, accent

inflexibility *n.* toughness, rigidity, stiffness, firmness

inflexible *adj.* rigid, unyielding, taut, firm, stiff

inflict *v.* impose, administer, deliver, strike, cause

influence *n.* power, authority, control, command, esteem, prominence, prestige, reputation

influence *v.* affect, impress, compel, urge, shape, convince, persuade, motivate

influential *adj.* prominent, substantial, powerful

inform *v.* tell, betray, instruct, relate, teach

informal *adj.* casual, intimate, relaxed

information *n.* **KNOWLEDGE:** facts, evidence, details, statistics, data; **NEWS:** report, notice, message

infraction *n.* violation, breach

infrequent *adj.* seldom, occasional, scarce, rare

infringe *v.* encroach, trespass, transgress, meddle

infuriate *v.* aggravate, enrage, provoke, anger

infuse *v.* fill, inspire; steep

ingenious

ingenious *adj.* able, clever, cunning, gifted, intelligent, original, resourceful, shrewd, skillful
ingenuity *n.* cleverness, imagination, inventiveness, originality, productiveness, resourcefulness
ingenuous *adj.* candid, innocent, straightforward
ingrain *v.* imbue, fix, instill, teach
ingratiate *v.* charm, seduce, disarm
ingredient *n.* component, constituent, element
inhabit *v.* dwell, occupy, reside, stay
inhabitant *n.* occupant, dweller, lodger, roomer, boarder, tenant, resident
inherent *adj.* inborn, inbred, inherited, innate, intrinsic, native, natural
inherit *v.* acquire, receive, succeed, get
inheritance *n.* bequest, legacy, heritage, gift
inhibit *v.* check, restrain, repress, frustrate, hinder
inhibition *n.* restraint, hindrance, interference
inhuman *adj.* mean, heartless, cruel, fierce, ruthless
iniquity *n.* crime, evil, injustice, sin, wickedness
initial *adj.* beginning, starting, basic, primary, elementary, first, fundamental
initiate *n.* beginner, learner, novice
initiation *n.* **BEGINNING:** introduction; **INDOCTRINATION:** induction, orientation
initiative *n.* enterprise, responsibility
injure *v.* harm, damage, wound, hurt
injurious *adj.* harmful, detrimental, damaging
injury *n.* hurt, abrasion, wound, laceration, affliction
injustice *n.* infringement, violation, transgression, breach, infraction, wrong
inkling *n.* hint, indication, notion, innuendo, suspicion, suggestion

inmate *n.* occupant, patient, convict, prisoner
inn *n.* tavern, hostel, hotel, motel, resort
innate *adj.* inborn, native
innermost *adj.* intimate, private, secret
innocence *n.* honesty, simplicity, purity, naïveté, chastity, ignorance, virtue
innocent *adj.* GUILTLESS: blameless, faultless, honest; OPEN: guileless, frank, childish, naïve, natural, simple; PURE: unblemished, wholesome, upright, virtuous, righteous, angelic; HARMLESS: innocuous, inoffensive, safe
innovation *n.* change, newness, addition
innuendo *n.* hint, insinuation, aside, intimation
innumerable *adj.* countless, incalculable
inopportune *adj.* disadvantageous, ill–timed, inappropriate, awkward, untimely
input *n.* data, information, knowledge, facts
input *v.* add, enter
inquest *n.* inquiry, investigation
inquire *v.* ask, investigate, probe, interrogate
inquiry *n.* probe, analysis, hearing, examination
inquisitive *adj.* curious, questioning, meddling, analytical, prying, snoopy, nosy, interested
inquisitor *n.* examiner, questioner
inroad *n.* encroachment, invasion
insane *adj.* DEMENTED: crazed, frenzied, lunatic, balmy, psychotic, raving, deluded, possessed, obsessed; FOOLISH: madcap, daft, idiotic, stupid
insanity *n.* abnormality, dementia, psychosis, neurosis, phobia, mania
insatiate *adj.* ravenous, voracious
inscribe *v.* address, carve, dedicate, engrave, write

inscription *n.* dedication, engraving, legend
insecure *adj.* anxious, vague, uncertain, troubled
insert *v.* introduce, place, inject, include
insidious *adj.* treacherous, deceitful, harmful
insight *n.* perspicacity, shrewdness, intelligence
insignia *n.* badge, rank, ensign, symbol, decoration, emblem
insignificant *adj.* trivial, unimportant, irrelevant, petty, trifling
insincere *adj.* deceitful, pretentious, shifty, dishonest, false, hypocritical, sly
insinuate *v.* hint, suggest, imply, purport, mention
insipid *adj.* dull, flat, tasteless, uninteresting
insist *v.* persist, demand
insolent *adj.* disrespectful, insulting, rude
insolvent *adj.* bankrupt, broke, failed, ruined
inspect *v.* examine, scrutinize, probe, examine
inspiration *n.* IDEA: notion, whim, fancy, impulse, thought; STIMULUS: spur, influence, incentive
inspire *v.* encourage, enthuse, fire, invigorate, motivate, stimulate
install *v.* establish, introduce, inaugurate
installation *n.* induction, ordination, inauguration, launching, establishment
installment *n.* payment, part
instance *n.* example, case, situation, occurrence
instant *adj.* momentary, quick, pressing, current
instantly *adv.* urgently, directly, immediately
instigate *v.* incite, initiate, spur, urge
instill *v.* infuse, indoctrinate, implant, teach
instinct *n.* impulse, sense, intuition, feeling
instinctive *adj.* intuitive, spontaneous, natural

institute *n.* establishment, organization
institute *v.* establish, found, launch, organize
institution *n.* establishment, organization, company, association, business, university
instruct *v.* inform, teach, order, direct, educate
instruction *n.* guidance, direction, education
instructor *n.* professor, tutor, lecturer, teacher
instrument *n.* UTENSIL: apparatus, implement, device, tool; CONTRACT: deed, document
insubordinate *adj.* disobedient, mutinous, treacherous, defiant, rebellious
insufferable *adj.* difficult, intolerable, unbearable
insufficient *adj.* skimpy, meager, inadequate
insular *adj.* detached, isolated, narrow, provincial
insult *n.* affront, indignity, abuse, impudence, insolence, mockery, derision, impertinence, invective
insult *v.* offend, mock, annoy, provoke, taunt, ridicule
insurance *n.* security, indemnity, assurance, warrant
insure *v.* secure, warrant, protect, guarantee
insurrection *n.* uprising, rebellion, insurgence, revolt
intact *adj.* entire, whole, together
intangible *adj.* indefinite, uncertain, vague
integral *adj.* WHOLE: entire; NECESSARY: essential
integrate *v.* blend, combine, mix
integrity *n.* morality, honesty, uprightness, honor
intellect *n.* understanding, intelligence, mentality
intellectual *adj.* smart, creative, intelligent, learned
intellectual *n.* highbrow, genius, philosopher, academician, egghead, brain
intelligence *n.* UNDERSTANDING: discernment, comprehension, judgment; INTELLECT: mind, brain, mentality; INFORMATION: statistics, facts, news

intelligent *adj.* clever, bright, smart, brilliant, perceptive, keen, imaginative, knowledgeable, understanding, quick, sharp, comprehending, discerning

intelligentsia *n.* intellectuals, elite

intelligible *adj.* understandable, comprehensible, plain, clear, obvious

intend *v.* PROPOSE: purpose, aspire, aim, plan; MEAN: indicate, signify, denote

intense *adj.* deep, profound, heightened, vivid, impassioned, exaggerated, violent, excessive, keen, piercing, cutting, severe

intensify *v.* enhance, heighten, sharpen, emphasize, increase, strengthen

intensity *n.* concentration, strength, power, force, passion, fervor, ardor, severity, depth, magnitude

intensive *adj.* accelerated, hard, fast, severe

intent *adj.* fixed, absorbed

intent *n.* design, plan

intention *n.* purpose, aim, end, plan

intentional *adj.* deliberate, planned

inter *v.* bury, entomb

intercept *v.* obstruct, ambush, block, hijack

intercession *n.* entreaty, petition, mediation, plea

interchange *n.* BARTER: trade, exchange, substitution; INTERSECTION: cloverleaf, off–ramp

interest *n.* CONCERN: attention, excitement, curiosity, enthusiasm; SHARE: claim, right, stake

interest *v.* arouse, involve, fascinate, intrigue, attract, amuse, please, entertain

interested *adj.* AROUSED: stimulated, curious, affected, responsive, roused, stirred, attracted; OCCUPIED: engrossed, obsessed, absorbed, involved

interesting *adj.* intriguing, fascinating, engaging, absorbing, captivating

interfere *v.* meddle, intervene, interpose, interlope

interference *n.* MEDDLING: interruption, trespassing, tampering; OBSTRUCTION: check, obstacle, restraint

interior *adj.* within, inside, inland, inner, internal, inward, central, inside

interlope *v.* interfere, intrude, meddle

intermediate *adj.* intervening, medium, intermediary, median, central, middle

intermediary *n.* mediator, agent

intermission *n.* pause, interval, interim, recess

intermix *v.* mix, mingle

intermittent *adj.* cyclic, recurring, periodic, recurrent, changing, irregular

intern *v.* CONFINE: detain, imprison; TEACH: train, apprentice, tutor

internal *adj.* interior, inner, domestic, inside, inward, intrinsic, innate, inherent

interpret *v.* translate, explain, render, delineate, define, describe

interpretation *n.* rendition, description, representation, presentation, explanation

interrogate *v.* question, ask, examine

interrogation *n.* inquiry, investigation, examination

interrupt *v.* intervene, interfere, infringe

intersperse *v.* scatter, strew

interval *n.* time, period, interlude, interim, pause

intervene *v.* intercede, mediate, negotiate, reconcile

intervention *n.* intercession, interruption, interference, intrusion

interview *n.* meeting, audience, conference

interview *v.* interrogate, question, examine
intimacy *n.* closeness, familiarity, affection
intimate *adj.* familiar, close, trusted, secret, special
intimate *n.* friend, associate, companion, lover
intimate *v.* hint, allude
intimidate *v.* frighten, threaten
intolerable *adj.* insufferable, unendurable, unbearable, impossible, offensive, painful, undesirable
intolerant *adj.* dogmatic, bigoted, prejudiced
intoxicate *v.* inebriate, muddle, befuddle
intransigence *n.* obstinacy, stubborness
intransigent *adj.* intolerant, uncompromising
intricacy *n.* elaborateness, complexity, difficulty
intricate *adj.* involved, complex, tricky, abstruse, difficult, obscure
intrigue *v.* plot, scheme, delight, please, attract, charm, entertain, fascinate
intrinsic *adj.* essential, inborn, inherent
introduce *v.* PRESENT: submit, advance, offer, propose, acquaint; ACQUAINT: present; INSERT: add, enter, include
introduction *n.* ADMITTANCE: initiation, installation, entrance; PRESENTATION: debut, acquaintance, start, awakening, baptism; PREFACE: preamble, foreword, prologue, overture
introductory *adj.* opening, early, starting, beginning, preparatory, primary, original
introvert *n.* loner, recluse
intrude *v.* encroach, trespass, interfere, meddle
intuition *n.* instinct, hunch, foreknowledge, feeling
intuitive *adj.* instinctive, automatic, natural
inure *v.* acclimate, accustom

inured *adj.* hardened, cold, unfeeling
invade *v.* attack, intrude. infringe, trespass, interfere
invader *n.* trespasser, alien, attacker, enemy
invalidate *v.* void, revoke, annul, refute, nullify
invaluable *adj.* priceless, expensive, dear, valuable
invariable *adj.* unchanging, uniform, static, constant
invective *adj.* railing, abusive
inveigh *v.* protest, rant
inveigle *v.* coax, entice, flatter
invent *v.* create, discover, originate, devise, fashion, form, design, improvise, contrive, build
invention *n.* contrivance, contraption, design
inventory *n.* **LIST:** itemization, register, index, record; **INSPECTION:** examination, summary
inverse *adj.* reversed, contrary
invert *v.* **UPSET:** overturn, tip; **REVERSE:** change, transpose, exchange
investigate *v.* inquire, review, examine, study
investigation *n.* inquiry search research examination
inveterate *adj.* addicted, well–established, persisting
invidious *adj.* envious, malicious, spiteful
invigorate *v.* animate, energize, enervate, enliven, excite, exhilarate, freshen, stimulate
invincible *adj.* impregnable, invulnerable, powerful, strong, unconquerable
inviolate *adj.* hallowed, holy, intact, pure, sacred
inviting *adj.* appealing, attractive, encouraging
invocation *n.* prayer, appeal
invoice *n.* notice, statement, bill, receipt
invoke *v.* implore, solicit, summon
involuntary *adj.* unintentional, uncontrolled, instinctive, automatic, habitual

involve *v.* associate, commit, connect, comprise, connect, entangle, implicate, include, link

involved *adj.* COMPLICATED: elaborate, entangled, intricate, sophisticated; IMPLICATED: connected, emotional, engrossed, incriminated

invulnerable *adj.* strong, invincible, secure, safe

iota *n.* jot, particle, trace, scrap, grain, bit, speck

irascible *adj.* irritable, temperamental, testy, touchy

irate *adj.* enraged, furious, incensed, angry

irk *v.* vex, annoy, harass, disturb, bother

irony *n.* satire, ridicule, mockery, derision, sarcasm

irrational *adj.* illogical, unreasoning, specious, fallacious, wrong, senseless, silly, ridiculous

irreconcilable *adj.* implacable, incompatible

irrefutable *adj.* conclusive, evident, indisputable, obvious, undeniable

irregular *adj.* UNEVEN: rough, fitful, random, occasional, fluctuating, wavering, intermittent, sporadic, variable, shifting; UNCUSTOMARY: unique, extraordinary, abnormal, unusual; QUESTIONABLE: strange, debatable, suspicious

irrelevant *adj.* immaterial, unrelated, extraneous, pointless, trivial, unnecessary

irreparable *adj.* incurable, hopeless, irreversible, destroyed, ruined

irresistible *adj.* compelling, overpowering, overwhelming, powerful

irresponsible *adj.* capricious, flighty, fickle, thoughtless, rash, unstable, lax, shiftless, unreliable

irrevocable *adj.* permanent, indelible, inevitable

irritable *adj.* cranky, testy, touchy, huffy, peevish, petulant, surly, moody, churlish, grouchy, grumpy

irritant *n.* annoyance, bother, burden, nuisance

irritate *v.* **BOTHER:** exasperate, pester, disturb, annoy; **INFLAME:** redden, chafe, sting, burn, hurt, itch

irritated *adj.* annoyed, disturbed, upset, bothered

island *n.* isle, bar, archipelago

isolate *v.* detach, insulate, confine, seclude, divide

isolation *n.* solitude, seclusion, segregation, confinement, separation

issue *n.* **DISTRIBUTION:** publication; **TOPIC:** subject, concern, argument; **EDITION:** number, copy

issue *v.* **EMERGE:** proceed, appear, begin; **RELEASE:** circulate, announce, advertise, declare, publish

itemize *v.* list, catalog, enumerate, number, detail

itinerant *adj.* traveling, roving, nomadic, wandering

itinerant *n.* wanderer, nomad, vagrant, tramp

jab *v.* poke, punch, hit, blow

jacket *n.* coat, tunic, jerkin, parka, cape

jackpot *n.* bonanza, winnings, luck, profit, success

jaded *adj.* cold, impassive, indifferent, nonchalant, world–weary

jail *n.* penitentiary, cage, cell, dungeon, bastille, stockade, prison, lockup

jam *n.* **PRESERVES:** conserve, marmalade, jelly; **TROUBLE:** dilemma, problem, difficulty

jam *v.* compress, bind, squeeze, push, pack, press

jar *n.* **CONTAINER:** crock, vessel, beaker, cruet, bottle, flagon, flask; **JOLT:** jounce, thud, thump, bump

jargon *n.* argot, patois, idiom, vernacular, colloquialism, localism, dialect, slang

jaunt *n.* excursion, trip, tour, journey, walk

jaunty *adj.* buoyant, chipper, dashing, frisky, rakish

jealous *adj.* envious, possessive, resentful

jeer *n.* derision, ridicule, taunt
jeer *v.* deride, insult, mock, ridicule, taunt
jell *v.* set, harden, stiffen, thicken
jeopardize *v.* endanger, imperil, expose, venture, risk
jeopardy *n.* danger, peril, hazard, chance
jerk *n.* TWITCH: tic, shake, quiver; DOLT: scamp, scoundrel, fool, rascal
jerk *v.* SPASM: quiver, shiver, shake, twitch; PULL: yank, snatch, seize
jest *v.* joke, tease
jester *n.* comedian, buffoon, joker, actor, clown, fool
jetty *n.* pier, wharf
jewel *n.* prize, bauble, gem, trinket
jewelry *n.* bangles, gems, baubles, trinkets, adornments, ornaments
jiggle *v.* shake, twitch, wiggle, jerk
jingle *n.* rhyme, verse
jingle *v.* tinkle, clink, rattle
jinx *n.* hex, spell
job *n.* EMPLOYMENT: situation, position, calling, vocation, career, pursuit, business, profession, trade; TASK: assignment, undertaking, project, chore, errand, duty; ASSIGNMENT: output, duty
jobber *n.* broker, wholesaler
jocular *adj.* comic, frolicsome, funny, witty
jocund *adj.* cheerful, happy, joyful, lighthearted
jog *v.* TROT: canter, lope, nudge, run; NUDGE: bump, jar, jostle, shake
join *v.* unite, blend, combine, connect, couple, attach, link, fuse, entwine, associate
joint *adj.* joined, shared, united
joint *n.* juncture, union, coupling, hinge, link,

connection, seam; **DIVE:** hangout, bar, tavern

joke *v.* jest, quip, banter, laugh, play, frolic, wisecrack

jolly *adj.* gay, merry, joyful, happy

jolt *n.* **BUMP:** jar, bounce, blow, jerk; **SURPRISE:** jar, start, shock, surprise

jostle *v.* push, elbow, nudge

jot *n.* bit, iota

jot *v.* write, note, scribble, record

journal *n.* **DIARY:** almanac, chronicle, record; **PERIODICAL:** publication, newspaper, magazine, daily

journalist *n.* columnist, commentator, reporter

journey *n.* trip, tour, excursion, jaunt, travel

jovial *adj.* affable, amiable, merry, happy

joy *n.* mirth, delight, playfulness, gaiety, geniality, merriment, levity, jubilation, laughter

joyful *adj.* elated, glad, happy, joyous, jubilant

joyous *adj.* blithe, glad, gay, happy

jubilant *adj.* ecstatic, elated, exuberant, delighted, rapturous, joyous

jubilee *n.* anniversary, celebration

judge *n.* **MODERATOR:** arbiter, referee, umpire; **CONNOISSEUR:** analyst, critic, expert, specialist

judge *v.* hear, decide, adjudicate, rule

judgment *n.* **DISCERNMENT:** discrimination, taste; **DECISION:** determination, analysis, pronouncement, conclusion, verdict

judgmental *adj.* biased, prejudiced, unfair

judicial *adj.* legalistic, administrative, lawful

judicious *adj.* prudent, discreet, sensible, discreet

jug *n.* crock, flask, pitcher, container

juice *n.* sap, extract, fluid, liquid

juicy *adj.* succulent, moist, watery, syrupy

jumble

jumble *n.* clutter, mess, hodgepodge, confusion
jump *v.* **LEAP:** vault, spring, lunge, bound, skip, hurdle; **PLUMMET:** plunge, dive, fall; **ACCOST:** attack
junction *n.* **MEETING:** joining, coupling, joint, union; **CROSSROADS:** crossing, intersection
juncture *n.* joining, junction
jungle *n.* tangle, wilderness, undergrowth, forest
junior *adj.* younger, lower
junk *n.* scrap, waste, garbage, filth, trash
junk *v.* abandon, discard
junket *n.* picnic, excursion, trip
jurisdiction *n.* authority, range, province, scope, domain, extent, empire, sovereignty
jurist *n.* judge, attorney, adviser, lawyer
jury *n.* council, committee, tribunal, panel
just *adj.* **PRECISELY:** exactly, correctly, perfectly, accurate; **HARDLY:** barely, scarcely; **ONLY:** merely, simply, plainly; **FAIR:** impartial, equal, righteous
justice *n.* **FAIRNESS:** right, truth, equity; **LAWFULNESS:** legality, legitimacy, sanction, constitutionality, authority, custom; **ADMINISTRATION:** adjudication, arbitration, hearing, trial, litigation, judgment; **JUDGE:** magistrate, umpire, chancellor
justification *n.* excuse, defense, reason, explanation
justify *v.* **VINDICATE:** absolve, acquit, clear, excuse, exonerate; **EXPLAIN:** apologize, excuse, defend
jut *adj.* extend, bulge, project
juvenile *adj.* childish, youthful, adolescent, teenage
juxtapose *v.* compare, contrast
keen *adj.* **SHARP:** pointed, edged; **ASTUTE:** clever, shrewd, intelligent; **EAGER:** ardent, intent, zealous
keep *v.* **HOLD:** retain, possess, have, seize, save;

MAINTAIN: preserve, conserve; **CONTINUE:** sustain, endure; **REMAIN:** stay, continue, abide, settle; **STORE:** hoard, preserve, reserve, stash, cache

keepsake *n.* memento, token, remembrance, reminder

keg *n.* cask, drum, vat, barrel

kernel *n.* seed, grain, core, nut, germ

kettle *n.* vessel, cauldron, saucepan, stewpot, pot

key *n.* **OPENER:** latchkey, passkey; **SOLUTION:** clue, code, indicator, answer

kickback *n.* **BRIBE:** grease, payback, payola, tribute; **BACKLASH:** backfire, reaction, recoil

kickoff *adj.* start, opening, beginning, launching

kid *n.* child, son, daughter, tot, boy, girl

kid *v.* mock, tease

kidnap *v.* abduct, capture, shanghai

kill *v.* **SLAY:** slaughter, murder, assassinate, massacre, butcher, dispatch, execute, liquidate, finish; **CANCEL:** annul, nullify, counteract; **VETO:** cancel, prohibit, refuse, forbid

killer *n.* murderer, gangster, assassin, cutthroat

killjoy *n.* grouch, sourpuss, spoilsport

kiln *n.* dryer, oast, oven

kind *adj.* accommodating, agreeable, charitable, compassionate, considerate, generous, kindhearted, loving, obliging, sensitive, tactful, tender

kind *n.* **CLASS:** classification, species, genus; **TYPE:** sort, variety, description, denomination, designation

kindhearted *adj.* amiable, generous, good, humane

kindle *v.* fire, excite, light, ignite

kindly *adj.* generous, helpful, good, humane, kind

kindness *n.* **TENDERNESS:** consideration, thoughtfulness, humanity, understanding, compassion, graciousness, kindheartedness; **SERVICE:** benevolence, philanthropy, lift, boost, help

kindred *adj.* alike, kin, connected, related, similar

kingdom *n.* realm, domain, country, empire, principality, dominions, territory

kink *n.* bend, obstacle, hitch

kinship *n.* affiliation, relationship, connection, alliance, family

kit *n.* **EQUIPMENT:** material, tools, outfit; **PACK:** poke, knapsack, satchel, bag, container

knack *n.* dexterity, trick, skill, faculty, ability

knapsack *n.* sack, bag, pack, kit, rucksack

knead *v.* work, shape, twist, press

kneel *v.* genuflect, bend, stoop, bow, curtsey

knickknack *n.* bric–a–brac, curio, ornament, trifle, bauble, trinket, showpiece, gewgaw

knife *n.* blade, dagger, stiletto, lancet, machete, scalpel, dirk

knit *v.* unite, join, intermingle, affiliate

knob *n.* **PROJECTION:** bulge, protuberance, bulge, node, bump; **HANDLE:** doorknob, latch

knock *v.* rap, strike, thump, whack, beat, tap, hit

knoll *n.* mound, hill, hillock

knot *n.* **FASTENING:** bond, tie, cinch, hitch, splice; **CLUSTER:** group; **SNARL:** snag tangle twist

know *v.* **UNDERSTAND:** comprehend, apprehend; **RECOGNIZE:** perceive, discern, acknowledge

knowing *adj.* **SHREWD:** acute, clever, intelligent, reasonable, sharp; **DELIBERATE:** conscious, intentional

knowledge *n.* information, learning, lore, wisdom, enlightenment, expertise, awareness, insight

label *n.* tag, marker, insignia, identification, name

label *v.* identify, mark, name, specify
labor *n.* **TASK:** work, activity, toil, operation, employment, undertaking, job; **EXERTION:** energy, industry, diligence, strain, stress, effort
labor *v.* work, toil, strive
laborious *adj.* arduous, difficult, exhausting, onerous
lace *v.* fasten, tie, adorn, strap, bind, close
lacerate *v.* tear, wound
lacing *n.* bond, hitch, tie, fastener, knot
lack *n.* **ABSENCE:** deficiency, scarcity, insufficiency, inadequacy; **WANT:** need, privation, poverty, distress
lack *v.* need, want, require
lackadaisical *adj.* halfhearted, indifferent, languid
lackey *n.* **MENIAL:** servant; **FLUNKY:** toady, underling
laconic *adj.* concise, curt, succinct, terse
lad *n.* fellow, youth, stripling, boy, child
ladle *n.* spoon, skimmer, scoop
lady *n.* woman, female, matron, gentlewoman
ladylike *adj.* cultured, well-bred, polite, refined
lag *v.* tarry, straggle, falter, delay
laggard *n.* loiterer, idler
lair *n.* den, cave, home, pen
lame *adj.* halt, impaired, handicapped, limping
lament *v.* grieve, deplore
lamentation *n.* dirge, mourning, tears, wailing
lampoon *v.* satirize, burlesque
lance *v.* foil, point, spear
land *n.* **PROPERTY:** estate, tract, ranch, farm, lot; **COUNTRY:** province, region, nation
landing *n.* **ARRIVING:** docking, anchoring, arrival; **DOCK:** marina, pier, wharf
landlord *n.* innkeeper, landowner, lessor, owner

landscape *n.* countryside, scenery, panorama, view

lane *n.* way, alley, passage, path, road

language *n.* expression, tongue, word, sign, signal, gesture, vocabulary, diction, dialect, idiom, patois, vernacular, speech, jargon

languid *adj.* spiritless, sluggish

languish *v.* weaken, decline

lank *adj.* angular, bony, gaunt. lean, slender, spare

lanky *adj.* lean, rangy

lantern *n.* light, torch, lamp

lap *n.* EXTENSION: fold, flap, projection; RACECOURSE: circuit, round, course, distance

lapidary *n.* jeweler, engraver

lapse *v.* pass, void, slip, deteriorate, decline, weaken

larceny *n.* theft, burglary, thievery, robbery, crime

large *adj.* huge, wide, grand, great, considerable, substantial, vast, massive, immense, spacious, bulky, extensive

largely *adv.* MOSTLY: mainly, chiefly, principally; EXTENSIVELY: abundantly, comprehensively, widely

lariat *n.* lasso, riata, tether, line, rope

lascivious *adj.* bawdy, carnal, immoral, lewd, licentious, lurid, sensual, sexual

lash *n.* whip, stroke

lash *v.* strike, flog, thrash, scourge, beat, hit

lass *n.* girl, woman, lady, damsel, maiden

lassitude *adj.* weariness, listlessness

lasso *n.* rope, lariat, tether, noose

lasso *v.* rope, catch

last *adj.* FINAL: ultimate, concluding, ending, terminal, decisive, crowning, climactic, closing; RECENT: latest, newest, freshest

last *v.* **ENDURE:** continue, maintain, persist, remain, stay, survive, sustain; **SUFFICE:** do, satisfy, serve
lasting *adj.* enduring, abiding, constant, permanent
latch *n.* catch, hasp, hook, bar, fastener, lock
latch *v.* fasten, lock, cinch, close
late *adj.* **OVERDUE:** tardy, lagging, delayed; **DEFUNCT:** deceased, departed, dead; **RECENT:** new, fresh
latent *adj.* potential, undeveloped, dormant
lather *n.* foam, froth, suds, bubbles
lather *v.* foam, froth, soap
latitude *n.* freedom, degree, measure
latter *adj.* after, following, late, last, recent
lattice *n.* arbor, framework, trellis
laud *v.* glorify, honor, praise
laugh *v.* chuckle, snicker, titter, chortle, cackle, guffaw, giggle, roar
launch *v.* initiate, originate, start, begin
launder *v.* cleanse, wash, clean
lavatory *n.* basin, privy, bathroom, washroom, toilet
lave *v.* clean, wash
lavish *adj.* profuse, extravagant, generous, unstinted, unsparing, plentiful
lawful *adj.* **LEGAL:** legitimate, decreed, permitted, constitutional; **LEGISLATED:** enacted, official, enforced, legitimized, established
lawless *adj.* **WILD:** untamed, uncivilized, savage, barbarous, disordered, uncontrolled; **UNRESTRAINED:** riotous, insubordinate, disobedient, unruly
lawsuit *n.* action, suit, case, prosecution, claim, trial
lawyer *n.* attorney, solicitor, jurist, defender, prosecuting, counsel, solicitor, barrister, advocate
lax *adj.* slack, loose, remiss, soft, careless, indifferent

laxity, laxness *n.* slackness, negligence
layer *n.* stratum, thickness, fold, lap, floor, story, tier
layman *n.* nonprofessional, novice, dilettante, amateur, recruit
layout *n.* arrangement, design, organization, plan
lazy *adj.* indolent, idle, sluggish, apathetic, loafing, flagging, slothful, lethargic
lead *n.* GUIDANCE: leadership, direction; CLUE: evidence, trace, hint, proof, sign; ROLE: part, character
lead *v.* CONDUCT: steer, pilot, show, guide; DIRECT: manage, supervise
leaden *adj.* heavy, burdensome, oppressive, weighty
leader *n.* GUIDE: conductor, pilot; DIRECTOR: manager, officer, captain, master, ruler, boss, brains
leading *adj.* foremost, chief, dominating, best
leaflet *n.* brochure, handbill, circular, pamphlet
league *n.* union, alliance, group, unit, organization
leak *n.* HOLE: puncture, chink, crevice; WASTE: loss, leakage, seepage, expenditure, decrease; NEWS: exposé, slip
leak *v.* ESCAPE: drip, ooze, drool, flow
lean *v.* INCLINE: slant, sag, list, tip, veer, droop, pitch, tilt; TEND: favor, prefer
lean *adj.* THIN: lank, meager, slim, skinny; FIBROUS: muscular, sinewy
leaning *n.* inclination, preference, tendency
lean–to *n.* shelter, shanty, hut, hovel
leap *v.* jump, bound, spring, vault, bounce
learn *v.* acquire, read, master, ascertain, determine, unearth, hear, memorize, study
learned *adj.* scholarly, erudite, accomplished, well–informed, professorial, cultured, educated

learning n. lore, training, education, knowledge

lease v. let, rent, charter

least adj. SMALLEST: tiniest; TRIVIAL: piddling, unimportant; MINIMAL: bottom, lowest

leave n. PARTING: departure, farewell; PERMISSION: consent, dispensation, indulgence, authorization, consent; LIBERTY: furlough, vacation

leave v. ABANDON: forsake, desert; DEPART: withdraw, part, defect, flee, embark, emigrate, scram, split, vacate, go; BEQUEATH: transmit, will, give, dower; OMIT: drop, forget, neglect

leaving n. departure, exodus

lecher n. debaucher, rake

lecture n. INSTRUCTION: address, discourse, lesson, oration, speech, talk; REPROOF: dressing–down, rebuke, reprimand

lecture v. INSTRUCT: address, instruct, talk, teach; REPROVE: rebuke, reprimand

ledge n. shelf, mantle, bar, step, ridge, rim

ledger n. accounts, books, records, journal

leech n. PARASITE: tapeworm, hookworm, bloodsucker; DEPENDENT: hanger–on, sponger, weakling

leer n. glance, grin, look, smirk

leery adj. distrustful, doubting, suspicious, wary

leeway n. space, margin, latitude, extent

left adj. REMAINING: staying, continuing, over, extra; RADICAL: left–wing, liberal, progressive, revolutionary; DEPARTED: gone, absent, lacking

legacy n. bequest, inheritance

legal adj. lawful, constitutional, permissible, allowable, legalized, sanctioned, legitimate, authorized

legality n. legitimacy, lawfulness, authority, law

legalize

legalize *v.* authorize, sanction, approve
legate *n.* ambassador, envoy
legation *n.* delegation, embassy
legend *n.* story, myth, saga, fable; inscription
legendary *adj.* fabulous, mythical, fanciful, allegorical
legerdemain *n.* deception, trickery
legible *adj.* readable, distinct, plain, sharp, clear
legion *n.* multitude, horde, throng, crowd
legislate *v.* enact, pass, constitute
legislation *n.* bill, enactment, act, law
legislature *n.* lawmakers, congress, parliament, senate, house, representatives
legitimate *adj.* LICIT: statutory, authorized, lawful, legal, honorable; LOGICAL: reasonable, probable, consistent, understandable; AUTHENTIC: real, verifiable, valid, reliable, genuine
leisure *n.* relaxation, recreation, holiday, vacation
leisurely *adj.* unhurried, lazily, calmly, listlessly
lend *v.* loan, advance, furnish, entrust, accommodate
length *n.* DISTANCE: measure, span, range, longitude, magnitude, dimension; DURATION: period, interval
lengthen *v.* extend, stretch, protract, increase;
lengthy *adj.* tedious, long, dull
lenient *adj.* mild, merciful, tolerant, kind
lesion *n.* abrasion, injury, tumor, wound
less *adj.* fewer, smaller, reduced, declined, inferior, secondary, subordinate, diminished, shortened
lessen *v.* diminish, dwindle, decline, decrease; reduce
lesser *adj.* inferior, minor, secondary, subordinate
lesson *n.* learning, precept, assignment
let *v.* PERMIT: approve, authorize, consent, tolerate, allow; LEASE: rent, hire, sublet

letdown *n.* frustration, setback, disillusionment, disappointment
lethal *adj.* deadly, fatal, mortal, malignant, harmful
lethargic *adj.* apathetic, listless, sluggish
lethargy *n.* stupor, dullness, drowsiness
letter *n.* MESSAGE: memo, note, memorandum, epistle, missive, line, mail; SYMBOL: character, type
letter *v.* inscribe, write
letup *n.* reduction, slowdown, pause, interval, respite
levee *n.* embankment, dike
level *adj.* SMOOTH: planed, even, flat; REGULAR: uniform, flush, straight, trim, precise, exact, matched, unbroken, aligned, continuous
level *v.* STRAIGHTEN: flatten, surface, bulldoze, smooth; DEMOLISH: destroy, ruin, wreck, raze
lever *n.* bar, fulcrum, pry, crowbar
leverage *n.* power, purchase; lift, hold, support
leviathan *n.* monster, beast
levity *n.* flippancy, frivolity
levy *n.* collection, seizure, toll, duty, custom, tax
levy *v.* collect, assess
lewd *adj.* RIBALD: smutty, indecent, sensual; LUSTFUL: wanton, lascivious, licentious, lecherous, dissolute, debauched, corrupt, depraved, vulgar
lexicon *n.* dictionary, vocabulary, glossary
liability *n.* obligation, responsibility, debt, indebtedness, responsibility
liable *adj.* RESPONSIBLE: accountable, answerable, exposed, obliged; APT: inclined, likely, tending
liaison *n.* LINK: agent, connection, emissary, proxy; AFFAIR: intrigue, romance, tryst
liar *n.* prevaricator, deceiver, perjurer, falsifier, fibber

libel *v.* defame, slander, smear, vilify

libelous *adj.* defamatory, derogatory, slanderous

liberal *adj.* **PROGRESSIVE:** broad–minded, nonconformist, permissive, radical, tolerant; **GENEROUS:** indulgent, lavish, magnanimous

liberate *v.* free, loose, release

liberation *n.* rescue, freedom, deliverance

libertine *n.* lecher, pervert, rake, roué

liberty *n.* **DELIVERANCE:** emancipation, enfranchisement, rescue, freedom; **LEAVE:** relaxation, rest, leisure, recreation; **PRIVILEGE:** permission, decision, selection; **RIGHTS:** freedom, independence

libretto *n.* lyric, words

license *n.* **CONSENT:** authorization, permission, sanction; **DOCUMENT:** permit, certificate, registration; **FREEDOM:** looseness, excess, immoderation, latitude

license *v.* grant, authorize, permit, allow

licit *adj.* authorized, lawful, sanctioned

lick *v.* beat, thrash, whip, defeat, overcome, vanquish, frustrate, conquer

lid *n.* cover, cap, top, roof, hood

lie *n.* falsehood, untruth, misrepresentation, prevarication, falsification, fabrication, distortion

lie *v.* **FIB:** falsify, prevaricate, deceive, misinform, exaggerate, distort, concoct, misrepresent, dissemble, delude; **PROSTRATE:** recline, retire, rest, sleep; **ABIDE:** remain, exist

lieu *n.* place, stead

life *n.* **BEING:** entity, presence, consciousness, vitality; **BIOGRAPHY:** story, memoir; **DURATION:** lifetime, span, career, generation, season, cycle; **SPIRIT:** animation, excitement, zeal

lifeless *adj.* **INERT:** inanimate, departed, dead; **LACKING SPIRIT:** lackluster, listless, heavy, dull, slow
lifetime *n.* existence, endurance, continuance
lift *v.* **ELEVATE:** raise, hoist; **STEAL:** filch, pilfer, swipe; **RESCIND:** repeal, reverse, revoke
light *adj.* **ILLUMINATED:** radiant, luminous, bright; **VIVID:** colorful, rich, clear; **SUPERFICIAL:** slight, frivolous, trivial, unimportant; **LIVELY:** spirited, animated, active; **ETHEREAL:** airy, fluffy, downy, dainty, thin, sheer, insubstantial, graceful
light *v.* **ILLUMINATE:** illumine, lighten, brighten; **IGNITE:** inflame, spark, kindle, burn; **REST:** stop, arrive
lighten *v.* unburden, lessen, uplift, alleviate, reduce, shift, change, unload
light-headed *adj.* **GIDDY:** inane, fickle, frivolous, silly; **FAINT:** tired, delirious, dizzy, weak
light-hearted *adj.* gay, joyous, cheerful, happy
lightly *adj.* delicately, airily, daintily, gently, subtly, softly, tenderly
like *adj.* similar, resembling, close, matching, related, analogous, corresponding, comparable
like *v.* **ENJOY:** relish, savor, fancy; **ADMIRE:** esteem, approve; **PREFER:** choose, desire, fancy
likelihood *n.* possibility, probability
likely *adj.* probable, conceivable, rational, plausible, apt, tending, prone, liable
likeness *n.* **SIMILARITY:** resemblance, correspondence; **REPRESENTATION:** image, effigy, portrait, picture
liking *n.* desire, fondness, devotion, affection, love
limb *n.* **BRANCH:** arm, bough, offshoot; **APPENDAGE:** arm, leg, part, wing, pinion, fin, flipper
limber *adj.* flexible, pliant, supple, nimble

limit *n.* boundary, frontier, border, extent, extremity

limit *v.* confine, bound, curb, restrict

limitation *n.* **RESTRICTION:** restraint, control; **CONDITION:** qualification, stricture, inhibition, constraint; **SHORTCOMING:** inadequacy, deficiency, weakness, failing, frailty, flaw

limp *adj.* weak, pliant, flaccid, flabby, pliable, slack, loose, flimsy

limp *n.* hitch, hobble

limp *v.* halt, stumble, shuffle, stagger, totter, falter

line *n.* **BORDER:** limit, boundary, edge, boundary; **ROW:** rank, file, order, arrangement, sequence, column, groove, thread; **JOB:** profession, career, vocation; **ROPE:** cord, filament; **DESCENT:** pedigree, lineage, family, heredity; **WARES:** goods, merchandise, produce, material; **TALK:** speech, patter

line *v.* **ARRANGE:** align, order, dress, array, fix, place; **BORDER:** edge, bound, fringe; **PROTECT:** face, back, bind, trim, pad; **TRACE:** delineate, outline, draw

linear *adj.* successive, direct, straight

linger *v.* remain, loiter, tarry, lag, delay, dawdle, wait

lingerie *n.* underwear, dainties, unmentionables

linguist *n.* lexicographer, translator, grammarian

liniment *n.* ointment, lotion, balm, medicine

lining *n.* interlining, filling, quilting, stuffing, padding

link *n.* **LOOP:** ring, coupling; **CONNECTION:** seam, weld, intersection, fastening, splice, articulation, joint

link *v.* connect, associate, combine, join

lint *n.* fluff, raveling, fiber, dust

liquid *adj.* **WATERY:** molten, moist, aqueous, liquefied, dissolved, melted, thawed, wet; **FLOWING:** running, splashing, thin, moving, viscous, fluid, juicy

liquidate *v.* **CHANGE:** sell, convert, exchange; **DESTROY:** eliminate, kill, annul, cancel

list *n.* roll, record, agenda, slate, inventory, account, tally, roster, muster, menu, docket

list *v.* **ARRANGE:** catalogue, register, tally, inventory, index; **LEAN:** pitch, slant, incline

listen *v.* hear, heed, attend, overhear

listless *adj.* languid, sluggish, indolent, indifferent

litany *n.* form, ritual

literacy *n.* scholarship, education, knowledge

literal *adj.* precise, exact, verbatim, accurate

literally *adj.* actually, exactly, strictly, verbatim

literary *adj.* scholarly, learned, bookish, literate

literate *adj.* lettered, learned, scholarly, educated

lithograph *n.* print, copy

lithograph *v.* engrave, print

litter *n.* **DEBRIS:** mess, jumble, hodgepodge, trash, clutter; **BROOD:** piglets, puppies, kittens, offspring

litter *v.* scatter, confuse, jumble

little *adj.* **SMALL:** diminutive, tiny, wee, slight, miniature, puny; **INADEQUATE:** inconsiderable, insufficient; **TRIFLING:** shallow, petty, superficial, frivolous, paltry, trivial; **BASE:** weak, shallow, mean, petty

livable *adj.* **HABITABLE:** inhabitable, comfortable; **BEARABLE:** acceptable, adequate, tolerable

live *adj.* **ACTIVE:** energetic, vital, vivid; **AWARE:** conscious, existing

live *v.* **EXIST:** subsist, survive, breathe, be; **RELISH:** savor, experience; **DWELL:** inhabit, abide; **CONTINUE:** remain, survive, endure, last

livelihood *n.* job, career, means, subsistence

lively *adj.* active, animated, brisk, energetic, spirited,

living

vigorous, vivacious

living *adj.* **ALIVE:** active, live, existing, breathing, being; **VIGOROUS:** awake, brisk, alert, active

living *n.* means, sustenance, maintenance, subsistence, work, vocation, business

load *n.* **BURDEN:** cargo, lading, payload, shipment, capacity, bundle; **RESPONSIBILITY:** charge, obligation, trust, duty

loaf *v.* loiter, idle, lounge, relax, shirk, dream

loafer *n.* malingerer, slacker, goldbrick, deadbeat

loan *v.* lend, provide, advance

loath *adj.* disinclined, unwilling

loathe *v.* detest, dislike

lobby *n.* **ENTRYWAY:** antechamber, foyer, hall, vestibule; **INFLUENCE:** pressure

lobby *v.* influence, promote

local *adj.* **LIMITED:** confined, restricted, bounded; **INDIGENOUS:** native, territorial, provincial, regional

locale *n.* vicinity, territory, district, area, region

locality *n.* district, section, sector, region, location, site, neighborhood, block, vicinity

locate *v.* **DISCOVER:** find, establish, determine, place; **SETTLE:** inhabit, dwell

lock *n.* **HOOK:** catch, latch, bolt, bar, hasp, bond; **TRESS:** tuft, ringlet, curl

lock *v.* fasten, unite, bolt, bar

locker *n.* cabinet, wardrobe, cupboard, closet

locket *n.* case, pendant, jewelry, necklace

lodge *n.* **RETREAT:** inn, hostel, chalet, hotel, motel, resort, cabin, cottage; **SOCIETY:** club, fraternity

lodge *v.* **SHELTER:** board, harbor, quarter; **PLACE:** fix, leave, deposit, embed

lodging *n.* accommodation, refuge, shelter, residence, home, hotel, motel, resort

lofty *adj.* **HIGH:** elevated, tall, towering, raised; **EXALTED:** arrogant, commanding, haughty, proud

log *n.* **WOOD:** limb, timber, stick **JOURNAL:** account, register, ledger, diary, record

logic *n.* reasoning, deduction, induction, thought

logical *adj.* coherent, consistent, probable, sound, congruent, reasonable

logistics *n.* procurement, distribution, management

logy *adj.* lethargic, sluggish

loiter *v.* linger, dawdle, idle, loll, tarry, wait

lone *adj.* solitary, deserted, alone

lonely *adj.* abandoned, homesick, forlorn, deserted, lonesome, solitary, secluded

lonesome *adj.* forlorn, alone, homesick, lonely

long *adj.* **ELONGATED:** extended, lengthy, outstretched; **PROLONGED:** protracted, meandering, lengthy, sustained; **TEDIOUS:** dull

long *v.* desire, yearn, wish, want

longing *n.* craving, yearning, pining, desire, wish

long–lived *adj.* perpetual, enduring, permanent

look *n.* **SIGHT:** glance, survey, glimpse, peek, peep, leer, stare; **APPEARANCE:** presence, mien, expression, looks, manner, aspect

look *v.* **EYE:** view, gaze, behold, contemplate, scrutinize, regard, inspect, observe, examine, watch; **SEEM:** resemble, appear

lookout *n.* **VIEW:** panorama, scene, observatory, station; **WATCHMAN:** watcher, sentinel, scout

loom *v.* **APPEAR:** rise, emerge; **MENACE:** threaten, hulk, hover, approach

loop *v.* curve, encircle, connect, bend

loophole *n.* escape, omission, avoidance

loose *adj.* SLACK: free, careless; LICENTIOUS: wanton, unrestrained, dissolute; UNBOUND: unattached, disconnected, baggy, free; VAGUE: random, obscure

loose *v.* FREE: release, liberate; RELAX: slack ease

loosen *v.* extricate, untie, undo, disentangle, free

loot *n.* plunder, spoils, take, booty

loot *v.* plunder, steal, thieve, rifle, rob

lop *v.* cut, trip, prune, chop

lope *v.* jog, run, trot

lopsided *adj.* uneven, unbalanced, tipped, irregular

lordly *adj.* grand, dignified, honorable, noble

lore *n.* enlightenment, wisdom, learning, knowledge

loss *n.* RUIN: destruction, calamity, disaster; DEPRIVATION: bereavement, destitution

lost *adj.* MISPLACED: mislaid, obscured, strayed, vanished; BEWILDERED: perplexed, puzzled; DESTROYED: demolished, wasted, ruined

lot *n.* FATE: destiny, fortune, doom, chance; PORTION: cluster, array, bunch, group; LAND: tract, parcel, division, patch, field; LOAD: consignment; ABUNDANCE: plenty, loads, oodles

lotion *n.* cream, balm, salve, unguent, cosmetic

loud *adj.* CLAMOROUS: noisy, vociferous, boisterous, cacophonous, raucous, harsh; BRASH: offensive, loud–mouthed, rude, vulgar; GARISH: gaudy, flashy, tawdry, ornate

lounge *n.* SOFA: couch, divan; ROOM: bar, lobby, parlor, salon

lounge *v.* recline, ease, idle, repose, loaf, rest

lovable *adj.* winning, winsome, lovely, friendly

love *n.* **DEVOTION:** attachment, infatuation, rapture, ardor; **ESTEEM:** respect, regard, admiration

love *v.* adore, idolize, prize, treasure, cherish

lovely *adj.* beautiful, attractive, comely, fair, handsome, engaging, enchanting, captivating, pleasing

lover *n.* suitor, sweetheart, admirer, escort, paramour, fiancé, boyfriend, girlfriend, steady

loving *adj.* devoted, thoughtful, passionate, amorous, affectionate, caring, considerate

low *adj.* **SQUAT:** flat, prostrate, crouched, sunken; **FAINT:** muffled, hushed, quiet; **SAD:** dejected, moody, blue; **VULGAR:** base, mean, coarse; **ECONOMICAL:** moderate, inexpensive, cheap

lower *adj.* inferior, beneath, under

lower *v.* diminish, fall, sink, depress, decrease, drop

lowering *adj.* threatening, dark, gloomy

lowly *adj.* unpretentious, meek, humble, unassuming

loyal *adj.* faithful, true, dependable, firm, faithful

loyalty *n.* fidelity, allegiance, faithfulness, constancy, attachment, support, devotion

lucid *adj.* **CLEAR:** obvious, unmistakable; **SHINING:** bright, luminous; **SANE:** rational, normal

luck *n.* **FORTUNE:** prosperity, wealth, windfall, blessings; **CHANCE:** fate, opportunity, break, accident

lucky *adj.* **BLESSED:** wealthy, favored, successful, prosperous, fortunate; **AUSPICIOUS:** providential, propitious, magic

lucrative *adj.* profitable, fruitful, productive, gainful

ludicrous *adj.* absurd, ridiculous, laughable, farcical, incongruous

lug *v.* carry, tug, lift, draw

luggage *n.* baggage, trunks, bags, valises

lukewarm *adj.* cool, tepid, chilly

lull *n.* pause, hiatus, stillness, hush, silence

lull *v.* soothe, quiet, calm

lumber *v.* slog, plod

luminescence *n.* fluorescence, fire, radiance, light

luminous *adj.* lighted, glowing, radiant, bright

lump *n.* mass, clump, block, chunk, hunk

lunacy *n.* **INSANITY:** madness, dementia, mania; **FOOLISHNESS:** silliness

lunatic *adj.* **INSANE:** demented, deranged, psychotic; **FOOLISH:** irrational, idiotic, daft, stupid

lunge *v.* thrust, surge, bound, jump

lurch *v.* roll, stagger, weave, sway, totter

lure *n.* bait, decoy, trick

lure *v.* entice, enchant, bewitch, allure

lurid *adj.* ghastly, gruesome, sensational

lurk *v.* skulk, slink, prowl, wait, crouch, conceal, hide

luscious *adj.* toothsome, palatable, delicious

lush *adj.* **GREEN:** verdant, dense, grassy; **DELICIOUS:** rich, juicy, succulent; **ELABORATE:** extravagant, luxurious, ornamental, ornate

lust *n.* desire, appetite, passion, sensuality

luster *n.* brightness, radiance, glow, brilliance, light

lusty *adj.* hearty, boisterous, robust, vigorous

luxuriant *adj.* exuberant, overabundant

luxuriate *v.* indulge, bask, revel

luxurious *adj.* comfortable, affluent, expensive, rich

luxury *n.* indulgence, idleness, leisure, lavishness, extravagance, excess

lying *adj.* **FRAUDULENT:** deceitful, double–dealing, dishonest; **FALSIFYING:** prevaricating, misrepresenting; **UNRELIABLE:** unsound, tricky, treacherous, false

lynch *v.* punish, hang, murder
lyrical *adj.* melodious, sweet, rhythmical, poetic
machination *n.* conspiracy, plot
machine *n.* contrivance, device, implement
machinist *n.* operator, engineer, workman
macrocosm *n.* universe, world
mad *adj.* INSANE: demented, deranged, psychotic;
  ANGRY: provoked, enraged, exasperated
madden *v.* craze, infuriate, enrage, anger
maddening *adj.* annoying, infuriating, disturbing
made *adj.* fashioned, built, formed, manufactured
made–up *adj.* invented, concocted, devised, fictitious
madhouse *n.* bedlam, confusion
madman *n.* lunatic, maniac, screwball, oddball
magazine *n.* periodical, journal, publication
magic *adj.* enchanting, mystic, enchanting
magic *n.* occultism, legerdemain, wizardry, sorcery,
  divination, witchcraft, voodooism, soothsaying
magical *adj.* occult, enchanting, mystic, mysterious
magician *n.* conjurer, sorcerer, wizard, shaman
magnanimous *adj.* charitable, noble, unselfish, forgiving, generous
magnate *n.* tycoon, mogul
magnetic *adj.* alluring, appealing, attractive, irresistible, captivating, fascinating, charming
magnetism *n.* attraction, lure, attraction
magnetize *v.* fascinate, attract
magnificence *n.* grandeur, majesty, stateliness, glory,
  radiance, luxuriousness, greatness, lavishness, brilliance, splendor, richness, pomp
magnificent *adj.* splendid, grand, exalted, majestic
magnify *v.* amplify, expand, increase, enlarge

magnitude *n.* SIZE: extent, quantity; IMPORTANCE: greatness, consequence, significance

maid *n.* GIRL: maiden, woman; SERVANT: nursemaid, housemaid, chambermaid

mail *v.* post, send, drop

maim *v.* disfigure, mutilate, disable, damage, hurt

main *adj.* principal, chief, leading, dominant, foremost

main *n.* conduit, channel, duct, pipe

mainly *adv.* chiefly, largely, essentially, predominantly, principally

maintain *v.* UPHOLD: support, sustain, affirm, defend; ASSERT: state, attest, declare, say; PRESERVE: keep, conserve, reserve, save, manage

majestic *adj.* stately, dignified, exalted, grand, noble

majesty *n.* grandeur, nobility, greatness

major *adj.* important, significant, main, principal

make *v.* MANUFACTURE: construct, fabricate, assemble, fashion, produce, build, form; CREATE: originate, generate, devise, conceive, invent; FORCE: constrain, compel, coerce; WAGE: conduct, engage, act; PREPARE: ready, arrange, adjust, cook; OBTAIN: earn, gain; ATTAIN: reach, arrive

makeshift *adj.* temporary, expedient, stopgap

make–up *n.* COSMETICS: paint, mascara, liner, powder; COMPENSATION: atonement, conciliation, payment; COMPOSITION: structure, arrangement, formation

maladroit *adj.* awkward, bungling, clumsy, inept

malady *n.* affliction, ailment, disease, sickness

malformation *n.* deformity, distortion

malfunction *n.* breakdown, slip, failure

malice *n.* hatred, spite, animosity, resentment

malicious *adj.* hateful, spiteful, bad

malign *v.* vilify, defame, slander
malignant *adj.* lethal, poisonous, deadly, harmful, destructive, deleterious, corrupt, dangerous
malinger *v.* lounge, loll
mall *n.* market, shop
malnutrition *n.* starvation, hunger
malodorous *adj.* stinking, fetid
malpractice *n.* negligence, neglect, carelessness
mammoth *adj.* huge, large
manacle *v.* chain, handcuff, shackle
manage *v.* DIRECT: control, lead, oversee, mastermind, engineer, handle, supervise; CONTRIVE: accomplish, effect, achieve; ENDURE: survive
manageable *adj.* docile, compliant, tractable, obedient, submissive, yielding
manager *n.* supervisor, administrator, director, superintendent, executive
managerial *adj.* executive, administrative
mandate *v.* decree, require
mandatory *adj.* imperative, compulsory, obligatory
mane *n.* hair, ruff, fur
maneuver *v.* plot, scheme, contrive, design, conspire
manger *n.* trough, tub
manhandle *v.* damage, maul, mistreat, abuse, beat
mania *n.* craze, lunacy, madness, desire, obsession
maniac *n.* madman, lunatic
manifest *adj.* apparent, clear, evident, obvious
manifest *v.* show, prove
manifestation *n.* evidence, indication, sign
manipulate *v.* control, shape, mold, form manage
mankind *n.* humanity, society, man
mannequin *n.* model, dummy, display

manner *n.* **CONDUCT:** deportment, demeanor, behavior; **CUSTOM:** habit, use, way, practice

mannerism *n.* peculiarity, idiosyncrasy, quirk

mannerly *adj.* polished, considerate, charming

mansion *n.* house, villa, hall, estate, home

mantel *n.* shelf, ledge

mantle *n.* cloak, blanket

manual *n.* handbook, guidebook, reference

manufacture *v.* make, fabricate, produce, build

manuscript *n.* book, paper, document, composition

many *adj.* numerous, multiple, innumerable, several

map *n.* chart, graph, drawing, portrayal, draft, plan

mar *v.* damage, spoil, disfigure, harm, scratch, deface

maraud *v.* raid, pillage

march *v.* parade, tramp, advance, proceed

margin *n.* edge, border, lip, shore, boundary

marina *n.* dock, mooring

marine *adj.* nautical, maritime, oceanic

maritime *adj.* nautical, marine, seafaring, aquatic

mark *n.* **STAMP:** imprint, impression

mark *v.* **BRAND:** imprint, label, identify, earmark; **SIGNIFY:** denote mean characterize, qualify

marker *n.* ticket, trademark, seal, brand, stamp, pencil, pen, boundary, inscription, label

market *v.* sell, trade, vend, exchange, barter

marquee *n.* awning, canopy

marry *v.* **WED:** espouse; **JOIN:** unite, combine

marsh *n.* swamp, morass, bog, quagmire

marshal *v.* arrange, gather, lead

martial *adj.* warlike, combative, aggressive

martyr *n.* saint, victim, sufferer, offering, scapegoat

marvel *v.* wonder, awe, stare

marvelous *adj.* fabulous, astonishing, spectacular

mash *v.* crush, bruise, squash, pulverize press

mask *v.* disguise, cloak, conceal, veil, hide

mass *n.* MATTER: piece, portion, wad, hunk, lump; HEAP: volume quantity; SIZE: magnitude, extent

massacre *v.* slaughter, kill, exterminate, annihilate

massage *v.* rub, knead, stimulate, caress

massive *adj.* weighty, bulky, huge, cumbersome, large

master *n.* lord, teacher, mentor, genius, maestro

master *v.* CONQUER: subdue, humble, succeed, overcome; LEARN: understand, comprehend

masterful *adj.* commanding, skillful, excellent

mastery *n.* CONTROL: dominance, sovereignty, superiority; SKILL: capacity, proficiency, ability

match *n.* EQUAL: peer, equivalent, counterpart, approximation; CONTEST: race, rivalry, competition

match *v.* equalize, liken, coordinate, even, balance

material *adj.* physical, real, tangible; essential

materialize *v.* form, become, actualize

maternal *adj.* motherly, protective

mathematics *n.* arithmetic, geometry, algebra, computation, trigonometry, calculus, logarithms

matrimony *n.* marriage, wedlock, union

matrix *n.* mold, die

matron *n.* dame, dowager, lady, wife, mother, woman

matter *n.* SUBSTANCE: material, constituents, object, thing, element; SUBJECT: interest, focus, theme; AFFAIR: undertaking, circumstance, concern

mature *adj.* developed, ripe, grown, cultured

maturity *n.* competence, development, cultivation; adulthood, majority

maudlin *adj.* tearful, sentimental

maxim *n.* saying, proverb, aphorism, adage, epithet
maximum *adj.* greatest, supreme, highest, best
maybe *adv.* perhaps, possibly, conceivable
mayhem *n.* crime, violence
maze *n.* labyrinth, tangle, convolution, intricacy
meadow *n.* grass, pasture, field
meager *adj.* lean, scanty, spare, wanting
meal *n.* FOOD: repast, feast, chow, spread, banquet tea; GRAIN: fodder, provender, forage, feed
mean *adj.* HUMBLE: servile, pitiful, shabby; VICIOUS: contemptible, despicable, degenerate, knavish, unscrupulous; BASE: low, vulgar, common
mean *v.* SIGNIFY: denote, symbolize, imply, suggest, designate, intimate; INTEND: propose, expect
meander *v.* wander, wind, roam, flow, ramble
meaning *n.* sense, import, definition, implication, intent, connotation, context, significance
meaningful *adj.* significant, essential, important
means *n.* INSTRUMENTALITY: machinery, method, system, agency; WEALTH: resources, substance, property
measure *n.* EXTENT: degree, dimension, capacity, weight, volume, distance, quantity, area, mass; STANDARD: rule, test, example, norm, criterion
measured *adj.* steady, systematic, deliberate, regular
mechanical *adj.* AUTOMATED: programmed, automatic; PERFUNCTORY: stereotyped, unchanging, monotonous
mechanism *n.* machine, device, process, tool
medal *n.* badge, award, commemoration, decoration
meddle *v.* interfere, interlope, intervene, encroach
meddlesome *adj.* intrusive, prying, snoopy, nosy
mediate *v.* arbitrate, negotiate
medication *n.* remedy, pill, vaccination

mediocre *adj.* middling, average, common, ordinary
meditation *n.* contemplation, reflection, thought
medium *n.* MEANS: mechanism, tool, agency, device;
SPIRITUALIST: seer, oracle, prophet
medley *n.* mixture, conglomeration, variety
meek *adj.* humble, unassuming, passive, docile
meet *v.* ENCOUNTER: engage, battle, match, face;
TOUCH: coincide, join, intersect; CONVENE: assemble,
gather, converge, congregate; SATISFY: fulfill, suffice
melancholy *adj.* gloomy, depressed, dispirited, sad
mellow *v.* ripen, mature, age
melodramatic *adj.* artificial, sensational, exaggerated
melody *n.* song, tune, air, lyric, strain
melt *v.* DISSOLVE: liquefy, thaw, soften, DWINDLE: vanish, go, pass; RELENT: forgive, yield
member *n.* LIMB: organ, arm, leg; ASSOCIATE: constituent, affiliate; PART: segment, fragment, division
memento *n.* keepsake, reminder, souvenir
memoir *n.* biography, autobiography, account
memorabilia *n.* memento, souvenir
memorable *adj.* unforgettable, notable, significant,
monumental, eventful, exceptional, singular
memorial *n.* monument, tablet, tombstone, mausoleum, statue; celebration, ceremony
memorize *v.* retain, learn, remember
memory *n.* recollection, retrospection, reminiscence
menace *v.* threaten, intimidate, portend
mend *v.* repair, patch, fix, aid, remedy, cure, correct
menial *n.* servant, domestic, maid, lackey
mental *adj.* thoughtful, rational, intellectual, subcon-
scious, telepathic, psychic, clairvoyant
mentality *n.* intellect, comprehension, reasoning

mention

mention *v.* remark, comment, infer, intimate, suggest
merchandise *n.* goods, wares, commodities, stock
merchandise *v.* advertise, sell
merchant *n.* trader, shopkeeper, dealer, jobber
merciful adj. lenient, softhearted, mild tolerant
mercurial *adj.* changeable, volatile
mere *adj.* minor, insignificant, little
merge *v.* combine, fuse, join, blend, mix, unite
merit *n.* worth, excellence, honor, character, virtue
merit *v.* earn, warrant, justify, deserve
merriment *n.* mirth, joy, gaiety, happiness, humor
mesh *v.* engage, coincide, suit, agree, fit
mess *n.* confusion, disorder, jumble, clutter
message *n.* communication, tidings, information
messenger *n.* courier, envoy, minister, herald, runner, emissary, angel, prophet
metamorphosis *n.* transformation, change
metaphorical *adj.* figurative, symbolical, allegorical
method *n.* procedure, process, technique, system
meticulous *adj.* mindful, cautious
metropolitan *adj.* cosmopolitan, modern, urban
mettlesome *adj.* spirited, active
middle *adj.* median, mean, midway, equidistant, central, halfway, intermediate
middleman *n.* wholesaler, jobber
miff *v.* offend, annoy
might *n.* power, ability, strength, force, sway
mighty *adj.* powerful, great, imposing, impressive
migrate *v.* move, emigrate, leave
migration *n.* voyage, departure, journey, movement
mild *adj.* moderate, gentle, meek, temperate
militant *adj.* aggressive, warlike, belligerent

millinery *n.* hats, bonnets

mimic *v.* IMITATE: copy, simulate, impersonate; MOCK: burlesque, caricature, ridicule

mind *n.* MENTALITY: perception, judgment, wisdom, intellect; INTENTION: inclination, determination

mind *v.* OBEY: heed, behave, attend, regard; OBJECT: complain, deplore, dislike

mindless *adj.* CARELESS: inattentive, oblivious, neglectful, indifferent; FOOLISH: senseless, rash

miniature *adj.* small, tiny, little, minute

minimize *v.* reduce, lessen, depreciate, decrease

minister *n.* clergyman, ambassador

minister *v.* attend, tend, help

ministration *n.* assistance, comfort, relief

minor *adj.* inferior, secondary, lesser, trivial

minor *n.* adolescent, child, infant, youth

minute *adj.* SMALL: microscopic, tiny; TRIVIAL: paltry, immaterial; EXACT: particular, detailed

minutiae *n.* particulars, details

miracle *n.* marvel, revelation, wonder

miraculous *adj.* supernatural, wonderful, marvelous, phenomenal, mysterious

mirage *n.* illusion, phantasm, hallucination, fantasy

mirth *n.* gaiety, laughter, frolic, jollity, fun

misbehave *v.* sin, trespass, err

miscalculate *v.* blunder, miscount, err, mistake

miscellaneous *adj.* DIVERSE: unmatched, unlike; MIXED: muddled, scattered, confused, disordered

mischievous *adj.* playful, roguish, naughty

misconduct *n.* misbehavior, wrongdoing, mischief

miser *n.* niggard, skinflint, money–grubber

miserable *adj.* wretched, distressed, troubled

misery *n.* **PAIN:** distress, suffering, agony; **DESPAIR:** depression, sadness; **TROUBLE:** grief, anxiety

misfortune *n.* calamity, adversity, unpleasantness

misgiving *n.* mistrust, doubt, uncertainty

misguided *adj.* misled, deceived, confused

misjudge *v.* miscalculate, overestimate, underestimate, mistake

mislead *v.* delude, trick, beguile, dupe, misrepresent

mismatched *adj.* incompatible, discordant, unfit

misrepresent *v.* distort, falsify, deceive, lie, mislead

miss *n.* **FAILURE:** slip blunder mishap mistake deviation **WOMAN:** lass maid female girl

mission *n.* purpose, charge, commission

missionary *n.* apostle, evangelist, messenger

mist *n.* vapor, cloud, rain, haze, fog

mistake *n.* **BLUNDER:** error, slip, omission, goof; **MISUNDERSTANDING:** confusion, misinterpretation

mistake *v.* err, blunder, misjudge, botch, bungle

mistreat *v.* harm, injure, wrong, abuse

mistrust *v.* suspect, distrust, doubt

misunderstanding *n.* **MISAPPREHENSION:** misinterpretation; **DISAGREEMENT:** quarrel, dispute

mix *v.* **BLEND:** combine, mingle, stir, unite; **CONFUSE:** jumble, tangle; **ASSOCIATE:** fraternize

mixture *n.* combination, blend, compound, amalgam, medley, potpourri, incorporation, hodgepodge

mix–up *n.* chaos, commotion, confusion, disorder

moan *v.* groan, wail, whine

mob *n.* throng, crowd, rabble, multitude, horde

mob *v.* attack, crowd, swarm, press, overwhelm

mobile *adj.* movable, loose, free

mock *adj.* imitation, counterfeit, sham

mock *v.* deride, taunt, mimic, caricature, imitate
mockery *n.* disparagement, ridicule
mode *n.* manner, fashion
model *n.* **EXAMPLE:** prototype, ideal; **PATTERN:** design, standard; **POSER:** sitter, mannequin, nude
model *v.* **FORM:** shape, fashion; **SIT:** pose; **DEMONSTRATE:** show, wear, display
moderate *adj.* **INEXPENSIVE:** cheap, economical; **MODEST:** temperate, calm, reserved; **TOLERANT:** restrained, cautious; **PLEASANT:** temperate, mild
moderate *v.* abate, decline, decrease
moderation *n.* restraint, temperance, balance
modern *adj.* **STYLISH:** chic, smart, fashionable; **CONTEMPORARY:** new, current, renovated, improved
modest *adj.* **HUMBLE:** unassuming, meek, diffident; **UNPRETENTIOUS:** plain, seemly, tasteful, unadorned, unaffected; **MODERATE:** reasonable, inexpensive, economical; **PROPER:** pure, chaste, seemly, decent; **LOWLY:** simple, unaffected
modify *v.* change, vary, alter
moist *adj.* wet, humid, dank, moistened, damp
mold *n.* **FORM:** matrix shape frame, pattern, die, cast; **GROWTH:** rust, parasite, fungus, lichen, decay
molest *v.* disturb, bother, annoy, irritate, badger
mollify *v.* assuage, pacify
molten *adj.* melted, liquefied
moment *n.* **TIME:** instant, jiffy; **IMPORTANCE:** significance, note, consequence
momentary *adj.* fleeting, passing, transient, cursory
momentum *n.* impetus, impulse, force, drive, energy
monetary *adj.* pecuniary, financial, fiscal
money *n.* currency, cash, notes, specie, funds

monologue *n.* speech, talk, discourse, address
monopolize *v.* dominate, engross, corner
monopoly *n.* trust, syndicate, cartel
monotonous *adj.* tiresome, tedious, wearying, dull
monster *n.* **MONSTROSITY:** chimera, werewolf; **FREAK:** abnormality; **BRUTE:** criminal, rascal, savage
monstrous *adj.* **HUGE:** stupendous, prodigious, enormous, large; **UNNATURAL:** abnormal, unusual
monument *n.* memorial, shrine, statue, monolith
monumental *adj.* lofty, impressive, majestic, grand
mood *n.* state, condition, temper, humor, disposition
moody *adj.* downcast, pensive, unhappy, sad
moot *adj.* disputable, arguable
mope *v.* fret, pine, sorrow, brood, sulk
moral *adj.* virtuous, proper, scrupulous, honorable, aboveboard, principled, chaste, noble
morale *n.* assurance, resolve, spirit, confidence
morality *n.* righteousness, uprightness, virtue
morals *n.* ethics, ideals, standards, mores, principles
moratorium *n.* delay, halt, suspension
morbid *adj.* **DISEASED:** sickly, unhealthy, ailing; **PATHOLOGICAL:** gloomy, melancholic, depressed
morning *n.* dawn, morn, daybreak, cockcrow, sun–up
morose *adj.* surly, downcast, gloomy
morsel *n.* piece, bite, chunk, bit, part
mortal *adj.* **FATAL:** malignant, lethal, deadly; **TEMPORAL:** human, transient, perishable, temporary
mostly *adv.* **FREQUENTLY:** often, regularly; **LARGELY:** chiefly, essentially, principally
motel *n.* hotel, cabin, inn, resort
motherly *adj.* maternal, devoted, protective, loving
motif *n.* theme, melody

motion n. **MOVEMENT:** change, act, action, passage; **PROPOSAL:** suggestion, proposition, plan

motivate v. inspire, stimulate, incite, spur, goad

motive n. cause, purpose, idea, reason

motto n. maxim, adage, saw, aphorism, sentiment, slogan, catchword, axiom, proverb, saying

mound n. pile, heap, knoll, hill

mount v. **RISE:** ascend; **CLIMB:** scale, clamber

mountainous adj. steep, lofty, craggy, rugged

mourn v. grieve, sorrow, bemoan, languish, pine

mournful adj. sorrowful, unhappy, sad

movable adj. portable, mobile, detachable, free

move v. **EXCITE:** arouse, stir, stimulate; **PROPEL:** impel, actuate; **PROPOSE:** introduce, submit; **ADVANCE:** go, walk, run, travel, progress, proceed, traverse

movement n. **CHANGE:** migration, evolution, transition, progression; **TREND:** drift, tendency, inclination

mow v. cut, scythe, reap, harvest

mud n. muck, mire, slush, silt, ooze

muddle v. confuse, disarrange, mix, jumble, snarl

muddy adj. **MURKY:** dull, cloudy, indistinct, obscure; **SWAMPY:** soggy, sodden, slushy, boggy

muffle v. deaden, mute, stifle, decrease, soften

muffler n. scarf, neckpiece, choker

mug n. vessel, stein, flagon, cup

muggy adj. damp, humid, moist

multitude n. throng, mob, crowd, gathering, people

mumble v. mutter, utter, murmur

munch v. chew, masticate, crunch, bite, eat

mundane adj. normal, ordinary, everyday

municipality n. community, district, village, town

murder n. homicide, carnage, slaying, butchery

murder *v.* kill, slay, assassinate, butcher
murky *adj.* gloomy, dark, dim, dusky, dingy, dirty
muscular *adj.* brawny, powerful, husky, strong
museum *n.* collection, archives, treasury, depository
music *n.* melody, harmony, tune, air, strain
musical *adj.* tuneful, sweet, pleasing, lyrical
musty *adj.* moldy, sour, stale, crumbling
mutation *n.* change, modification, deviation
mute *adj.* speechless, silent, bewildered, unspoken
mutilate *v.* maim, damage, injure, deface, disfigure
mutiny *n.* insurrection, revolt, resistance, revolution
mutter *v.* mumble, murmur, grumble, complain
mutual *adj.* reciprocal, common, joint, shared
muzzle *v.* gag, muffle, silence, suppress, hush, quiet
myriad *n.* variable, innumerable, endless, multiple
mysterious *adj.* PUZZLING: enigmatic, strange, unnatural; SECRET: veiled, obscure, hidden, ambiguous
mystical *adj.* occult, spiritual, mysterious, secret
mystify *v.* puzzle, perplex, hoodwink, deceive
myth *n.* legend, fable, lore, saga, parable, tale, story
mythological *adj.* whimsical, fantastic, imaginary
nab *v.* grab, take, snatch, seize
nag *v.* scold, vex, annoy, pester, bother
naïve *adj.* unaffected, artless, innocent, unsophisticated, gullible, credulous, trusting, inexperienced
naïveté *n.* inexperience, innocence
naked *adj.* uncovered, unclad, bare, exposed
name *n.* REPUTATION: renown, fame; TITLE: designation; STAR: hero, lion, celebrity
name *v.* appoint, nominate, select, delegate, designate
nameless *adj.* undistinguished, obscure, unknown
namely *adv.* specifically, particularly

nap *n.* REST: sleep, siesta, doze; PILE: shag, texture
napkin *n.* serviette, linen, towel
narrate *v.* tell, recite, describe, reveal, report
narrow *adj.* CRAMPED: close, confined; DOGMATIC: intolerant, prejudiced; CLOSE: precarious, dangerous
nasty *adj.* OFFENSIVE: foul, gross, vulgar; INDECENT: immodest, smutty, lewd; UNKIND: sarcastic, mean
nation *n.* PEOPLE: populace, community, society; STATE: realm, country, domain
nationalism *n.* chauvinism, jingoism, loyalty
native *adj.* NATURAL: innate, inborn, hereditary; INDIGENOUS: aboriginal, primeval, domestic, local
natty *adj.* trim, spruce
natural *adj.* INTRINSIC: original, fundamental, inherited, native; TYPICAL: characteristic, usual, customary; UNSTUDIED: ingenuous, artless, spontaneous; REAL: actual, tangible, physical
naughty *adj.* bad, mischievous, wayward, roguish
nausea *n.* sickness, queasiness, vomiting, illness
nauseate *v.* sicken, repulse, bother, disgust, disturb
nauseous *adj.* ill, queasy, squeamish, sick
navigable *adj.* passable, open, safe
near, nearby *adj.*, *adv.* BORDERING: adjacent, adjoining, neighboring; EXPECTED: approaching, coming
neat *adj.* TIDY: trim, prim, spruce, dapper, orderly, precise; CLEVER: dexterous, skillful, agile
nebulous *adj.* vague, cloudy, hazy
necessary *adj.* essential, important, requisite, required, imperative, compulsory, mandatory
necessitate *v.* compel, constrain, oblige, force
necessity *n.* requirement, need, requisite
nectar *n.* drink, juice, fluid

need *n.* POVERTY: indigence, penury; LACK: shortage, inadequacy; REQUIREMENT: necessity

needy *adj.* destitute, indigent, penniless, poor

nefarious *adj.* vile, wicked

negate *v.* repeal, retract, neutralize, cancel, nullify

negative *n.* REFUSAL: contradiction, disavowal, refutation, denial; PICTURE: film, image, plate

neglect *v.* SLIGHT: disregard, disdain, affront, ignore, spurn; EVADE: defer, procrastinate, postpone

negligent *adj.* careless, indifferent, inattentive

negotiate *v.* bargain, mediate, conciliate, arbitrate

negotiation *n.* compromise, intervention, mediation

neighborhood *n.* vicinity, environs, locality

neophyte *n.* convert, novice, apprentice

nerve *n.* COURAGE: resolution, mettle, boldness; IMPUDENCE: temerity, audacity, effrontery, rudeness

nervous *adj.* EXCITABLE: impatient, restless, uneasy, unstable; EXCITED: fidgety, jittery, agitated, bothered

nestle *v.* snuggle, cuddle, huddle

neurosis *n.* compulsion, nervousness, obsession

neurotic *adj.* disturbed, unstable, troubled

neutral *adj.* UNBIASED: impartial; DULL: drab, vague

new *adj.* RECENT: current, late; MODERN: contemporary, fashionable; NOVEL: unique, original, unusual; INEXPERIENCED: unseasoned, unskilled, incompetent

newcomer *n.* outsider, alien, stranger

newfangled *adj.* novel, unique, fashionable, modern

news *n.* information, tidings, report, account

next *adj., adv.* FOLLOWING: succeeding, subsequent; ADJACENT: beside, adjoining, neighboring, touching

nibble *v.* nip, gnaw, snack, bite, eat

nice *adj.* likable, pleasant, agreeable, amiable

niche *n.* recess, cranny, corner, cubbyhole
nick *v.* indent, notch, slit, cut, dent
night *n.* evening, nightfall, twilight, bedtime
nimble *adj.* AGILE: light, quick, spry, active, graceful; ALERT: bright, clever, intelligent
noble *adj.* EXALTED: courtly, lordly, dignified, distinguished; MERITORIOUS: virtuous, refined, chivalrous; TITLED: aristocratic, patrician; GRAND: stately, impressive, imposing
nobody *n.* nonentity, upstart, cipher
nod *v.* SIGNAL: bow, acknowledge; NAP: drowse, sleep
noise *n.* sound, clamor, racket, fracas, din, uproar
noisome *adj.* unhealthy, disgusting
noisy *adj.* clamorous, vociferous, boisterous, loud
nomad *n.* wanderer, migrant, vagabond, traveler
nominate *v.* name, appoint, propose, designate
nonchalant *adj.* CASUAL: unconcerned, impassive, detached, indifferent; CARELESS: negligent, trifling
nonconformist *n.* radical, rebel, eccentric, maverick
nonprofit *adj.* charitable, altruistic, humane
nonsense *n.* INANITY: trash, senselessness, buncombe; FUN: jest, absurdity
nonviolent *adj.* passive, calm, quiet
nook *n.* niche, cubbyhole, cranny, hole
noose *n.* loop, hitch, lasso, rope
normal *adj.* USUAL: ordinary, typical, common REGULAR: routine, orderly, methodical; SANE: lucid, rational, reasonable; HEALTHY: whole, sound
nostalgia *n.* longing, homesickness, wistfulness
nosy *adj.* snoopy, curious, inquisitive, interested
notable *adj.* remarkable, distinguished, striking
notch *n.* nick, indent, cut, dent, groove

note *n.* memo, reminder, memorandum
note *v.* **NOTICE:** perceive, see; **RECORD:** transcribe
noted *adj.* well–known, celebrated, notorious, famous
notice *n.* warning, notification, announcement
noticeable *adj.* appreciable, conspicuous, obvious
notion *n.* whim, fancy, idea, assumption
notorious *adj.* infamous, known, disreputable
notwithstanding *adv.* despite, although, but
nourish *v.* feed, encourage, sustain
nourishing *adj.* healthy, nutritious
novel *adj.* new, strange, odd, unique, unusual
novelist *n.* writer, narrator, author
novelty *n.* fad, innovation, creation
novice *n.* beginner, neophyte, amateur
now *adv.* momentarily, promptly, instantly
noxious *adj.* injurious, harmful
nuance *n.* subtlety, distinction, difference
nucleus *n.* essence, core, kernel, center, hub, focus
nudge *v.* poke, bump, tap, push, touch
nugget *n.* lump, ingot, chunk, rock
nuisance *n.* **BOTHER:** annoyance, vexation, trouble;
  CRIME: breach, infraction, affront
null *adj.* void, invalid, vain, unsanctioned
numb *adj.* deadened, unfeeling, senseless
numb *v.* deaden, stupefy, paralyze, stun, dull
numerous *adj.* many, copious, diverse, infinite
nuptials *n.* wedding, marriage, matrimony
nurse *v.* tend, minister, aid, treat
nurture *v.* nourish, feed, sustain
nutriment *n.* food, nourishment, provisions, victuals
nutritious *adj.* nourishing, wholesome, healthful
nuzzle *v.* caress, cuddle, snuggle, nestle

oasis *n.* refuge, retreat

oath *n.* PROMISE: vow, pledge; PROFANITY: curse, swearword, blasphemy

obdurate *n.* stubborn, hardhearted

obedient *adj.* DUTIFUL: loyal, devoted, deferential, faithful; DOCILE: submissive, compliant

obese *adj.* fat, corpulent, plump, stout

obey *v.* yield, conform, submit, serve comply

object *n.* THING: article, gadget; GOAL: aim, objective

object *v.* disapprove, protest, dispute, complain

objective *adj.* impartial, impersonal

objective *n.* goal, aim, target, mission, destination

obligate *v.* bind, restrict, constrain, force

obligatory *adj.* required, essential, binding, necessary

oblige *v.* ACCOMMODATE: assist, aid, contribute, help; REQUIRE: constrain, bind, force, compel, coerce

obliging *adj.* amiable, accommodating, helpful, kind

oblivion *n.* obscurity, void, emptiness, nothing

oblivious *adj.* distracted, preoccupied, absorbed

obnoxious *adj.* offensive, annoying, disagreeable

obscene *adj.* indecent, lewd, wanton, lascivious

obscure *adj.* vague, indistinct, unclear, hazy, arcane

obscure *v.* DIM: cloud, screen; CONCEAL: cover, veil

observable *adj.* perceptible, noticeable, discernible

observance *n.* CUSTOM: ritual, practice, rite; AWARENESS: observation, notice

observant *adj.* alert, discerning, perceptive, bright

observe *v.* WATCH: scrutinize, see, notice; COMMENT: remark, note, mention; COMMEMORATE: dedicate, solemnize; ABIDE BY: comply, follow, obey

obsessed *adj.* haunted, beset, controlled, troubled

obsession *n.* fixation, fascination, passion, mania

obsessive *adj.* compulsive, preoccupied
obsolete *adj.* antiquated, archaic, out–of–date
obstacle *n.* hindrance, restriction, obstruction
obstinate *adj.* stubborn, headstrong, opinionated
obstreperous *adj.* noisy, unruly
obstruct *v.* block, interfere, bar, hinder, prevent
obtain *v.* get, take, acquire, seize, procure
obtuse *adj.* blunt, stupid
obvious *adj.* apparent, perceptible, open, clear, intelligible, comprehensible, understandable
occasion *n.* event, occurrence, incident, happening
occasional *adj.* sporadic, random, infrequent
occult *adj.* hidden, mysterious, supernatural, secret
occupancy *n.* possession, occupation
occupation *n.* vocation, employment, job, profession
occupy *v.* SEIZE: conquer, invade; FILL:, pervade, permeate; ENGAGE: absorb, engross, involve, fascinate
occur *v.* happen, transpire, befall
oceanic *adj.* marine, aquatic, maritime, nautical
odd *adj.* UNUSUAL: unique, strange; SINGLE: sole, unpaired, unmatched, lone
odious *adj.* hateful, offensive, repulsive
odor *n.* smell, perfume, fragrance, bouquet
offal *n.* refuse, rubbish
offend *v.* displease, annoy, affront, outrage, bother
offense *n.* MISDEED: transgression; ATTACK: assault, aggression; RESENTMENT: pique, indignation, anger
offensive *adj.* AGGRESSIVE: assaulting, attacking, invading; REVOLTING: disgusting, repulsive, detestable
offer *v.* present, proffer, tender, propose, submit
offering *n.* contribution, donation, present, gift
offhand *adj.* impromptu, informal, improvised

officer *n.* executive, manager, director, president
official *adj.* **FORMAL:** proper, accepted; **AUTHORIZED:** endorsed, sanctioned; **RELIABLE:** authentic, genuine
official *n.* **ADMINISTRATOR:** comptroller, director, executive; **UMPIRE:** referee, linesman
offspring *n.* child, progeny, issue, descendant, heir
ointment *n.* salve, unguent, lotion, cream, balm
old *adj.* **AGED:** venerable, seasoned, enfeebled; **WORN:** thin, faded; **ANCIENT:** archaic, prehistoric, antique
ombudsman *n.* investigator, mediator
omen *n.* warning, portent, augury, indication, sign
ominous *adj.* threatening, forbidding, menacing
omission *n.* exclusion, lack, need, want
omit *v.* exclude, ignore, slight, overlook, disregard
omnipotent *adj.* all–powerful, almighty
omnipresent *adj.* universal, pervasive
once *adj., adv.* formerly, previously, earlier
oncoming *adj.* impending, imminent, approaching
only *adj.* **SOLELY:** exclusively, entirely, totally; **MERELY:** simply, barely, hardly; **SOLE:** single, isolated, unique
onset *n.* beginning, opening, start, origin
ooze *v.* leak, seep, exude, flow
opaque *adj.* dim, dusky, darkened, murky, gloomy
open *adj.* **CLEAR:** divulged, revealed, unobstructed; **UNRESTRICTED:** free, public; **UNGUARDED:** accessible; **UNDECIDED:** debatable, questionable; **FRANK:** plain, candid, straightforward
open *v.* **BEGIN:** inaugurate, initiate; **UNLOCK:** undo, unbolt; **BREACH:** penetrate, pierce; **EXPOSE:** reveal
openly *adv.* **FRANKLY:** candidly, honestly, sincerely; **SHAMELESSLY:** immodestly, flagrantly, wantonly
operate *v.* **FUNCTION:** work, serve, run, percolate;

MANAGE: manipulate, conduct, administer

operation *n.* **ACTION:** act, deed, undertaking, work; **METHOD:** process, formula, procedure

operative *adj.* effective, functioning

opinion *n.* belief, view, sentiment, conception

opinionated *adj.* obstinate, bigoted, stubborn, unyielding, prejudiced

opponent *n.* rival, competitor, adversary, antagonist

opportunity *n.* chance, circumstance, moment

oppose *v.* **CONTRADICT:** dispute, defy, confront, resist; **FIGHT:** compete, encounter, assail, storm, clash

opposite *n.* opposition, antithesis, counterpart

opposition *n.* **CONFLICT;** hostility, resistance; **DISLIKE:** antagonism, defiance, antipathy, abhorrence

oppress *v.* harass, maltreat, abuse, bother

oppression *n.* tyranny, domination, persecution

opprobrium *n.* disgrace, shame

optimal *adj.* favorable, desirable, optimum

optimism *n.* faith, cheerfulness, confidence, enthusiasm, expectation, certainty

option *n.* choice, selection, alternative

optional *adj.* discretionary, elective, voluntary

opulence *n.* riches, wealth

oracle *n.* prophet, seer, sage, fortuneteller

oral *adj.* spoken, vocal, verbal, uttered, voiced

orbit *v.* revolve, encircle, encompass

ordain *v.* **ESTABLISH:** install, appoint; **DESTINE:** foreordain, intend; **CONSECRATE:** invest, bless

ordeal *n.* trial, test, distress, calamity, difficulty

order *n.* **ARRANGEMENT:** plan, system; **ORGANIZATION:** fraternity, society; **COMMAND:** stipulation mandate, injunction; **CLASS:** kind, hierarchy, classification;

SEQUENCE: progression, succession, series
order *v.* **ARRANGE:** classify, organize; **COMMAND:** direct, instruct, require; **BUY:** secure, reserve, request
orderly *adj.* **NEAT:** tidy, arranged; **METHODICAL:** systematic, thorough, precise, careful
orderly *n.* aide, assistant
ordinance *n.* law, direction, mandate
ordinarily *adv.* usually, generally, habitually
ordinary *adj.* **USUAL:** normal, common; **AVERAGE:** mediocre, accepted, typical, characteristic
ordination *n.* investment, investiture, induction
organization *n.* **SYSTEM:** arrangement, classification; **ASSOCIATION:** federation, institute, alliance
organize *v.* **ARRANGE:** systematize, coordinate, classify; **ESTABLISH:** build, found, plan, formulate
orientation *n.* familiarization, introduction
origin *n.* birth, start, foundation, beginning, source
original *adj.* **FIRST:** fundamental; **CREATIVE:** imaginative, inventive; **GENUINE:** authentic, real
originate *v.* introduce, found, start, begin
ornament *n.* decoration, embellishment, adornment, beautification
ornate *adj.* showy, gaudy, adorned, embellished
orphan *n.* foundling, waif, stray
ostensible *adj.* professed, apparent
other *adj.* separate, distinct, opposite, extra
oust *v.* eject, expel, discharge, evict, dislodge
out *n.* escape, excuse, explanation
outbreak *n.* **ERUPTION:** explosion, outburst, commotion, tumult; **VIOLENCE:** mutiny, revolution
outburst *n.* discharge, eruption, outbreak
outcast *n.* exile, fugitive, pariah, refugee

outcome *n.* upshot, consequence, result
outcry *n.* complaint, clamor, objection
outdated *adj.* outmoded, antiquated, old
outdo *v.* surpass, best, beat, exceed
outfit *v.* supply, equip, provide
outflank *v.* surround, outmaneuver, defeat
outgrowth *adj.* end, result, outcome, effect, result
outing *n.* excursion, airing, drive, vacation
outlandish *adj.* **STRANGE:** foreign; **BARBARIC:** rude
outlast *v.* outlive, outwear, endure, survive
outlaw *v.* forbid, ban, banish, condemn
outline *n.* **PLAN:** framework, draft; **CONTOUR:** boundary, frame; **SILHOUETTE:** profile, shape, formation
outlook *n.* **VIEWPOINT:** scope, vision; **PROSPECT:** likelihood, possibility, opportunity, probability
outlying *adj.* exterior, frontier, distant
outnumbered *v.* exceeded, bested, overcome, beaten
outrage *v.* offend, wrong, affront, insult
outrageous *adj.* shameless, disgraceful, scandalous, flagrant, contemptible, ignoble, atrocious
outright *adj.* unmitigated, unconditional, obvious
outside *adj.* outermost, external, outer
outsider *n.* foreigner, stranger, refugee, alien
outskirts *n.* suburbs, limits, boundary, edge
outspoken *adj.* blunt, candid, artless, frank
outstanding *adj.* distinguished, conspicuous, notable
outwit *v.* trick, bewilder, confuse, deceive
ovation *n.* outburst, applause
over *adj.* **ABOVE:** overhead, higher; **AGAIN:** afresh; **BEYOND:** past, farther; **DONE:** accomplished, finished
overbearing *adj.* domineering, tyrannical, dictatorial
overcast *adj.* cloudy, gloomy, dark

overcome *v.* conquer, overwhelm, best, vanquish
overconfident *n.* reckless, impudent, heedless, rash
overdo *v.* **MAGNIFY:** amplify, overreach, exaggerate, enhance; **WEARY:** tire, fatigue, exhaust, overtax
overdue *adj.* late, delayed, belated, tardy
overestimate *v.* overvalue, overrate, exaggerate
overflow *v.* **SPILL OVER:** waste, cascade, spout, gush, surge; **FLOOD:** inundate
overhaul *v.* recondition, modernize, fix, renew, repair
overpower *v.* overwhelm, master, subjugate, defeat
overrate *v.* overvalue, magnify, exaggerate
overrule *v.* invalidate, override, cancel, revoke, reject
overrun *v.* **DEFEAT:** overwhelm, invade, occupy; **INFEST:** ravage, invade, overwhelm
oversee *v.* superintend, supervise, manage
oversight *n.* failure, overlooking, mistake, error
overt *adj.* apparent, open
overtake *v.* catch, exceed, overhaul, reach
overthrow *v.* upset, overcome, overrun, overpower
overtone *n.* inference, hint, suggestion
overture *n.* **SUGGESTION:** advance, tender, negotiations; **PRELUDE:** prologue, preface, introduction
overturn *v.* subvert, ruin, overthrow, reverse, overthrow, upset
overwhelm *v.* **DEFEAT:** overcome, overthrow, conquer; **ASTONISH:** bewilder, confound, confuse, surprise
overwrought *adj.* excited, overexcited
owed *adj.* owing, due, indebted, unpaid
own *v.* **ACKNOWLEDGE:** grant, admit, declare; **POSSESS:** hold, have, enjoy, retain, keep
owner *n.* proprietor, landlord, landlady, partner
ownership *n.* possession, claim, deed, title, control

pace *n.* step, gait, movement, speed
pacify *v.* calm, soothe, conciliate, appease, placate
package *n.* bundle, parcel, packet, box, carton
pact *n.* contract, agreement, bargain, treaty
pad *n.* **TABLET:** stationery, notebook; **STUFFING:** cushion, wadding, waste, filling
pad *v.* **STUFF:** pack, fill, **INCREASE:** inflate, increase
padding *n.* stuffing, wadding, waste, filling
paddle *v.* spank, thrash, rap, punish
padlock *n.* lock, latch, fastener, catch
pagan *adj.* heathen, unchristian, idolatrous
pagan *n.* heathen, gentile, unbeliever, infidel
page *n.* leaf, sheet, folio, side, surface, recto, verso
page *v.* call, summon
pageant *n.* parade, celebration, pomp
pail *n.* vessel, bucket, pot, receptacle, jug, container
pain *n.* **SUFFERING:** anguish, distress, misery, wretchedness, torment; **HURT:** ache, spasm, cramp, agony, sting, burn; **GRIEF:** despondency, worry, anxiety, depression, sadness
pain *v.* distress, hurt, grieve, trouble
painful *adj.* **SORE:** raw, throbbing, burning, hurtful, piercing, smarting, sensitive, tender
paint *v.* **PORTRAY:** sketch, picture, depict; **COAT:** brush, swab, daub, cover, spread
pair *n.* set, two, brace, couple
pair *v.* join, couple, combine, match, balance
palace *n.* manor, mansion, castle
pale *adj.* wan, pallid, sickly, anemic, cadaverous, haggard, deathlike, ghostly
palpitate *v.* tremble, quiver, pulsate
paltry *adj.* worthless, small, insignificant, trifling

pamper *v.* overindulge, spoil, indulge, pet, humor, gratify, coddle, please

pamphlet *n.* booklet, leaflet, brochure, bulletin, circular, broadside, handbill, announcement

pan *n.* vessel, kettle, pail, bucket, container

pandemonium *n.* noise, disorder, uproar, anarchy, riot, confusion

pane *n.* panel, window, glass

panel *n.* ornament, tablet, inset, decoration

pang *n.* pain, throb, sting, bite

panhandle *v.* solicit, ask, bum, beg

panic *n.* dread, alarm, fright, fear

panorama *n.* view, spectacle, scenery, prospect

pant *v.* gasp, desire, wheeze, throb, palpitate

pantomime *n.* sign, charade, mime

pantry *n.* storage, provisions, storeroom, larder, cupboard, closet, room

pants *n.* trousers, breeches, slacks, jeans, overalls, cords, shorts, corduroys, pantaloons, chaps, knickers, bloomers, rompers

paper *n.* DOCUMENT: record, abstract, affidavit, bill, certificate, contract, credentials, deed, diploma; NEWSPAPER: journal, daily; ESSAY: article, theme

par *n.* equality, standard, level, norm, model

parable *n.* fable, allegory, moral, story, tale

parade *n.* PROCESSION: spectacle, ceremony, demonstration, review, pageant, ritual

parade *v.* march, demonstrate, display, exhibit

paradox *n.* mystery, enigma, ambiguity, puzzle

paragon *n.* model, example, ideal, perfection, best

parallel *n.* match, correspond, correlate, equal

paraphernalia *n.* trappings, equipment, gear

parasite

parasite *n.* dependent, sponger, hanger–on, toady
parcel *n.* package, bundle, packet, carton
parch *v.* scorch, dry, shrivel, desiccate, dehydrate
pardon *v.* exonerate, clear, absolve, reprieve, acquit, liberate, discharge, free, release, forgive, condone, overlook, exculpate, excuse
pare *v.* cut, diminish, shave, skin
parentage *n.* birth, descent, parenthood
parental *adj.* paternal, maternal, familial, genetic
park *n.* plaza, square, lawn, green, promenade, boulevard, tract, grounds, woodland, meadow
parochial *adj.* limited, restricted, narrow, provincial, insular, sectional, local, regional
parody *v.* mimic, copy, caricature, imitate, joke
parole *v.* release, discharge, pardon, liberate, free
parson *n.* clergyman, cleric, preacher, minister
part *n.* **PORTION:** piece, fragment, fraction, section, sector, segment, particle, component, share; **ROLE:** character, hero, heroine, constituent
part *v.* **DIVIDE:** separate, sever; **DEPART:** withdraw
partial *adj.* **INCOMPLETE:** unfinished; **PREJUDICED:** unfair, influenced, biased, inclined
partiality *n.* fondness, inclination, preference
participate *v.* compete, play, strive, engage
particle *n.* jot, scrap, atom, molecule, fragment, piece, shred, bit, part
particular *adj.* **SPECIFIC:** distinct, singular, appropriate, special; **ACCURATE:** precise, minute, exact
particularly *adj.* expressly, especially
partisan *n.* adherent, supporter, disciple, follower
partition *n.* **DIVISION:** apportionment, distribution, **BARRIER:** separation, wall, obstruction

partly *adj.* partially, somewhat
partner *n.* associate, co–worker, ally, comrade
partnership *n.* alliance, union, brotherhood, society
party *n.* **AFFAIR:** social, reception, gathering, function; **GROUP:** company, crowd, assembly; **ORGANIZATION:** bloc, faction; **PERSON:** someone, somebody
pass *v.* **ELAPSE:** transpire; **TRANSFER:** relinquish, give; **ENACT:** legislate, establish; **EXCEED:** excel, transcend; **PROCEED:** progress, advance; **THROW:** toss, fling
passable *adj.* open, navigable, accessible
passage *n.* **JOURNEY:** voyage, crossing, trek; **PASSAGEWAY:** entrance, hall; **READING:** excerpt, section, portion, paragraph, quote
passenger *n.* traveler, commuter
passion *n.* feeling, craving, desire, emotion
passionate *adj.* excitable, tempestuous, impassioned, fervent, moving, inspiring, dramatic, stirring, eloquent, spirited, intense
passive *adj.* complacent, inert, lifeless, idle
passport *n.* pass, permit, visa, identification
password *n.* countersign, watchword, identification
past *adj.* former, preceding, foregoing, earlier
past *n.* antiquity, history
paste *n.* adhesive, cement, glue, mucilage
paste *v.* fasten, affix, patch, stick
pastime *n.* amusement, recreation, sport, hobby
pastor *n.* priest, rector, clergyman, minister
pastry *n.* dessert, delicacy
pasture *n.* grass, grazing, meadow, field
pat *v.* tap, touch, stroke, pet, rub
patch *n.* piece, bit, scrap, spot
patch *v.* repair, darn, mend

path *n.* trail, way, track, byway

pathetic *adj.* sad, touching, affecting, moving, pitiful

pathos *n.* pity, sorrow, grief

patience *n.* forbearance, fortitude, composure, endurance, perseverance, persistence

patient *adj.* submissive, forbearing, unruffled, imperturbable, passive, persevering, calm

patio *n.* porch, courtyard, square, yard

patriarch *n.* ruler, master, ancestor, chief

patriot *n.* statesman, nationalist, loyalist, chauvinist

patrol *v.* watch, walk, inspect, guard

patron *n.* protector, sponsor, benefactor, backer

patronize *v.* condescend, stoop, snub

pattern *n.* model, original, guide, copy

pause *n.* delay, respite, suspension, hiatus, interim, lapse, cessation, interval

pause *v.* STOP: halt, cease, interrupt, suspend; REFLECT: deliberate

pawn *v.* deposit, pledge, hock, sell

pay *n.* PROCEEDS: return, recompense, indemnity, reparation, settlement, reimbursement; WAGES: compensation, salary, remuneration, earnings

pay *v.* COMPENSATE: recompense, remunerate, repay, reimburse; RETURN: yield, profit, pay, dividends

payment *n.* REIMBURSEMENT: restitution, refund, reparation; INSTALLMENT: portion, part

peace *n.* ARMISTICE: pacification, conciliation, agreement; CALM: tranquillity, harmony, silence, stillness; COMPOSURE: contentment

peaceful *adj.* quiet, tranquil, serene, calm

peak *n.* summit, top, crown, zenith, height, summit

peasant *n.* laborer, farmer, worker, workman

peculiar *adj.* **UNUSUAL:** wonderful, singular, outlandish, strange; **UNIQUE:** characteristic, eccentric

peddle *v.* hawk, vend, trade, sell

pedestal *n.* base, stand, foundation, support

pedestrian *adj.* common, ordinary

peek *n.* sight, glimpse, glance, look

peek *v.* glance, peep, glimpse

peel *n.* skin, rind, husk, bark, shell

peel *v.* strip, skin, pare, flay, uncover

peep *v.* **CHIRP:** cheep; **PEEK:** glimpse, glance

peer *n.* equal, match, rival, companion

peer *v.* gaze, inspect, scrutinize

peeve *v.* irritate, annoy, anger, bother

peevish *adj.* cross, fretful, angry

pen *n.* cage, coop, sty, enclosure

pen *v.* **ENCLOSE:** confine; **WRITE:** compose

penalize *v.* chasten, castigate, punish

penalty *n.* punishment, fine, discipline

penance *n.* repentance, atonement, reparation

penchant *n.* inclination, taste, bias

pencil *v.* write, sketch, mark,

pendant *n.* locket, lavaliere, decoration, jewelry

pending *adj.* continuing, awaiting, ominous

penetrable *adj.* permeable, open, accessible, porous

penetrate *v.* pierce, perforate, puncture

penetrating *adj.* keen, astute, shrewd, sharp, intelligent, perceptive

penitentiary *n.* prison, reformatory, pen, jail

pension *n.* annuity, payment, allowance, retirement

perceive *v.* **OBSERVE:** note, look, notice; **UNDERSTAND:** comprehend, sense, grasp

perceptible *adj.* discernible, recognizable, obvious

perception *n.* judgment, understanding, apprehension, discernment, insight, observation
perceptive *adj.* alert, incisive, keen, observant
perch *v.* roost, land, rest, sit
peremptory *adj.* decisive, final, imperious, dictatorial
perfect *adj.* COMPLETE: absolute, whole; FAULTLESS: impeccable, immaculate, untainted, ideal, sublime, excellent; EXACT: precise, sharp, distinct, accurate
perfect *v.* finish, fulfill, realize, achieve, complete
perfectly *adj.* flawlessly, faultlessly, ideally
perforate *v.* bore, pierce, drill, slit, stab, penetrate
perforation *n.* break, aperture, slit, hole
perform *v.* ACCOMPLISH: do, achieve, fulfill, discharge, effect, complete, finish, realize; PRESENT: enact, show, exhibit, display, dramatize, execute
performance *n.* exhibition, appearance, offering, representation, revue, play, concert, drama
perfume *n.* scent, fragrance, aroma, odor
perhaps *adj.* maybe, possibly, conceivably, reasonably
perilous *adj.* precarious, unsafe, dangerous
perimeter *n.* boundary, margin, outline, border, edge
period *n.* EPOCH: era, age; END: limit, conclusion
periodical *adj.* rhythmic, regular, recurrent
periodical *n.* publication, magazine, newspaper
periphery *n.* circumference, perimeter, border
perish *v.* die, pass, depart
perjure *v.* prevaricate, falsify, lie
permanence *n.* continuity, durability, stability
permanent *adj.* fixed, enduring, abiding, continuing, lasting, imperishable, persevering, constant
permeate *v.* penetrate, pervade, saturate, fill
permissible *adj.* allowable, sanctioned, permitted

permission *n.* liberty, consent, license, authorization, approval, sanction, endorsement, affirmation

permit *n.* permission, warrant, license, grant

permit *v.* consent, sanction, tolerate, let, allow

perpetrate *v.* perform, commit, act, do

perpetual *adj.* **UNENDING:** continual, unceasing, constant, endless; **REPETITIOUS:** repeating, recurrent

perplex *v.* puzzle, confound, bewilder, confuse

perplexed *adj.* troubled, uncertain, bewildered

persecute *v.* oppress, harass, victimize, abuse

persecution *n.* torture, torment, teasing, provoking

perseverance *n.* grit, resolution, pluck, determination

persevere *v.* persist, remain, pursue, endure

persist *v.* persevere, pursue, strive, continue, endure

person *n.* individual, being, character, personage

personable *adj.* agreeable, pleasant, charming

personage *n.* someone, individual, person

personal *adj.* **PRIVATE:** secret, confidential; **INDIVIDUAL:** peculiar, particular, individual, special

personality *n.* **CHARACTER:** disposition, nature, temper, individuality; **CELEBRITY:** star, luminary

personify *v.* represent, symbolize, exemplify

personnel *n.* employees, workers, group, staff

perspective *n.* view, vista, aspect, attitude, outlook

persuade *v.* influence, induce, convince, cajole

persuasion *n.* **INFLUENCE:** inducing, enticing; **BELIEF:** creed, tenet, religion, faith

persuasive *adj.* convincing, influential, winning, enticing, compelling, potent, powerful, forceful, plausible

pertain *v.* belong, relate, refer, concern

pertinent *adj.* relevant, pertaining, related

perturb *v.* disturb, pester, worry, irritate, bother

pervade *v.* penetrate, spread, suffuse, permeate
perverse *adj.* deviant, wayward, delinquent, bad
perversion *n.* DISTORTION: deception, lie; CORRUPTION: depravity, wickedness, vice
pervert *v.* corrupt, ruin, vitiate, divert
pessimism *n.* unhappiness, gloom, sadness
pessimistic *adj.* DISCOURAGING: worrisome, troubling, dismal; CYNICAL: hopeless, gloomy, sad
pester *v.* annoy, harass, provoke, bother
pestilence *n.* disease, epidemic, sickness, illness
pet *n.* darling, lover, favorite, idol, adored
pet *v.* caress, fondle, cuddle, touch embrace
petition *n.* request, prayer, supplication, appeal
petrified *adj.* stone, hardened, mineralized, firm
petty *adj.* small, contemptible, insignificant, frivolous, trivial, unimportant
phantasm *n.* vision, illusion, specter
phenomenal *adj.* extraordinary, unique, remarkable
philanthropic *adj.* benevolent, humanitarian, kind
philosophic *adj.* thoughtful, reflective, cogitative, rational, profound, erudite, deep, learned
philosophy *n.* STUDY: wisdom, theory, explanation; PRINCIPLE: truth, axiom, conception, basis; BELIEF: outlook, view, position, opinion, viewpoint
phlegmatic *adj.* calm, sluggish, indifferent
phobia *n.* avoidance, aversion, hatred, resentment
phony *adj.* affected, imitation, artificial, false
photograph *n.* print, portrait, likeness, snapshot
photographic *adj.* accurate, detailed, exact, graphic
physical *adj.* material, corporeal, visible, tangible, palpable, substantial, real
physician *n.* healer, practitioner, surgeon, doctor

physique *n.* structure, build, constitution, body

pick *v.* CHOOSE: select, separate; GATHER: pluck, pull

picket *n.* STAKE: pole, post; WATCHMAN: guard, sentry

picket *v.* strike, blockade, boycott, protest

picture *n.* REPRESENTATION: view, photograph, image, portrait; DESCRIPTION: depiction, portrayal

picture *v.* DEPICT: sketch, portray, draw, paint, represent, describe; IMAGINE: create, conceive

picturesque *adj.* charming, pictorial, scenic, graphic, striking, arresting, quaint

piece *n.* part, portion, share, section

pierce *v.* penetrate, stab

piety *n.* reverence, devotion, devoutness, veneration

pigment *n.* coloring, paint, dye, color

pile *n.* heap, collection, mass, quantity

pile *v.* amass, stack, gather, accumulate, store

pilgrim *n.* traveler, wayfarer, wanderer, sojourner

pill *n.* tablet, capsule, pellet, medicine, drug

pillage *v.* plunder, loot, rob, destroy, steal

pillar *n.* COLUMN: pedestal, mast, shaft, post; SUPPORT: mainstay, prop

pillow *n.* cushion, pad, support, headrest

pilot *v.* guide, conduct, manage, lead

pin *v.* close, clasp, bind, fasten

pinnacle *n.* apex, zenith, crest, summit, climax

pious *adj.* reverent, devout, divine, holy, religious

pipe *n.* tube, conduit, culvert, duct

piracy *n.* robbery, theft, pillage, holdup

pirate *n.* plunderer, marauder, privateer, buccaneer

pit *n.* hole, abyss, cavity, depression

pitch *n.* SLOPE: slant, incline, angle, grade; THROW: toss, hurl, cast; FREQUENCY: tone, sound

pitfall *n.* snare, mesh, deadfall, trap
pith *n.* center, essence, heart, core
pitiful *adj.* sorry, mean, despicable, miserable, distressed, pathetic, pitiable, depressing
pity *n.* compassion, charity, tenderness, kindliness, benevolence, clemency, humanity, sympathy
pity *v.* **COMMISERATE:** sympathize, console, grieve, weep, comfort; **FORGIVE:** pardon, reprieve, spare
pivot *v.* turn, whirl, swivel, rotate
place *n.* **POSITION:** point, spot; **LOCALITY:** locus, site, area, region; **RANK:** status, position
place *v.* **PUT:** locate, deposit; **ARRANGE:** fix, order
placement *n.* situation, position, arrangement
plague *n.* pestilence, illness, epidemic
plague *v.* afflict, vex, disturb, trouble, irk, bother
plain *adj.* **OBVIOUS:** open, manifest, clear, understandable; **SIMPLE:** unadorned, unpretentious, modest; **ORDINARY:** everyday, commonplace; **BLUNT:** outspoken, candid, impolite, rude
plan *n.* **DRAFT:** diagram, design, schematic, drawing; **SCHEME:** project, idea, undertaking, plot, conspiracy, strategy; **ARRANGEMENT:** layout, disposition, order,
plan *v.* **SCHEME:** plot, devise, contrive, intrigue, conspire, calculate; **OUTLINE:** draft, sketch, map; **INTEND:** propose, think, expect
plane *n.* level, horizontal, flat
plane *v.* finish, smooth, level, flatten
planned *adj.* projected, budgeted, programmed
plantation *n.* farm, acreage, estate, ranch
plateau *n.* tableland, mesa, elevation, hill
platform *n.* **STAGE:** dais, rostrum, stand, terrace; **PROGRAM:** principles, policies

plausible *adj.* convincing, probable, credible, likely

play *n.* **AMUSEMENT:** enjoyment, diversion; **REC-REATION:** games, sports; **THEATER:** drama, musical

play *v.* revel, carouse, gambol, cavort, participate

player *n.* athlete, contestant, actor, performer

playful *adj.* joking, whimsical, comical, funny

playmate *n.* comrade, neighbor, companion, friend

playwright *n.* writer, author, tragedian

plea *n.* appeal, request, supplication, pleading

plead *v.* **BEG:** implore, beseech, solicit, ask; **ARGUE:** present, allege, cite, declare

pleasant *adj.* affable, agreeable, obliging, charming, gracious, amiable, polite, civil, cordial, sociable

please *v.* gratify, delight, satisfy

pleasing *adj.* charming, agreeable, delightful, pleasant

pleasure *n.* enjoyment, delight, happiness, amusement, preference, desire

pledge *n.* security, surety, guarantee, agreement

pledge *v.* promise, swear, vow, vouch

plentiful *adj.* bountiful, prolific, profuse, lavish, extravagant, copious, abundant, abounding

plenty *n.* abundance, lavishness, deluge, torrent, bounty, profusion, flood, avalanche

pliable, pliant *adj.* flexible, limber, supple, plastic

plight *n.* condition, dilemma, state

plod *v.* trudge, hike, walk

plot *v.* **INTRIGUE:** frame, contrive, scheme, conspire; **PLAN:** sketch, outline, draft

plump *adj.* obese, stout, fleshy, fat

plunder *v.* seize, burn, steal, raid, ravage

plunge *v.* cast, fall, rush, dive, jump

plus *adj.* increase, additionally, surplus, extra

poach *v.* steal, filch, pilfer, smuggle
pocket *n.* CAVITY: hollow; POUCH: poke, sac
pocket *v.* take, conceal, hide, enclose, steal
poetic *adj.* lyrical, romantic, imaginative
poetry *n.* verse, rhythm, rhyme, poesy
poignant *adj.* penetrating, moving, touching
point *n.* POSITION: location, locality; PURPOSE: aim,
object, intent; MEANING: force, drift, import
point *v.* INDICATE: show, name, denote; DIRECT: guide,
steer, influence, lead
pointer *n.* INDICATOR: dial, gauge; HINT: clue, tip
pointless *adj.* DULL: prosaic, trivial, unnecessary;
INEFFECTIVE: useless, impotent, incompetent, weak
poise *n.* carriage, bearing, grace, composure, dignity
poisonous *adj.* noxious, venomous, toxic, harmful
poke *v.* jab, punch, crowd, push,
policy *n.* principle, doctrine, scheme, design
polish *v.* smooth, burnish, finish, shine
polite *adj.* polished, mannerly, amiable, gracious,
cordial, diplomatic, civil, sociable, respectful
politeness *n.* refinement, culture, civility, courtesy
poll *v.* sample, canvass, question, register, enroll, list
pollute *v.* soil, defile, stain, dirty
pollution *n.* dirt, grime, smog, sewage, garbage,
waste, exhaust, pesticides, smoke
poltergeist *n.* ghost, spirit, apparition, specter, spook
pomp *n.* pageantry, magnificence, splendor
pompous *adj.* pretentious, arrogant, haughty, proud
ponder *v.* meditate, think, deliberate, consider
ponderous *adj.* weighty, dull, lifeless, heavy
pool *n.* WATER: puddle; STAKES: ante, pot, kitty
pool *v.* merge, unite, consolidate, combine, blend, join

poor *adj.* **INSOLVENT:** indigent, penniless, destitute, needy, starved, beggared, broke, **WEAK:** puny, feeble, infirm; **INFERIOR:** mediocre, trashy, shoddy, deficient, cheap, flimsy

pop *n.* **SODA:** beverage, seltzer, cola; **NOISE:** report, burst, shot, crack, detonation

poppycock *n.* drivel, nonsense, gibberish

populace *n.* people, multitudes, masses, people

popular *adj.* liked, favorite, beloved, celebrated, admired, famous, widespread

popularity *n.* acceptance, notoriety, prevalence

populated *adj.* inhabited, occupied, peopled, urban

population *n.* inhabitants, citizenry, populace, society

porous *adj.* absorbent, pervious, permeable

port *n.* harbor, haven, refuge, anchorage, dock

portable *adj.* movable, transportable, transferable

portal *n.* entrance, archway, gateway, opening

portend *v.* foretell, predict, herald

porter *n.* doorkeeper, custodian, caretaker

portfolio *n.* **CASE:** briefcase, folder; **ASSETS:** holdings, stocks, bonds

portion *n.* **PART:** scrap, fragment, piece; **ALLOTMENT:** share, quota

portrait *n.* likeness, painting, picture

portray *v.* draw, describe, depict, characterize

portrayal *n.* description, replica, likeness

pose *n.* position, attitude, affectation, pretense

pose *v.* **MODEL:** sit; **PRETEND:** profess, feign, act:

posh *adj.* rich, smart, comfortable

position *n.* **LOCATION:** whereabouts, bearings; **OPINION:** view, belief; **PROFESSION:** job, office, occupation; **STATION:** status, rank; **POSTURE:** carriage, bearing

positive

positive *adj.* decisive, clear, emphatic, assertive, resolute, certain, confident, sure
possess *v.* have, hold, own, occupy, control, maintain
possessions *n.* belongings, effects, estate, property
possessor *n.* owner, holder, proprietor, occupant
possibility *n.* plausibility, feasibility, chance, hazard, hope, prospect
possible *adj.* likely, conceivable, imaginable
possibly *adv.* likely, maybe, perhaps, potentially
post *n.* column, pillar, pedestal, upright, mast
poster *n.* advertisement, sign, card, note
posterior *adj.* **SUBSEQUENT:** coming, after, succeeding, next, following, later; **BEHIND:** back
posterity *n.* eternity, descendants, children, offspring
postpone *v.* defer, table, delay, suspend, retard, withhold, shelve, adjourn, pause
postscript *n.* appendix, addition, supplement
posture *n.* **STANCE:** pose, carriage, aspect, presence; **ATTITUDE:** feeling, sentiment, disposition
pot *n.* **KITTY:** jackpot, ante; **CONTAINER:** vessel, kettle, pan, crock, receptacle, urn, bowl
potable *adj.* clean, fresh, unpolluted
potency *n.* **STRENGTH:** power, energy, vigor; **AUTHORITY:** influence, control, dominion, command
potential *adj.* possible, latent, implied, likely
pouch *n.* bag, sack, receptacle, container
pounce *v.* seize, spring, attack, bound, surge, jump
pound *v.* beat, crush, pulverize, strike, crush, hit
pour *v.* **FLOW:** discharge, emit, issue, drain, rush; **EMPTY:** spill, splash; **RAIN:** stream, flood, drench
poverty *n.* **DESTITUTION:** indigence, want, privation, insolvency; **LACK:** shortage, inadequacy, scarcity

power *n.* STRENGTH: vigor, stamina; AUTHORITY: jurisdiction, dominion, dominance, control, sway, sovereignty, supremacy; FORCE: compulsion, coercion, duress; ENERGY: horsepower, potential, dynamism
powerful *adj.* mighty, omnipotent, influential,
authoritative, potent, forceful, compelling
powerless *adj.* helpless, feeble, weak, impotent, infirm
practical *adj.* useful, feasible, workable, rational,
utilitarian, serviceable, efficient, effective
practically *adv.* effectively, virtually, nearly, almost
practice *n.* CUSTOM: usage; METHOD: mode, manner,
fashion; REPETITION: exercise, rehearsal
practice *v.* drill, train, exercise, rehearse
practiced *adj.* skilled, able, experienced, trained
pragmatic *adj.* logical, sensible, practical, realistic
praise *v.* commend, applaud, acclaim, endorse, eulo-
gize, compliment, celebrate, honor, glorify, extol
prance *v.* strut, caper, cavort, frisk, gambol, dance
prank *n.* trick, antic, game, escapade, caper, joke
pray *v.* ask, petition, plead, beseech, beg, implore
prayer *n.* appeal, request, petition, plea, entreaty,
preach *v.* lecture, teach, sermonize, discourse, exhort,
moralize, talk, harangue, inform, address
preacher *n.* missionary, parson, evangelist, minister
preamble *n.* preface, prelude, introduction
precarious *adj.* uncertain, unsafe, risky, doubtful,
dubious, dangerous, unstable
precaution *n.* care, prudence, anticipation, forethought, regard, foresight
precede *v.* lead, antedate, preface, introduce, herald
precedence *n.* superiority, preference, priority
preceding *adj.* foregoing, former, previous, earlier

233

precious *adj.* **VALUABLE:** costly, expensive; **BELOVED:** cherished, prized; **REFINED:** delicate, fragile, dainty
precipice *n.* cliff, crag, bluff, hill, mountain
precipitate *v.* cause, accelerate, press, hasten, speed
precipitous *adj.* sheer, steep, sharp, abrupt
precise *adj.* exact, accurate, definite, careful
precision *n.* exactness, correctness, accuracy
preconception *n.* prejudice, bias, assumption
predecessor *n.* forerunner, antecedent, ancestor
predicament *n.* difficulty, strait, plight, scrape, circumstance, mess, pinch, crisis
predict *v.* foretell, prophesy, prognosticate, divine
predominance *n.* dominance, supremacy, control
predominant *adj.* **SUPREME:** almighty, powerful; **FIRST:** transcendent, surpassing, superlative, principal
preeminent *adj.* distinguished, eminent, outstanding
preface *v.* introduce, commence, precede, begin
preference *n.* choice, election, option, selection, pick
preferred *adj.* chosen, selected, favored
prehistoric *adj.* ancient, primitive, antiquated, old
prejudice *n.* bias, inclination, partiality
prejudiced *adj.* predisposed, opinionated, partisan, narrow, intolerant, parochial, provincial
preliminary *adj.* preparatory, preceding, introductory
prelude *n.* introduction, preamble, prologue, preface
premature *adj.* rash, precipitate, untimely, early
premise *n.* supposition, assumption, proposition
premium *adj.* excellent, select, prime, superior
premium *n.* reward, prize, remuneration, bonus
premonition *n.* foreboding, portent, sign, warning
preoccupied *adj.* distracted, absorbed, engrossed, disturbed, troubled,

preparation *n.* **READYING:** rehearsal, anticipation, build–up; **PREPAREDNESS:** readiness, fitness, training, education; **MIXTURE:** compound, medicine, poultice

prepare *v.* **READY:** fix, fabricate, devise, anticipate, plan, arrange, make; **OUTFIT:** equip; **COOK:** concoct

prepossessing *adj.* winning, captivating, charming

prerequisite *n.* requirement, necessity, essential

prerogative *n.* privilege, advantage, exemption, right

prescription *n.* remedy, formula, medicine

presence *n.* **ATTENDANCE:** occupancy, residence, inhabitancy; **PROXIMITY:** nearness, closeness; **DE-MEANOR:** appearance, behavior, carriage

present *adj.* now, existing, contemporary, immediate, instant, today, nowadays, already, current

present *n.* gift, grant, donation, offering

present *v.* **EXHIBIT:** do, act, perform; **BESTOW:** give, grant, confer donate, proffer, offer

presentable *adj.* proper, satisfactory, attractive

presently, *adv.* soon, directly, shortly, immediately

preservation *n.* protection, conservation, keeping, storage, curing, refrigeration

preserve *v.* **GUARD:** protect, shield; **KEEP:** process, cure

preside *v.* superintend, direct, lead, control, manage

press *n.* haste, urgency, rush, confusion, strain

pressing *adj.* important, urgent, demanding

pressure *n.* **TENSION:** burden, stress, squeeze; **PERSUASION:** compulsion, coercion

pressure *v.* press, compel, constrain, urge, persuade

prestige *n.* influence, reputation, fame, esteem

presume *v.* believe, consider, suppose, assume

presumption *n.* **ASSUMPTION:** conjecture, supposition; **IMPUDENCE:** arrogance, audacity, effrontery

pretend *v.* feign, affect, imitate, simulate, represent
pretense *n.* simulation, fabrication, imitation; deception, affectation, subterfuge, pretext
pretentious *adj.* presumptuous, arrogant, pompous
pretty *adj.* ATTRACTIVE: comely, lovely, beautiful; PLEASANT: delightful, cheerful, pleasing
prevalent *adj.* prevailing, common, widespread
prevent *v.* preclude, block, stop, thwart, halt, impede, check, frustrate, obstruct, inhibit, restrain, hinder
previous *adj.* former, antecedent, prior, preceding
prey *v.* hunt, spoil, pillage, loot, victimize
price *n.* expense, cost, worth, payment
price *v.* appraise, assess, rate, value
priceless *adj.* invaluable, inestimable, valuable
prick *v.* pierce, stick, cut, hurt, puncture
prickly *adj.* thorny, pointed, spiny, sharp
pride *n.* egotism, haughtiness, disdain, condescension
prim *adj.* exact, stiff, formal, demure, decorous, polite
primary *adj.* EARLIEST: primitive, first, original; FUNDAMENTAL: elemental, basic; PRINCIPAL: chief, prime, main
primitive *adj.* SIMPLE: rough, rude, fundamental; ANCIENT: primeval, old, beginning, uncivilized
primp *v.* dress, prepare, paint, powder
princely *adj.* lavish, sumptuous, luxurious, expensive, handsome, rich
principal *adj.* chief, leading, first, main, foremost, preeminent, dominant, prevailing
principle *n.* FUNDAMENTAL: law, origin, source, postulate; BELIEF: opinion, teaching, faith
prior *adj.* before, antecedent, foregoing, preceding
priority *n.* preference, precedence, advantage

prisoner *n.* captive, convict, detainee, hostage

privacy *n.* seclusion, solitude, isolation, aloofness, separation, concealment, secrecy

private *adj.* personal, separate, secluded, clandestine

privilege *n.* right, perquisite, prerogative, concession

prize *n.* reward, premium, bonus, booty, plunder, loot, award, medal, trophy, crown

probable *adj.* likely, seeming, presumable, feasible

problem *n.* **DIFFICULTY:** dilemma, quandary, obstacle; **QUESTION:** query, intricacy, enigma, puzzle

procedure *n.* fashion, mode, method, system, order

proceed *v.* move, progress, continue, advance

proceeding *n.* performance, undertaking, venture, happening, operation, procedure, exercise

proceeds *n.* gain, interest, yield, return

process *n.* operations, means, manner, method

process *v.* treat, ready, concoct, prepare

prod *v.* provoke, crowd, shove, push

produce *v.* **CREATE:** originate, conceive, design, devise, compose, invent; **CAUSE:** effect, occasion; **MAKE:** assemble, build, construct, manufacture;

product *n.* result, output, outcome

productive *adj.* rich, fruitful, prolific, fertile

profanity *n.* irreverence, abuse, cursing, swearing

profession *n.* **CAREER:** occupation, calling, avocation, vocation, position; **DECLARATION:** avowal, vow, oath

professional *adj.* skillful, expert, adept, able, qualified

professor *n.* teacher, educator, instructor, lecturer

proficiency *n.* learning, skill, knowledge, ability

proficient *adj.* adept, expert, skilled, skillful, able

profit *n.* gain, return, proceeds, remuneration

profitable *adj.* lucrative, beneficial, advantageous

profound *adj.* SCHOLARLY: learned, sagacious, intellectual; HEARTFELT: great, intense

program *n.* SCHEDULE: agenda, calendar, curriculum, plan, outline; ENTERTAINMENT: performance, show

progress *n.* headway, impetus, motion, improvement, advancement, development, growth

progressive *adj.* tolerant, lenient, open–minded

prohibit *v.* forbid, interdict, obstruct, prevent, ban

project *n.* plan, scheme, outline, design

projection *n.* BULGE: prominence, protuberance; FORECAST: prognostication, prediction, guess

prolong *v.* extend, lengthen, continue, increase

prominent *adj.* FAMOUS: notable, leading, distinguished; CONSPICUOUS: striking, noticeable

promiscuous *adj.* indiscriminate, unrestricted, lewd

promise *n.* agreement, pact, covenant, contract

promise *v.* pledge, declare, vow, swear, profess, guarantee, warrant, insure, underwrite, subscribe

promising *adj.* likely, encouraging, hopeful

promote *v.* further, encourage, help, aid, assist, support, back, champion, advocate, bolster, nourish, nurture, subsidize, boost, advance

prompt *adj.* timely, precise, punctual

prompt *v.* instigate, arouse, inspire, incite, urge

prone *adj.* disposed, inclined, predisposed, likely

pronounced *adj.* noticeable, clear, definite, obvious

pronouncement *n.* report, declaration, statement

proof *n.* verification, confirmation, substantiation, corroboration, testimony

propensity *n.* talent, capacity, ability, inclination

proper *adj.* decent, conventional, decorous, prudish: prim, precise, strait–laced

property *n.* possessions, belongings, assets, holdings
prophecy *n.* prediction, forecast, prognostication
prophesy *v.* foretell, predict, divine
prophet *n.* seer, oracle, soothsayer, astrologer
propitious *adj.* auspicious, encouraging, promising
proponent *n.* defender, advocate, champion, protector
proposal *n.* **OFFER:** overture, proposition, suggestion, **PLAN:** scheme, program, prospectus
propose *v.* offer, recommend, submit, volunteer
proposition *n.* offer, scheme, project, plan
propriety *n.* accordance, compatibility, congruity, modesty, dignity, pleasantness
prospect *n.* expectation, promise, outlook, possibility
prospective *adj.* promised, planned, proposed
prosper *v.* thrive, flourish, flower, succeed
protect *v.* shelter, shield, guard, preserve, defend
protection *n.* shield, screen, shelter, defense, safeguard, security, guaranty
protector *n.* champion, defender, patron, sponsor, benefactor, supporter, advocate
protest *n.* meeting, rally, demonstration, dissent
protest *v.* object, demur, disagree, oppose
proud *adj.* **DIGNIFIED:** stately, lordly; **EGOTISTICAL:** vain, vainglorious, haughty, arrogant
prove *v.* demonstrate, substantiate, authenticate, corroborate, validate, confirm, establish
provide *v.* furnish, equip, outfit, stock, supply
provincial *adj.* narrow, backward, rude, unpolished
provision *v.* requirement, stipulation, prerequisite
provisional *adj.* transient, passing, temporary
provoke *v.* **VEX:** irritate, aggravate, bother; **INCITE:** stir, rouse, arouse; **CAUSE:** make, produce, begin

prowl *v.* slink, lurk, rove, sneak

proxy *n.* agent, broker, representative, delegate

prudent *adj.* CAREFUL: cautious, circumspect, wary, discreet; PRACTICAL: sensible, wise, discerning

pry *v.* snoop, spy, nose, inquire, meddle

pseudo *adj.* imitation, quasi, sham, false

publication *n.* broadcasting, announcement, advisement, disclosure

publicize *n.* announce, broadcast, promulgate

publish *v.* DISTRIBUTE: print, issue; ADVERTISE: announce, promulgate, proclaim

pudgy *adj.* fat, chubby, chunky, stout

pull *n.* TOW: drag, haul; INFLUENCE: power, authority

pulpy *adj.* soft, smooth, thick, fleshy

pulse *n.* beating, pulsation, vibration, throb, beat

pun *n.* witticism, quip, joke

punch *v.* HIT: thrust, blow, strike, knock; PERFORATE: pierce, puncture, bore, penetrate, prick

punctual *adj.* prompt, precise, exact, meticulous

puncture *v.* pierce, prick, perforate, penetrate

punish *v.* correct, discipline, chasten, reprove, penalize, fine, incarcerate, chastise

puny *adj.* small, feeble, inferior, diminutive, weak

purchase *v.* obtain, acquire, buy

pure *adj.* UNMIXED: unadulterated, simple, clear, undiluted; CLEAN: immaculate, germ–free, sterilized, sanitary, refined; CHASTE: virginal, continent, celibate; ABSOLUTE: sheer, utter, complete

purge *v.* cleanse, evacuate, eliminate

purpose *n.* aim, intention, end, goal, mission, objective, expectation, intent, aspiration

pursue *v.* chase, seek, hound, track, stalk

push *n.* shove, force, bearing, propulsion, drive, exertion, weight, straining, inducement, reserve, impact, blow, pressure

push *v.* PRESS: thrust, shove, ram, jostle, elbow; PROMOTE: advance, launch, start, sell

put *v.* PLACE: set, plant, lodge, situate, deposit

putrid *adj.* rotten, corrupt, putrefied, decayed

puzzle *v.* PERPLEX: obscure, bewilder, complicate, confuse; WONDER: marvel, surprise, astonish

puzzling *adj.* OBSCURE: uncertain, ambiguous, mystifying; DIFFICULT: perplexing, abstruse, hard

quaint *adj.* odd, strange, fanciful, cute, whimsical

quake *v.* tremble, shrink, cower, shake

qualified *adj.* LIMITED: conditional, confined, restricted; COMPETENT: adequate, equipped, able

quality *n.* ATTRIBUTE: trait, endowment, condition, property; CHARACTER: nature, essence; GRADE: class, merit, worth, excellence, variety, rank

qualm *n.* scruple, suspicion, doubt, uncertainty

quantity *n.* amount, number, measure

quarantined *adj.* isolated, restrained, separated,

quarrel *v.* dispute, wrangle, contend, squabble, clash, bicker, contest, disagree, argue, feud, oppose

quarrelsome *adj.* factious, irritable, pugnacious, unruly, contentious, churlish, cantankerous

queasy *adj.* squeamish, sick, uneasy, uncomfortable

queer *adj.* odd, peculiar, strange, curious

question *v.* ASK: inquire, interrogate, petition, solicit, quiz, probe, investigate; DOUBT: challenge, dispute

questionable *adj.* CONTROVERSIAL: vague, unsettled, debatable, ambiguous, indefinite; DUBIOUS: disreputable, notorious, suspicious quick

quick *adj.* **RAPID:** swift, fleet, fast; **IMMEDIATE:** instantaneous, prompt; **HASTY:** impetuous, quick–tempered, rash; **ALERT:** ready, sharp, vigorous, active

quicken *v.* **HASTEN:** speed, hurry, accelerate, move, **EXPEDITE:** urge, promote

quiet *adj.* silent, calm, peaceful, hushed, muffled, noiseless, still, reserved, reticent

quiet *n.* **REST:** calm, tranquillity, relaxation, peace, repose; **SILENCE:** hush, stillness

quip *n.* retort, remark, jest, repartee, banter, language

quirk *n.* whim, caprice, fancy, peculiarity

quit *v.* **ABANDON:** surrender, renounce, relinquish; **CEASE:** discontinue, halt, desist, stop; **LEAVE:** go, depart, vacate, resign

quiver *v.* vibrate, shudder, wave, shiver, tremble

quiz *v.* question, examine, test, cross–examine, query

quote *v.* **EXCERPT:** extract, say, repeat; **PRICE:** request, demand, value

rabble *n.* crowd, mob, masses, riffraff, people

rabid *adj.* **FANATICAL:** obsessed, zealous; **INSANE:** raging, deranged, mad;

race *v.* hurry, run, tear, bustle, fly, dash, sprint

racket *n.* **UPROAR:** clatter, din, disturbance, noise, **CONSPIRACY:** scheme, corruption, crime, theft

racketeer *n.* criminal, extortionist, trickster

radial *adj.* branched, outspread, spreading

radiant *adj.* shining, luminous, radiating, bright

radiate *v.* spread, diffuse, disperse, disseminate

radiation *n.* fallout, pollution, radioactivity, heat

radical *adj.* **FUNDAMENTAL:** original, primitive, native, organic; **EXTREME:** progressive, militant, seditious, riotous, rebellious, revolutionary, heretical

242

raffle *n.* lottery, sweepstakes, pool

raft *n.* flatboat, barge, float, catamaran, boat

rag *n.* cloth, remnant, wiper, shred

rage *n.* **FURY:** frenzy, tantrum, uproar, storm, outburst; **FAD:** fashion, style, mode, vogue, craze, mania

rage *v.* rave, splutter, scream, bluster, storm, rant

ragged *adj.* tattered, frayed, frazzled, threadbare

raid *n.* attack, invasion, foray, assault, roundup

rain *v.* pour, drizzle, shower, sprinkle, mist, storm

raise *v.* **LIFT:** elevate, hoist, boost; **REAR:** breed, cultivate, produce; **ERECT:** construct, build

rake *n.* **RASCAL:** lecher, drunkard, scoundrel

rally *n.* gathering, meeting, celebration, session

ram *v.* butt, bump, collide, thrust, drive

ramble *v.* **SAUNTER:** stroll, roam, wander; **DRIFT:** stray, diverge, meander, digress

ramp *n.* incline, slope, grade, hill, inclination

rampant *adj.* raging, uncontrolled, violent, turbulent, tumultuous, unruly, unrestrained

rancid *adj.* unpleasant, tainted, stale, bad, rotten

random *adj.* aimless, haphazard, casual, unpredictable, irregular

range *n.* **SCOPE:** extent, area, expanse; **MOUNTAINS:** highlands; **DISTANCE:** reach, span, projection

range *v.* **VARY:** differ, fluctuate, diverge; **TRAVERSE:** wander, ramble, explore, traverse

rank *adj.* foul, smelly, fetid, putrid, stinking, rancid, offensive, noxious, gamy, disgusting, malodorous

rank *n.* **ROW:** column, file, string, line; **EMINENCE:** position, distinction, standing, status, ancestry

rank *v.* **ARRANGE:** assign, order; **EVALUATE:** judge, fix, valuate, classify

ransack v. SEARCH: rummage, scour, seek; LOOT: pillage, plunder, ravish, strip, rifle

rant v. rave, fume, rail, rage, yell

rap n. knock, thump, slap, blow

rapid adj. swift, speedy, accelerated, hurried, fast

rapt adj. awed, transported, entranced, enchanted

rapture n. delight, ecstasy, pleasure, satisfaction

rare adj. UNCOMMON: exceptional, singular, extraordinary, unusual; SCARCE: expensive, precious; CHOICE: select, superlative, excellent

rascal n. scoundrel, rogue, rake, knave, shyster, cad, scalawag, reprobate, miscreant

rash adj. hasty, impetuous, impulsive, foolish, heedless, foolhardy, brash

rasping adj. hoarse, grating, grinding, harsh

rate v. rank, judge, evaluate, grade

ratify v. substantiate, endorse, approve, sanction

rating n. grade, class, degree, rank

ration n. allowance, allotment, portion, quota, share

rational adj. LOGICAL: stable, thoughtful, sensible, impartial, objective, sober; REASONABLE: intelligent, sensible, wise; SANE: normal, lucid, responsible

rattle v. disconcert, bother, unnerve, confuse, disturb, embarrass

raucous adj. hoarse, harsh, loud, gruff, rough

ravage v. pillage, devastate, despoil, plunder, sack

rave v. TALK: babble, gabble, jabber; RAGE: storm, splutter, rail, rant

ravel v. untwist, disentangle, unsnarl, free, loosen

ravenous adj. voracious, starved, hungry

ravine n. hollow, gully, gorge, canyon, gulch, valley, gap, chasm, abyss, break, crevice, crevasse

raw *adj.* **UNFINISHED:** natural, crude, rough; **UN-TRAINED:** immature, inexperienced; **COLD:** biting, windy, bleak; **SCRAPED:** chafed, bruised

reach *n.* compass, range, scope, grasp, stretch, extension, orbit, horizon, gamut, ability, limit, extent

reach *v.* **EXTEND:** span, encompass, overtake; **STRETCH:** lunge, strain, seize; **ARRIVE:** gain, enter

react *v.* respond, reciprocate, behave, answer

reaction *n.* response, rejoinder, repercussion

read *v.* **UNDERSTAND:** comprehend, perceive, apprehend, grasp, learn; **INTERPRET:** decipher, explain, expound, construe

readable *adj.* **LEGIBLE:** distinct, comprehensible, decipherable; **INTERESTING:** absorbing, fascinating, engrossing, entertaining, engaging, stimulating

readily *adv.* quickly, promptly, eagerly, willingly

reading *n.* **INTERPRETATION:** commentary, translation; **EXCERPT:** passage, section, quotation

ready *adj.* **PREPARED:** alert, handy, expectant, available; **ENTHUSIASTIC:** eager, willing, ardent, zealous

real *adj.* **GENUINE:** authentic, original; **EXISTING:** actual, substantive, tangible

realism *n.* authenticity, naturalness, actuality, reality

realization *n.* understanding, comprehension, consciousness, awareness

realize *v.* **FULFILL:** complete, accomplish; **UNDERSTAND:** recognize, apprehend, discern; **OBTAIN:** receive get

realm *n.* kingdom, province, domain, sphere

rear *n.* back, hindmost, tail, posterior, rump, butt

reason *n.* **JUDGMENT:** intelligence, sanity; **LOGIC:** speculation, rationalism, analysis; **MOTIVE:** end, rationale, aim, intent; **MIND:** brain, mentality, intellect

reason *v.* **THINK:** reflect, deliberate, contemplate; **ASSUME:** suppose, gather, conclude; **DISCUSS:** persuade, argue, contend, debate

reasonable *adj.* **RATIONAL:** sane, conscious, sensible, unbiased; **JUST:** fair, right, honest; **LIKELY:** feasible, sound, plausible; **MODERATE:** inexpensive, fair, cheap

reassure *v.* console, comfort, encourage, guarantee

rebel *n.* revolutionary, agitator, insurgent, seditionist, malcontent, dissenter, renegade, radical

rebel *v.* rise, revolt, resist, mutiny, riot, oppose

rebellion *n.* insurrection, revolt, revolution

rebound *v.* recoil, reflect, ricochet, bounce

rebuke *v.* chide, reprove, condemn, reprimand

recede *v.* retreat, shrink, ebb, lower, abate, decline, drop, lessen, decrease, fall

receipt *n.* **ACQUISITION:** receiving, acceptance, arrival; **VOUCHER:** acknowledgment, notice, stub

receive *v.* **ACCEPT:** admit, inherit, acquire, obtain, secure; **EXPERIENCE:** undergo, suffer; **WELCOME:** accommodate, accept, greet

recent *adj.* modern, fresh, novel, contemporary, late

receptacle *n.* repository, holder, container

reception *n.* gathering, party, soiree, entertainment

receptive *adj.* alert, sensitive, perceptive, observant

recess *n.* **ALCOVE:** nook, cell, cubicle; **SUSPENSION:** intermission, interlude

recipe *n.* formula, compound, instructions, directions

recipient *n.* receiver, legatee, heir

recite *v.* render, enact, dramatize, interpret, soliloquize, narrate, recount, portray

reckless *adj.* heedless, thoughtless, wild, rash

reckon *v.* account, consider, evaluate, judge, estimate

reclaim *v.* recover, redeem, regain, mend, improve

recognition *n.* acknowledgment, verification, appreciation, esteem, attention, regard, honor

recognize *v.* DISTINGUISH: place, recall, remember, perceive;, ACKNOWLEDGE: appreciate, realize

recoil *v.* shrink, retreat, bounce, spring

recommend *v.* commend, praise, endorse, suggest, prescribe, urge, advise

reconcile *v.* ADJUST: adapt, arrange, regulate; HARMONIZE: pacify, mitigate, mediate, intercede

reconciliation *n.* conciliation, adjustment, agreement

record *n.* DOCUMENT: manuscript, account, history, deed; RECORDING: disk, phonograph, record, cut

record *v.* write, transcribe, catalogue, tabulate, chronicle, preserve

recover *v.* SALVAGE: redeem, rescue, reclaim; RALLY: convalesce, heal, mend, revive, recuperate

recreation *n.* pastime, amusement, relaxation

recuperate *v.* recover, convalesce, heal

recur *v.* return, reappear, happen, repeat

redecorate *v.* refurbish, refresh, restore, recondition, remodel, renovate, revamp

redeem *v.* RECOVER: repay, purchase, atone, compensate; SAVE: liberate, free, deliver, rescue

redemption *n.* regeneration, salvation, rebirth, rescue

redress *n.* compensation, payment, reparation

reduce *v.* LESSEN: dilute, diminish, decrease, lower; DEFEAT: conquer, overcome, subdue; HUMBLE: degrade, demote, abase, humiliate

redundant *adj.* superfluous, wordy, verbose, dull

referee *n.* arbitrator, umpire, conciliator, judge

reference *n.* allusion, mention, relation, implication

refine *v.* **PURIFY:** rarefy, strain, filter, clean, separate; **IMPROVE:** better, clarify, explain

refined *adj.* genteel, cultivated, polished, elegant, gracious, mannerly, courteous, polite

refinement *n.* **CULTURE:** cultivation, sophistication, breeding, enlightenment, scholarship, learning; **POLITENESS:** polish, manners, tact, civility, affability

reflect *v.* ponder, contemplate, concentrate, weigh, consider, think

reflection *n.* thought, consideration, contemplation, rumination, speculation, deliberation, meditation

reform *n.* reformation, betterment, improvement

reform *v.* revise, redeem, rectify, rehabilitate, remedy, restore, rebuild, reclaim, regenerate, amend, correct

refrain *v.* avoid, cease, forbear, abstain

refresh *v.* invigorate, animate, exhilarate, renew, replenish, restore

refuge *n.* shelter, sanctuary, retreat, haven

refugee *n.* exile, expatriate, fugitive, renegade, derelict, foundling, alien, outcast

refund *n.* return, reimbursement, repayment, remuneration, compensation, rebate, settlement

refuse *n.* rubbish, leavings, remains, residue, trash

refuse *v.* reject, decline, rebuff, spurn, deny

refute *v.* disprove, answer, deny

regain *v.* recapture, retrieve, reacquire, recover

regard *n.* **LOOK:** gaze, glance; **OPINION:** estimation, appreciation, affection, admiration

regard *v.* **OBSERVE:** notice, mark; **CONSIDER;** view, think; **RESPECT:** esteem, value, admire

regimentation *n.* organization, regulation, uniformity

region *n.* territory, area, realm, locale, domain, sphere

regress *v.* backslide, relapse, revert, retreat, sink

regret *n.* REMORSE: compunction, repentance, misgiving, qualm; GRIEF: pain, anxiety, sorrow

regret *v.* MOURN: lament, rue, repent, grieve, sorrow

regular *adj.* CUSTOMARY: conventional, usual; ORDERLY: methodical, precise, systematic, organized, consistent, rhythmic, periodic, measured

regularly *adv.* customarily, habitually, usually, commonly, ordinarily, normally

regulate *v.* CONTROL: rule, legislate, direct, govern, manage; ADJUST: adapt, standardize, rectify, correct

regulation *n.* rule, law, statute, ordinance, command

rehabilitate *v.* restore, reinstate, change, reestablish

reign *v.* rule, govern, manage

reimburse *v.* repay, compensate, refund

reinforce *v.* buttress, strengthen, support

reject *v.* REFUSE: repudiate, decline, renounce, deny; DISCARD: expel, eliminate

rejoice *v.* exult, enjoy, revel, celebrate

rejoinder *n.* answer, reply, rebuttal, refutation

rejuvenate *v.* reinvigorate, refresh, strengthen

relapse *v.* backslide, revert, regress, deteriorate, degenerate, weaken, sink

relate *v.* TELL: recount, recite, retell, describe, report; CONNECT: associate, correlate, compare

related *adj.* associated, linked, affiliated, akin, parallel, correlated, similar

relax *v.* slacken, repose, recline, unbend, rest

relaxed *adj.* untroubled, carefree, comfortable

relay *n.* communicate, transmit, deliver, carry, send

release *v.* liberate, acquit, loose, free

relent *v.* soften, comply, relax, yield

relentless *adj.* unmerciful, vindictive, hard, ruthless
relevance *n.* connection, pertinence, importance
relevant *adj.* pertinent, pertaining, applicable, related, concerning, connected
reliable *adj.* unimpeachable, trustworthy, reputable, irrefutable, incontestable, dependable, unfailing
reliance *n.* confidence, hope, faith, trust, dependence
relic *n.* vestige, trace, heirloom, antique, keepsake, memento, curiosity, token
relief *n.* SOFTENING: alleviation, comforting; AID: assistance, support, help, succor; RELAXATION: comfort, contentment, restfulness
relieve *v.* REPLACE: discharge, dismiss; LESSEN: ease, alleviate, allay, lighten, mitigate
religion *n.* FAITH: belief, persuasion, theology, doctrine, communion, piety
religious *adj.* DEVOUT: pious, sanctimonious, reverential; SCRUPULOUS: methodical, thorough, careful
relish *v.* fancy, like, enjoy
reluctance *n.* unwillingness, disinclination, qualm, hesitation, doubt
remain *v.* STAY: inhabit, stop, settle; ENDURE: prevail, continue; SURVIVE: outlive, outlast
remainder *n.* residue, remains, remnant, dregs, surplus, leavings, excess, scrap, fragment, salvage
remark *v.* say, state, speak, mention, observe
remarkable *adj.* exceptional, extraordinary, unusual
remedy *v.* help, aid, heal, counteract, repair, cure
remember *v.* RECALL: recollect, reminisce; MEMORIZE: learn, master, retain
remembrance *n.* MEMORY: recollection, recognition, reminder; GIFT: reward, token, keepsake

remind *v.* hint, caution, mention, prompt, prod, stress, emphasize, note, warn

remit *v.* transmit, pay, tender, forward

remnant *n.* remainder, residue, leavings, dregs

remodel *v.* renovate, refurbish, redecorate, modernize

remorse *n.* anguish, guilt, compunction, contrition, grief, regret

remote *adj.* DISTANT: removed, secluded, isolated; ANCIENT: aged, old; SEPARATED: unrelated, irrelevant

removal *n.* dismissal, discharge, expulsion, exile, deportation, banishment, elimination, ejection

rend *v.* tear, burst, rip, sever, sunder, break

rendition *n.* interpretation, translation, version

renew *v.* refresh, regenerate, rehabilitate, invigorate, restore, freshen, stimulate

renounce *v.* disown, disavow, deny, discard

renovate *v.* remake, rehabilitate, renew

rent *n.* LEASE: lend, sublet; HIRE: charter, engage

reorganize *v.* renovate, regenerate, reconstruct

repair *v.* restore, fix, correct, refurbish, mend

reparation *n.* amends, compensation, indemnity, retribution, payment

repay *v.* REIMBURSE: recompense, refund, indemnify, compensate; RETALIATE: reciprocate, revenge

repeal *v.* revoke, abrogate, annul, abolish, cancel

repeat *v.* iterate, echo, recite, recapitulate

repel *v.* REBUFF: resist, oppose, repulse; OFFEND: revolt, disgust; REJECT: disown, dismiss, refuse

repentance *n.* sorrow, remorse, self–reproach, regret

repentant *adj.* penitent, regretful, contrite, sorry

repetition *n.* recurrence, duplication, renewal, reiteration, wordiness

repetitious *adj.* boring, wordy, repeating, dull
replace *v.* substitute, supplant, restore, reinstate
replenish *v.* refill, restock, renew
replica *n.* copy, likeness, model, duplicate, imitation
reply *v.* answer, retort, rejoin, return
report *v.* narrate, recount, inform, advise, relate, tell
reporter *n.* journalist, newsman, correspondent
represent *v.* DEPICT: render, portray, enact, symbolize, describe; IMITATE: substitute, impersonate
representative *n.* emissary, deputy, agent, delegate, congressman, deputy, diplomat
repress *v.* check, restrain, control, curb, hinder
reprieve *n.* delay, respite, suspension
reprimand *v.* reprove, rebuke, chide, reproach, denounce, criticize, scold
reproach *v.* censure, upbraid, condemn, scold, blame
reproduce *v.* COPY: duplicate, mimeograph; REPEAT: recreate, re–enact, relive, mirror, echo; MULTIPLY: procreate, breed, propagate
reproduction *n.* copy, imitation, print, blowup
repudiate *v.* reject, retract, repeal, revoke, abandon
repulse *v.* resist, repel, rebuff, spurn, snub
repulsive *adj.* offensive, disgusting: odious, forbidding, horrid
reputable *adj.* distinguished, celebrated, honorable, trustworthy, honest, worthy, brave, noble
reputation *n.* character, honor, standing, prestige, prominence, eminence, notoriety
request *v.* ask, solicit, beseech, entreat, sue, beg
require *v.* NEED: want; DEMAND: exact, expect
requirement *n.* PREREQUISITE: condition, provision, stipulation, qualification; NEED: necessity, demand

rescue *v.* **SAVE:** recover, redeem, salvage, retrieve; **FREE:** deliver, liberate, release

research *n.* search, investigation, analysis, experimentation, examination, study

resemblance *n.* likeness, correspondence, coincidence, similarity

resentment *n.* annoyance, irritation, anger

reserve *n.* **SECURITY:** savings, insurance, resources, provisions, assets, hoard; **CALM:** caution, restraint, reticence, inhibition, demureness

reserve *v.* retain, keep, possess, have, hold, own

reserved *adj.* **BOOKED:** saved, claimed, held; **WITHHELD:** preserved, conserved; **RESTRAINED:** composed, sedate, collected, serene, placid

reservoir *n.* supply, store, reserve, pool, cistern

reside *v.* dwell, live, stay, lodge, occupy

residence *n.* habitation, quarters, apartment, home

residue *n.* remainder, leavings, scraps, shavings

resign *v.* **RELINQUISH:** yield, surrender, capitulate, abandon, submit; **QUIT:** retire, leave

resigned *adj.* quiet, peaceable, docile, submissive, yielding, relinquishing, obedient, passive

resilient *adj.* rebounding, elastic, springy, flexible

resist *v.* oppose, endure, bear, persist, suffer, abide, persevere, last, repel

resolute *adj.* constant, determined, steadfast, firm

resolution *n.* **DETERMINATION:** fortitude, perseverance, resolve; **PROPOSAL:** recommendation, declaration

resolve *v.* decide, determine, conclude, decree

resource *n.* reserve, support, means, stratagem

resourceful *adj.* ingenious, capable, active, intelligent

resources *n.* means, money, riches, assets, capital,

respect

property, reserve, wealth

respect *n.* regard, relation, esteem, honor, admiration

respectable *adj.* presentable, tolerable, passable, virtuous, honorable

respectful *adj.* deferential, courteous, reverent, attending, venerating, deferring, polite

respite *n.* delay, postponement, reprieve, pause, delay

respond *v.* reply, rejoin, acknowledge, answer

response *n.* reply, rejoinder, acknowledgment, answer

responsibility *n.* STABILITY: loyalty, faithfulness, competence, honesty; DUTY: obligation, trust

responsible *adj.* ACCOUNTABLE: liable, obligated, obliged, pledged, bound, answerable; ABLE: reliable, capable, dutiful, dependable, competent

rest *n.* REPOSE: quiet, slumber, peacefulness, relaxation, doze, nap, respite; REMAINDER: residue, surplus, remnant, balance; CESSATION: intermission, interval, inactivity, pause, recess

restful *adj.* tranquil, calm, peaceful, quiet, serene, soothing, relaxing, refreshing

restitution *n.* restoration, amends, compensation

restless *adj.* fidgety, jumpy, nervous, uneasy, agitated, unsettled, restive, impatient, jittery

restore *v.* RETURN: replace; RECREATE: revive, recover, renew; REBUILD: reconstruct, rehabilitate, repair; HEAL: refresh, cure

restrain *v.* curb, bridle, rein, regulate, muzzle, inhibit, deter, hamper, restrict, gag, limit, contain, check

restraint *n.* SELF–CONTROL: reserve, reticence, forbearance, abstinence, abstention; LIMITATION: hindrance, restriction, impediment

restrict *v.* limit, circumscribe, contract, shorten

restricted *adj.* limited, confined, hampered, bridled, blocked, barred, decreased, diminished, reduced

result *n.* consequence, outcome, aftermath, upshot, settlement, determination, payoff, end

resurrection *n.* transformation, rebirth, renewal

retain *v.* **HOLD:** grasp, clutch; **EMPLOY:** maintain, engage, hire; **REMEMBER:** recall, recollect, recognize

retaliate *v.* repay, requite, return, revenge

retard *v.* hinder, postpone, delay, impede

retire *v.* **LEAVE:** withdraw, part, retreat; **REST:** sleep; **RESIGN:** relinquish

retort *n.* reply, counter, repartee, response, answer

retort *v.* reply, rejoin, answer

retraction *n.* denial, revocation, cancellation

retreat *n.* refuge, sanctuary, port, haven, resort

retreat *v.* withdraw, depart, reverse, backtrack, leave

retribution *n.* punishment, reprisal, retaliation

retrieve *v.* recover, regain, reclaim

return *n.* **HOMECOMING:** arrival, reappearance; **RESTORATION:** restitution, recompense; **PROCEEDS:** profit, income, results, gain, revenue, yield, interest

return *v.* **REAPPEAR:** recur, repeat, revive, rebound; **REINSTATE:** restore, replace; **ANSWER:** reply, respond, retort; **REPAY:** reimburse, recompense, refund; **YIELD:** interest, profit

reveal *v.* disclose, publish, betray, announce, declare

revelation *n.* **DISCLOSURE:** discovery, announcement, betrayal; **WORD:** truth, apocalypse, doctrine, faith

revenge *n.* retaliation, reprisal, retribution

revenue *n.* income, return, earnings, yield, receipts, proceeds, profits

reverence *n.* veneration, respect, admiration, regard,

esteem, adoration, praise

reverse *n.* **OPPOSITE:** converse, contrary; **DEFEAT:** vanquishment, downfall, annihilation

review *v.* **CORRECT:** criticize, revise; **INSPECT:** examine, analyze, check

revise *v.* improve, correct, reconsider, rewrite, edit

revival *n.* renewal, rebirth, resurrection, restoration, freshening, awakening

revive *v.* enliven, refresh, renew, resuscitate, invigorate; freshen, rouse, arouse, strengthen

revoke *v.* annul, reverse, recall, retract, cancel

revolt *n.* rebellion, uprising, mutiny, revolution

revolting *adj.* awful, loathsome, repulsive, offensive

revolutionary *adj.* **REBELLIOUS:** mutinous, insurgent, subversive; **NOVEL:** new, unusual, advanced, forward

revolve *v.* roll, spin, rotate, twirl, turn

reward *n.* **PAYMENT:** compensation, remuneration, pay, recompense; **PRIZE:** premium, bonus, award

rhythmic *adj.* measured, balanced, regular

rich *adj.* **WEALTHY:** moneyed, affluent; **SUMPTUOUS:** luxurious, magnificent, resplendent, lavish, ornate, splendid, elegant; **FERTILE:** lush, fruitful, luxuriant

riches *n.* wealth, fortune, possessions, money

rickety *adj.* infirm, shaky, fragile, weal

ricochet *v.* carom, rebound, reflect, bounce

rid *v.* clear, relieve, shed, free

riddle *n.* enigma, puzzle, dilemma, complexity

ride *n.* excursion, drive, trip, transportation, journey

rider *n.* addition, codicil, addendum, amendment, appendix, supplement

ridicule *v.* mock, gibe, scoff, sneer, taunt, mimic, deride, scorn, caricature, satirize

ridiculous *adj.* absurd, ludicrous, preposterous, funny, unusual

rig *n.* tackle, apparatus, gear, equipment

right *adj.* **CORRECT:** precise, accurate, exact, factual, true, valid; **JUST:** lawful, legitimate, honest, fair

right *n.* **PREROGATIVE:** immunity, exemption, license; **JUSTICE:** equity, fairness

right *v.* correct, repair, restore, remedy, rectify, mend

righteous *adj.* **VIRTUOUS:** just, honorable, exemplary, noble, trustworthy, ethical, impartial; **RELIGIOUS:** devout, pious, saintly, angelic, devoted, reverent, spiritual, holy

rightful *adj.* proper, just, honest, fair, legal

rigid *adj.* **STIFF:** unyielding, inflexible, solid, firm; **STRICT:** exact, rigorous, severe; **FIXED:** set, unmoving, definite, determined

rigorous *adj.* harsh, austere, uncompromising, severe

rim *n.* margin, edge, border, verge, brim, lip, brink

rind *n.* covering, skin, peel, hull, shell

ring *n.* **CIRCLE:** circlet, girdle, rim; **JEWELRY:** band, signet, bracelet; **GROUP:** party, bloc, faction, group, gang, band; **SOUND:** clangor, jangle

rinse *v.* cleanse, clean, flush, dip, soak, wash

riot *n.* uproar, tumult, confusion, disorder, disturbance, protest

rip *v.* divide, tear, cut, rend, split, cleave, rive, shred

ripe *adj.* matured, grown, developed

ripen *v.* develop, evolve, advance, grow

rise *v.* **ASCEND:** mount, climb, scale; **HEIGHTEN:** grow, enlarge, extend, raise; **BEGIN:** spring, emanate, issue; **IMPROVE:** prosper, flourish, thrive; **SWELL:** inflate, billow, bulge

risk *n.* DANGER: hazard, peril, jeopardy; CHANCE: contingency, prospect, uncertainty

risky *adj.* perilous, precarious, hazardous, dangerous

rite *n.* ceremony, observance, service, ritual, custom

rival *n.* competitor, antagonist, opponent

rival *v.* approach, match, equal

rivalry *n.* competition, contention, opposition, dispute

roam *v.* ramble, range, meander, saunter, traipse

rob *v.* burglarize, plunder, defraud, cheat, pilfer, purloin, filch, embezzle, pillage, sack, loot

robbery *n.* burglary, larceny, thievery

robust *adj.* vigorous, husky, hale, hearty, sound

rock *v.* totter, sway, reel, quake, convulse, tremble

rogue *n.* knave, outlaw, miscreant, criminal

roll *n.* LIST: register, index, record; BREAD: pastry, bun; ROTATION: turn, revolution

roll *v.* rotate, circle, turn, revolve, spin

romantic *adj.* poetic, fanciful, chivalrous, courtly

romp *v.* play, skip, gambol, celebrate, frolic

room *n.* SPACE: vastness, sweep, extent; OPENING: place, vacancy; QUARTERS: lodgings, apartment

roomer *n.* lodger, occupant, dweller, renter, tenant

rooted *adj.* grounded, based, fixed, firm

rosy *adj.* promising, optimistic, favorable, cheerful

rot *n.* DECAY: decomposition, corruption, disintegration, NONSENSE: trash, silliness, foolishness

rotate *v.* turn, twist, wheel, revolve, move

rotation *n.* turn, circumrotation, circle, revolution

rotten *adj.* SPOILED: putrefying, decaying, rancid; UNSOUND: defective, impaired, weak; CORRUPT: contaminated, polluted, tainted, defiled, dirty

rough *adj.* UNEVEN: irregular, bumpy, jagged, coarse;

SEVERE: harsh, strict, stern; **CRUDE:** boorish, uncivil, uncultivated, rude; **TURBULENT:** buffeting, stormy, tumultuous; **UNFINISHED:** incomplete, imperfect; **APPROXIMATE:** inexact, unprecise, uncertain

round *adj.* **SPHERICAL:** circular, globular, cylindrical; **CURVED:** arched, rounded, bowed, curled

rouse *v.* **WAKEN:** arouse, raise, awaken; **STIMULATE:** urge, stir, provoke, animate, excite

routine *adj.* usual, customary, conventional, habitual

rove *v.* walk, meander, wander, roam

row *n.* line, series, order, file

rowdy *adj.* noisy, rebellious, mischievous, unruly

royal *adj.* **REGAL:** imperial, sovereign, supreme, noble; **STATELY:** dignified, majestic, courtly, aristocratic, lordly, imposing, resplendent

rub *v.* stroke, smooth, scrape, scour, polish

rubbish *n.* waste, debris, nonsense, litter, trash

rude *adj.* **BOORISH:** loutish, brutish, uncouth, vulgar, ribald; **HARSH:** gruff, abusive, brazen, audacious, hostile, insensitive, rough, violent; **COARSE:** rough, unrefined, unpolished, crude; **PRIMITIVE:** ignorant, uncivilized, barbarous

ruffle *v.* **DISARRANGE:** rumple, tousle; **ANGER:** irritate, fret, bother, agitate

rug *n.* mat, carpet, carpeting, linoleum

rugged *adj.* **ROUGH:** uneven, hilly, broken, mountainous; **STRONG:** vigorous, hale, sturdy, hardy, healthy

ruin *v.* **DESTROY:** demolish, wreck, ravage; **BANKRUPT:** impoverish, beggar

ruins *n.* remains, debris, wreckage, destruction

rule *v.* govern, control, dictate, manage, regulate

ruling *n.* order, decision, precept, law

rumble *n.* reverberation, resounding, roll, noise

rumor *n.* report, gossip, tidings, hearsay, tale

rumple *v.* wrinkle, crumple, crush, fold

run *n.* **SPRINT:** pace, bound, flow, amble, gallop, canter, lope, spring, trot, dart, rush, dash, flight, escape, break, charge, swoop, race, scamper, tear, whisk, fall, drop, **SERIES:** continuity, succession, sequence, **SCORE:** record, tally, point, **AVERAGE:** par, norm, **COURSE:** way, route, field, track

run *v.* **FLOW:** pour, tumble, drop, melt; **RUSH:** hurry, scurry, scramble, dash, speed, scamper, scuttle; **FUNCTION:** move, work, go; **MANAGE:** control, govern; **CONTINUE:** last, persevere

runoff *n.* drainage, surplus, flow, water

rupture *v.* break, burst, crack, tear

rural *adj.* country, rustic, agrarian, suburban

rush *n.* haste, dash, charge, hurry

rut *n.* **GROOVE:** hollow, trench, furrow, track; **HABIT:** custom, course, routine, practice

ruthless *adj.* cruel, savage, brutal, merciless, fiendish, unmerciful, ferocious, vengeful, barbarous

sabotage *v.* subvert, undermine, attack, destroy

sack *v.* plunder, ravage

sacrifice *n.* **OFFERING:** tribute, atonement; **LOSS:** discount, deduction, reduction

sacrifice *v.* forfeit, forgo, relinquish, yield, renounce

sad *adj.* **UNHAPPY:** downcast, gloomy, sorrowful, glum, dispirited, depressed, melancholy, blue; **PITIABLE:** disheartening, discouraging, dreary, disquieting

safe *adj.* **SECURE:** protected, guarded, shielded, sheltered; **INNOCENT:** innocuous, harmless; **RELIABLE:** trustworthy, dependable, competent

safe *n.* chest, strongbox, coffer, repository, vault, case

sag *v.* sink, settle, stoop, bend, lean

saint *n.* paragon, martyr, altruist, believer

salary *n.* wages, recompense, payroll, pay

sale *n.* COMMERCE: traffic, exchange, barter, trade; DEAL: transaction, purchase, auction, disposal; CLEARANCE: bargain, reduction, unloading

salute *v.* greet, recognize, praise

salvage *v.* save, retrieve, recover, regain

salvation *n.* deliverance, liberation, emancipation, rescue, safeguard, assurance

same *adj.* equivalent, identical, corresponding, equal

sample *v.* try, examine, taste, test, experiment

sanction *v.* approve, confirm, authorize, countenance

sanctuary *n.* CHURCH: shrine, temple; SHELTER: refuge, asylum, resort, haven

sane *adj.* rational, normal, lucid, sober, sound, balanced, sensible, reasonable, wise

sanitary *adj.* hygienic, wholesome, sterile, healthful

sap *n.* FLUID: secretion, essence, liquid; DUPE: dolt, gull, simpleton, fool

sarcastic *adj.* scornful, mocking, ironical, satirical, taunting, derisive, sneering, snickering, cynical

satire *n.* irony, sarcasm, mockery, ridicule, caricature

satisfaction *n.* GRATIFICATION: fulfillment, achievement; COMFORT: pleasure, contentment, serenity

satisfy *v.* please, delight, amuse, entertain, gladden, gratify, indulge, humor, fascinate, fill

saturate *v.* soak, overfill, drench, steep, immerse

savage *adj.* PRIMITIVE: crude, simple; CRUEL: barbarous, inhuman, brutal; WILD: untamed, uncivilized, uncultured, uncontrolled

save *v.* DELIVER: rescue, extricate, liberate, ransom, redeem; HOARD: collect, store, accumulate, gather; PRESERVE: conserve, keep

savor *v.* partake, enjoy, relish, appreciate, like

say *v.* utter, speak, state, announce, declare, assert

saying *n.* aphorism, maxim, proverb, adage

scaffold *n.* platform, gallows, framework, structure

scald *v.* burn, steam, char, blanch, parboil

scale *v.* MOUNT: climb, ascend, surmount; MEASURE: compare, balance, compute

scamper *v.* hasten, speed, haste, hurry, run

scan *v.* examine, scrutinize, browse, consider, look

scandal *n.* gossip, slander, defamation, gossip

scanty *adj.* scarce, meager, small, inadequate, thin, skimpy, sparse, diminutive

scarcity *n.* deficiency, inadequacy, insufficiency, lack

scare *v.* panic, terrify, alarm, frighten

scatter *v.* DISPERSE: disband, spread; DIFFUSE: dispel, dissipate, strew, distribute; WASTE: dissipate, spend

scene *n.* occurrence, spectacle, view, display

scenic *adj.* beautiful, spectacular, dramatic

scent *v.* smell, perfume, odor, fragrance, redolence

scheme *v.* plan, contrive, intrigue, devise

scholarly *adj.* erudite, cultured, studious, learned

schooling *n.* education, learning, nurture, discipline

scientific *adj.* ACCURATE: precise, exact, clear, objective; LOGICAL: deductive, methodical, sound

scoff *v.* mock, deride, jeer, ridicule

scold *v.* chide, admonish, rebuke, censure, reprove, reprimand, criticize, denounce, chasten

scoot *v.* run, dart, speed, rush, hasten, hurry

scope *n.* range, reach, field, extent

scorching *adj.* fiery, searing, sweltering, burning, hot

score *n.* tally, reckoning, account, summary

score *v.* **COMPOSE:** orchestrate, arrange, adapt; **PURCHASE:** get, procure, secure, buy

scorn *v.* refuse, despise, disdain

scornful *adj.* contemptuous, disdainful, haughty

scoundrel *n.* rogue, scamp, villain, rascal

scour *v.* scrub, cleanse, rub, clean, wash

scowl *v.* frown, glower, disapprove, grimace

scramble *v.* **MIX:** combine, blend, beat; **CLIMB:** clamber, push, struggle

scrap *n.* **TRASH:** junk, waste, cuttings, chips; **BIT:** fragment, particle, piece, morsel; **FIGHT:** quarrel, brawl, squabble

scrape *v.* rub, abrade, scour, rasp

scratch *v.* wound, hurt, cut, mark, injure, scar

scrawl *v.* write, scribble, scratch, doodle

scrawny *adj.* lean, lanky, gaunt, thin

scream *v.* shriek, screech, squeal, cry, yell

screen *v.* **HIDE:** veil, conceal, mask, shelter; **CHOOSE:** select, eliminate

screwy *adj.* odd, crazy, inappropriate, insane, wrong

scribble *n.* scrawl, scrabble, scratch, handwriting

scrub *v.* rub, cleanse, scour, clean, wash

scrupulous *adj.* exact, punctilious, strict, careful

scrutinize *v.* examine, view, study, stare, watch

scrutiny *n.* analysis, inspection, examination

scuffle *n.* struggle, shuffle, strife, fight

sealed *adj.* secured, fixed, firm, tight

seam *n.* joint, union, stitching, closure, suture

sear *v.* dry, scorch, brown, toast, cook

search *v.* seek, examine, rummage, hunt, quest

seasonal *adj.* periodically, biennial, annual, yearly

seasoned *adj.* **SPICY:** tangy, sharp, aromatic; **EX-PERIENCED:** established, settled, mature, able

seated *adj.* situated, located, established, rooted, set

secede *v.* withdraw, retract, leave, retreat

seclude *v.* screen, conceal, cover, hide

seclusion *n.* solitude, aloofness, privacy, retirement

secondary *adj.* **DERIVED:** dependent, subsequent, subsidiary, subordinate; **MINOR:** inconsiderable, petty, small, trivial, unimportant

secondhand *adj.* used, reclaimed, borrowed, derived

secrecy *n.* concealment, hiding, seclusion, privacy, mystery, dark, darkness, isolation, reticence, stealth

secret *adj.* unknown, mysterious, arcane, cryptic, occult, mystical, veiled, obscure, shrouded, hidden, concealed, clandestine, underhanded, stealthy

secretary *n.* **ASSISTANT:** clerk, typist, stenographer, correspondent; **OFFICER:** director, executive

secrete *v.* **HIDE:** conceal, cover, disguise; **EMIT:** discharge, produce, exude

secretive *adj.* reticent, taciturn, undercover, reserved

sector *n.* section, district, quarter, area, division

secure *adj.* **SAFE:** guarded, defended; **SELF–CONFIDENT:** assured, determined, confident

secure *v.* **FASTEN:** bind, tighten; **OBTAIN:** achieve, acquire, grasp, get

security *n.* guarantee, token, pawn, pledge, collateral, bail, warranty, convenant, agreement, hostage

sediment *n.* dregs, silt, grounds, residue

see *v.* **PERCEIVE:** observe, regard, view, gaze, detect, notice, contemplate; **UNDERSTAND:** comprehend, discern, recognize; **WITNESS:** observe, regard seniority

seek *v.* search, delve, dig, ransack, look, sniff, prowl
seem *v.* appear, look, resemble, show
seep *v.* percolate, trickle, leak, flow, drain
seethe *v.* boil, simmer, stew
segment *n.* part, portion, section, fragment, division
segregate *v.* separate, isolate, sever, divide
seize *v.* GRASP: take, catch, grip, grab, clutch, snatch; CAPTURE: conquer, overwhelm, apprehend, arrest; UNDERSTAND: comprehend, perceive
seizure *n.* spasm, spell, convulsion, breakdown, fit
seldom *adv.* rarely, infrequently, occasionally, uncommonly, scarcely, hardly
select *v.* pick, decide, elect, choose
selective *adj.* discriminating, judicious, particular
self–conscious *n.* unsure, uncertain, shy, doubtful
self–control *n.* poise, restraint, reserve, discretion, stability, dignity, constraint
self–esteem *n.* pride, vanity, haughtiness, egotism
self–evident *n.* obvious, plain, visible, apparent
self–restraint *n.* patience, endurance, control
sell *v.* market, vend, barter, exchange, trade, bargain, peddle, retail, wholesale, contract, retail
seller *n.* dealer, tradesman, salesman, retailer, agent, vender, merchant, auctioneer, shopkeeper, peddler, trader, marketer, storekeeper
sellout *n.* betrayal, deception, deal, trick
semblance *n.* resemblance, aspect, appearance
send *v.* DISPATCH: convey, ship, post, convey; BROADCAST: transmit, relay
senile *adj.* aged, infirm, feeble, old, sick
senior *adj.* older, elder, higher, superior
seniority *n.* standing, ranking, station

sensation

sensation *n.* consciousness, perception, feeling
sensational *adj.* **FASCINATING:** exciting, marvelous, incredible, impressive; **MELODRAMATIC:** exaggerated, excessive, emotional
sense *n.* **SENSATION:** feeling, touch, sight, hearing, taste, smell; **INTELLECT:** perception, reason, cleverness, knowledge, thought; **REASONABLENESS:** judgment, discretion, fairness; **INSIGHT:** tact, understanding, discernmen
senseless *adj.* ridiculous, silly, foolish, illogical, stupid
sensible *adj.* reasonable, prudent, perceptive, careful, aware, capable, rational, intelligent
sensitive *adj.* **TENDER:** delicate, sore, painful; **TOUCHY:** tense, nervous, irritable, unstable
sensitivity *n.* awareness, delicacy, feelings, sympathy
sensuality *n.* appetite, ardor, desire, emotion, love
sensuous *adj.* passionate, physical, exciting, sensual
sentence *n.* judgment, decree, punishment, verdict
sentiment *n.* feeling, emotion, opinion, thought
sentimental *adj.* emotional, tender, romantic, idealistic, visionary, affected
sentry *n.* sentinel, watch, protector, watchmen
separate *v.* **ISOLATE:** divide, seclude; **DEPART:** leave
separated *adj.* apart, disconnected, disjointed, removed, scattered, severed
sequel *n.* continuation, progression, sequence, series
sequence *n.* **SUCCESSION:** order, continuity, progression, flow; **ARRANGEMENT:** distribution, classification; **SERIES:** chain, string, array
serene *adj.* calm, unruffled, tranquil, composed, sedate, placid
series *n.* rank, file, line, row, set, range, string, order,

sequence, succession, array, gradation

serious *adj.* **GRAVE:** solemn, pressing, important; **THOUGHTFUL:** earnest, somber, reflecting, sincere

sermon *n.* discourse, lesson, doctrine, lecture

serve *v.* help, aid, assist, attend

service *v.* maintain, sustain, repair

session *n.* sitting, assembly, gathering

set *adj.* **FIRM:** stable, settled, fixed, rigid; **DETERMINED:** steadfast, decided

set *n.* **GROUP:** clique, circle, faction; **COLLECTION:** assemblage, assortment

set *v.* **PLACE:** put, plant, situate, deposit; **ESTABLISH:** anchor, fix, install; **JELL:** solidify, congeal, harden

setback *n.* hindrance, check, delay, difficulty

setting *n.* environment, surroundings, mounting, backdrop, frame, background, context

settle *v.* **PROVE:** establish, verify; **FINISH:** end, achieve; **LOCATE:** reside, dwell, colonize

settlement *n.* **AGREEMENT:** covenant, compact, contract; **COMPENSATION:** remuneration, reimbursement

setup *n.* composition, plan, order, organization

sever *v.* separate, part, split, cleave, cut, divide

several *adj.* some, sundry, various, numerous, many

severe *adj.* exacting, inflexible, harsh, cruel, oppressive, rigid, rigorous, difficult, oppressive, relentless

sew *v.* join, fasten, stitch, tack, bind, piece, baste

sewage *n.* refuse, excrement, offal, waste, residue

shabby *adj.* threadbare, worn, ragged, faded, dilapidated, deteriorated, seedy

shade *n.* **DARKNESS:** blackness, shadow; **TINT:** color, brilliance, saturation, hue; **VARIATION:** difference, hint, suggestion; **SCREEN:** shelter, covering, curtain shake

shake *n.* tremble, shiver, pulsation, movement
shaken *adj.* unnerved, upset, overcome, excited
shaky *adj.* INFIRM: trembling, unsteady, tottering, unstable; UNRELIABLE: uncertain, questionable
shallow *adj.* SLIGHT: inconsiderable, superficial; SILLY: trifling, inane, frivolous, petty, foolish
sham *adj.* pretended, false, misleading, untrue
shame *v.* humiliate, mortify, dishonor, disgrace
shameful *adj.* IMMODEST: immoral, debauched, degraded, indecent, lewd, vulgar; DISHONORABLE: scandalous, infamous, outrageous, disreputable
shameless *adj.* brazen, bold, forward, rude, lewd
shape *v.* CAST: mold, form, fashion, DEVELOP: adapt, regulate, become, grow
shape *n.* FORM: contour, configuration; PATTERN: frame, mold; CONDITION: fitness, health
shapely *adj.* symmetrical, comely, proportioned, trim
share *v.* DIVIDE: allot, apportion; PARTAKE: participate, receive; GIVE: yield, bestow, accord
sharp *adj.* EDGED: honed, cutting, keen; CLEVER: astute, bright, intelligent; DISTINCT: explicit, clear, definite; INTENSE: piercing, shrill; STYLISH: dressy, chic, fashionable
shatter *v.* break, sliver, split, burst
shears *n.* clippers, cutters, snips, scissors
sheath *n.* scabbard, case, covering
shed *n.* shelter, hut, outbuilding, lean-to, woodshed
shed *v.* drop, molt, slough, discard, exude, emit
sheer *adj.* ABRUPT: steep, precipitous, perpendicular; THIN: transparent, delicate, fine
shelter *n.* protection, refuge, haven, sanctuary
shelter *v.* cover, defend, screen, hide, conceal, harbor,

protect, shield, safeguard, surround, enclose
shine *v.* **RADIATE:** glitter, sparkle, twinkle, glimmer, glow, blaze; **REFLECT:** glisten, gleam, mirror; **POLISH:** scour, brush, burnish, wax
ship *v.* transport, send, consign
shirk *v.* avoid, elude, malinger, evade
shiver *v.* shake, tremble, vibrate, quiver
shock *v.* **STARTLE:** astound, disturb; **OFFEND:** disgust, outrage, horrify, abash, dismay; **JAR:** rock, jolt
shocking *adj.* repulsive, revolting, offensive
shoddy *adj.* cheap, flimsy, tacky, inferior, poor
shore *n.* **COAST:** beach, seaside, bank; **SUPPORT:** prop, buttress, strut
short *adj.* **CONCISE:** brief, condensed; **ABRUPT:** curt, inconsiderate, rude, testy; **DEFICIENT:** inadequate substandard
shortage *n.* lack, deficiency, failure, dearth, shortfall
shortcoming *n.* fault, defect, flaw, drawback
shoulder *v.* bear, support; shove, crowd
shove *v.* push, nudge, jostle, press
show *v.* display, explain, indicate, reveal, demonstrate
show *n.* **PRODUCTION:** play, ceremony; **DISPLAY:** appearance, plausibility, pretext
showy *adj.* conspicuous, flamboyant, pretentious
shower *n.* rainfall, sprinkle, drizzle, mist
shred *n.* strip, fragment, splinter, rag
shred *v.* cut, mince, grate, tear
shrew *n.* scold, nag, harridan
shrewd *adj.* cunning, sharp, keen, intelligent, perceptive, sly, canny, crafty, cagey
shriek *v.* scream, yell, shout, howl, squawk
shrill *adj.* piercing, sharp, harsh

shrine *n.* temple, altar, church, sanctuary
shrink *v.* **CONTRACT:** shrivel, constrict, lessen; **RECOIL:** cringe , wince, retreat, withdraw
shrivel *v.* wither, shrink, decrease
shroud *v.* hide, cover, conceal, obscure, veil, screen
shudder *v.* tremble, shake, shiver, quiver
shun *v.* avoid, ignore, eschew, evade
shut *v.* close, bar, secure, fasten, enclose
shy *adj.* timid, reserved, distrustful, suspicious
sick *adj.* ill, diseased, infected, afflicted, queasy, nauseous, feeble, unhealthy
side *n.* **EDGE:** border; **FACTION:** team, party
siege *n.* attack, assault, onslaught, blockade
sieve *v.* strain, purify, filter
sift *v.* separate, strain, filter, screen
sigh *n.* moan, groan, gasp, cry
sight *n.* view, spectacle, scene, display, show, vision
sign *n.* **SYMPTOM:** indication, hint, clue, suggestion; **EMBLEM:** badge
sign *v.* **GESTURE:** indicate, signal; **ENDORSE:** confirm, acknowledge, initial, autograph
signal *v.* signify, motion, gesture, wave
significant *adj.* important, notable, momentous, symbolic, meaningful
signify *v.* mean, indicate, communicate, denote, imply, intimate, portend
silence *n.* serenity, hush, tranquillity, quiet
silence *v.* hush, still, quiet, muzzle, stifle, suppress
silent *adj.* quiet, hushed, still, reserved, dormant
silly *adj.* foolish, imprudent, ridiculous, absurd, inane, frivolous
similar *adj.* resembling, like, comparable, related

similitude *n.* resemblance, likeness
simple *adj.* unaffected plain clear, unadorned, uncomplicated, bare, innocent, artless
simplify *v.* clarify, explain, elucidate, interpret
simulate *v.* feign, fake, pretend, disguise, fabricate
simultaneous *adj.* concurrent, coexisting
sin *v.* transgress, misbehave, offend, trespass
sincere *adj.* honest, genuine, earnest, faithful
singe *v.* scorch, burn, sear, char
single *adj.* individual, lone
singular *adj.* unique, unusual, remarkable, individual
sinister *adj.* ominous, menacing, base, bad, evil
sink *v.* submerge, depress, fall, slump, lower, droop
sip *v.* drink, imbibe, taste, sample, savor
sit *v.* PERCH: seat, squat; MEET convene, assemble
site *n.* location, place, spot, position
situation *n.* circumstances, predicament, state, job, profession, trade, status, station, rank
size *n.* bulk, magnitude, extent, mass, dimensions
skeleton *n.* bones, framework, outline, structure
skeptic *n.* doubter, cynic, unbeliever, agnostic
skeptical *adj.* doubtful, cynical, incredulous
sketch *v.* draw, outline, design, plan, draft, picture
skid *v.* slip, slide, swerve, veer, glide
skill *n.* DEXTERITY: ability, expertise, competence, talent; OCCUPATION: craft, vocation, trade, job
skillful *adj.* adept, adroit, proficient, accomplished
skin *v.* strip, peel, husk, scale, scalp
skinny *adj.* thin, lean, bony, gaunt, emaciated
skirmish *n.* scuffle, scrimmage, engagement, combat
skirt *v.* circumvent, bypass, detour, sidestep
skittish *adj.* jumpy, nervous, fidgety, timid, bashful

skulk *v.* sneak, lurk, prowl
slab *n.* hunk, block, chunk
slack *adj.* lax, loose, lazy, indolent, sluggish, slow
slacken *v.* decrease, abate, diminish
slander *n.* gossip, libel, scandal, misrepresentation
slander *v.* malign, vilify, besmirch, disparage
slang *n.* jargon, lingo, dialect, colloquialism
slant *n.* slope, incline, grade, inclination, bent
slant *v.* LEAN: angle, tilt; DISTORT: misrepresent, color
slap *v.* smack, strike, hit, spank, cuff, buffet
slash *v.* cut gash, slice, slit, wound
slaughter *n.* slaying, bloodshed, carnage, massacre
slay *v.* kill, murder, butcher, destroy, annihilate
sleazy *adj.* flimsy, shoddy, cheap, trashy, run–down
sleek *adj.* smooth, glossy, glassy, shiny, neat
sleep *v.* slumber, rest, doze, snooze, nod, nap
sleepy *adj.* drowsy, tired, sluggish
slender *adj.* thin, slim, slight, spare, fragile, flimsy
slight *adj.* TRIVIAL: trifling, insignificant, petty, unimportant, superficial; DELICATE, dainty, flimsy, slender, fragile, frail, insubstantial
slight *v.* disregard, insult, snub, neglect, overlook
slim *adj.* slender slight trifling, dainty, slender
slime *n.* mire, muck, mud, ooze
sling *v.* hurl, throw, chuck, pitch, launch
slink *v.* skulk, cower, creep, lurk, sneak, steal, prowl
slip *n.* error, mistake, blunder, indiscretion
slip *v.* slide, totter, stumble, fall
slipshod *adj.* slovenly, careless, sloppy, untidy
slit *v.* cut, gash, slash, rip, slice, split, tear, pierce
sloppy *adj.* careless, lax, untidy, messy, disorderly
slope *n.* incline, hill, grade, slant, inclination

slouch *v.* slump, droop, bend, stoop, loll

slovenly *adj.* messy, careless, sloppy, disorderly, disheveled, bedraggled, untidy, slipshod

slow *adj.* LEISURELY: gradual, deliberate, lethargic; DENSE: dull, stupid

sluggish *adj.* languid, lethargic, indolent, slothful

slumber *v.* sleep, rest, nap, doze, snooze

slump *n.* decrease, drop, depression, setback, decline

slur *n.* insult, innuendo, slight, affront, blemish

sly *adj.* cunning, wily, deceitful, deceptive, tricky, artful, shifty, evasive, elusive, shrewd, clever, calculating, treacherous, shady, slick, smooth, slippery

small *adj.* INCONSEQUENTIAL: little, insignificant, trivial, unimportant; SELFISH: stingy, mean, petty

smart *adj.* CLEVER: intelligent, keen, penetrating, alert, bright; STYLISH: sharp, dashing, neat, elegant

smash *v.* break, shatter, crush, pound, destroy, demolish, wreck, ruin

smear *v.* SLANDER: libel, , sully, slur; SMUDGE: daub, plaster, spread, apply

smell *n.* odor, aroma, fragrance, scent, stench, stink

smile *v.* grin, smirk, beam, laugh

smirk *n.* sneer, leer, grimace

smoky *adj.* hazy, foggy, smoggy, dingy, frosted, filmy

smooth *adj.* EVEN: level, flat, flush, polished, sleek, uniform; SUAVE: glib, polite, courteous

smother *v.* suffocate, stifle, asphyxiate, strangle, subdue, suppress

smudge *n.* smear, blot, blur, stain, blemish, streak

smug *adj.* conceited, egotistical, satisfied

smutty *adj.* pornographic, lewd, indecent, obscene, vulgar, suggestive, raunchy

snag *n.* hindrance, impediment, obstacle, impasse
snare *v.* catch, entangle, trap, trick, lure
snatch *n.* fragment, scrap, shred, snippet, tatter
snatch *v.* grab, pluck, seize, steal, filch, swipe, take
sneak *v.* lurk, prowl, creep, slink, steal, skulk
sneer *v.* criticize, deride, ridicule, scoff, gibe, taunt
snicker *v.* giggle, laugh, chortle, chuckle, titter
snide *adj.* underhanded, sarcastic, derogatory, insinuating, vicious, nasty, mean, malicious
snip *v.* clip, pare, cut, lop, nip, slice, slit
snivel *v.* weep, whine, bawl, bemoan, blubber
snobbery *n.* contempt, arrogance, insolence
snobbish *adj.* snooty, condescending, patronizing
snub *n.* insult, affront, slight, slur, rebuke
snug *adj.* comfortable, cozy, secure, safe
snuggle *v.* cuddle, nestle, nuzzle, burrow, hug
soak *v.* steep, saturate, douse, permeate, infuse
sob *v.* cry, moan, weep, wail, lament, whimper, bewail
sober *adj.* serious, solemn, subdued, restrained, sedate, composed, rational, reasonable, sound, somber
social *adj.* genial, pleasant, polite, civil, pleasant
society *n.* ORGANIZATION: fellowship, association, brotherhood, fraternity, club; CULTURE: community, civilization, people, nation
soft *adj.* malleable, pliant, yielding, fluffy
soggy *adj.* saturated, damp, wet, soaked, sodden
sojourn *n.* stay, visit, stopover, vacation, abide
solace *v.* comfort, console, soothe, cheer, relieve, alleviate, assuage, allay, soften, mitigate
sole *adj.* one, single, lone, exclusive, individual, unique, unshared
solemn *adj.* sacred, grave, serious, grim, imposing,

thoughtful, dignified, formal, somber, austere

solemnize *v.* commemorate, honor, celebrate, hallow

solicit *v.* supplicate, beg, implore, urge, request, ask, inquire, question, proposition

solicitation *n.* request, petition, suit, claim, appeal

solicitor *n.* attorney, petitioner, supplicant

solicitous *adj.* concerned, anxious, heedful, kind, devoted, tender, loving, thoughtful

solid *adj.* whole, regular, unbroken, firm, substantial, sound, hard, stable, dense, stout

solidify *v.* harden, crystallize, set, coagulate, congeal

solitary *adj.* single, sole, individual, singular, isolated, lonely, remote, separate

solitude *n.* isolation, seclusion, privacy

solution *n.* answer, resolution, conclusion, explanation, settlement

solve *v.* answer, resolve, explain, decipher, decode

somber *adj.* dull, gloomy, dark, dim, drab, dismal, depressing, dreary, melancholy

sonorous *adj.* resonant, reverberating, vibrant

sooty *adj.* blackened, dirty, grimy, dingy, filthy

soothe *v.* calm, comfort, ease, quiet, refresh, soften, alleviate, assuage, mitigate, pacify

soothsayer *n.* prognosticator, diviner, oracle, prophet, astrologer, seer, mystic

sophisticated *adj.* worldly, refined, cultured

sorcery *n.* magic, witchcraft, alchemy, enchantment

sordid *adj.* vile, dirty, squalid, foul, low, base, abject

sore *adj.* sensitive, raw, tender, painful, inflamed

sorrow *n.* grief, affliction, anguish, remorse, misery, sadness, woe, trouble, affliction

sorrow *v.* grieve, mourn, weep, lament, deplore

sorry *adj.* regretful, repentant, apologetic
sort *v.* order, arrange, classify, distribute, assort
sot *n.* drunkard, lush, drunk, alcoholic, wino
soul *n.* spirit, essence, ghost, being
sound *adj.* safe, whole, healthy, strong, complete, vigorous, stable, sensible, rational, sane, hale
sound *n.* tone, noise, vibration, resonance, intonation
source *n.* origin, beginning, inception, cause, root
souvenir *n.* keepsake, token, memento, relic, trophy
sow *v.* scatter, disseminate, disperse, plant
space *n.* room, area, gap, expanse, distance, interval
spacious *adj.* roomy, capacious, large, ample, commodious, vast, huge, voluminous, extensive
span *n.* distance, measure, length, extent, stretch
span *v.* cross, traverse, reach, connect, link, bridge
spare *adj.* LEAN: thin, gaunt, slight, emaciated; EXTRA: excess, additional
sparkle *v.* glitter, gleam, twinkle, glisten, shine
sparse *adj.* meager, inadequate, scanty, thin, spare
spasm *n.* convulsion, fit, contortion, seizure
spatter *v.* splash, slosh, spray, shower, speckle
speak *v* talk, articulate, say, utter, lecture, address
special *adj.* specific, certain, particular, designated, unique, distinctive, uncommon, unusual
specialist *n.* expert, professional, authority
specie *n.* coin, money, currency
species *n.* type, kind, class, breed, variety, category
specific *adj.* precise, particular, distinct, explicit
specify *v.* stipulate, designate, cite, name, define
specimen *n.* sample, example, model, type, pattern
specious *adj.* deceptive, misleading, false
speck *n.* bit, particle, trace, grain, iota

speckle *n.* spot, speck, dot, mote, fleck
spectacle *n.* sight, show, demonstration, wonder
spectacular *adj.* amazing, marvelous, impressive, sensational, dramatic, splendid, striking, fabulous
spectator *n.* onlooker, observer, witness, bystander
specter *n.* ghost, spook, phantom, spirit, apparition
spectrum *n.* range, scale, sweep, extent
speculate *v.* **CONSIDER:** theorize, contemplate, consider, infer; **RISK:** gamble, venture, chance
speech *n.* language, oration, communication
speed *v.* hasten, hurry, expedite, precipitate
speedy *adj.* quick, fast, hasty, brisk, swift, hurried
spend *v.* give, waste, disburse, dissipate, deplete
sphere *n.* **GLOBE:**, orb, shell, planet; **DOMAIN:** province realm, environment
spill *v.* slop, splash, drop, flow
spin *v.* turn, rotate, twirl, whirl, gyrate
spindle *n.* shaft, beam, axle, arbor
spirit *n.* **GHOST:** apparition, phantom, specter; **VITALITY:** vivacity, vigor, zeal, ardor; **SIGNIFICANCE:** intent, meaning, sense
spite *n.* malice, malevolence, rancor, grudge
spiteful *adj.* vindictive, malicious, cruel, malevolent
splash *v.* spatter, douse, spray, swash
spleen *n.* anger, petulance, wrath, rancor
splendid *adj.* grand, magnificent, impressive, dazzling
splendor *n.* glory, magnificence, grandeur
splice *v.* join, implant, unite, graft
splinter *n.* sliver, shaving, fragment, chip, piece
splinter *v.* crumble, shatter, fracture, break, smash
split *v.* divide, sever, break, separate, cleave
spoil *v.* decay, ruin, damage, decompose, putrefy

sponsor

sponsor *n.* patron, mentor, supporter, backer
spontaneous *adj.* impromptu, impulsive, natural
sporadic *adj.* occasional, infrequent, scattered
spot *n.* STAIN: blot, blemish; LOCATION: locale, site
spout *v.* pour, discharge, emit, flow, spill, gush
sprawl *v.* recline, lounge, relax, slouch
sprightly *adj.* lively, frisky, nimble, animated, agile
spring *v.* bound, leap, issue, jump, hop, vault
sprinkle *v.* disperse, distribute, scatter, spatter
sprint *v.* run, race, zip, dash, tear
sprout *v.* germinate, bud, burgeon, grow, develop
spry *adj.* nimble, agile, active, vigorous, animated, brisk, lively, quick, energetic
spunk *n.* pluck, mettle, courage, daring, nerve, spirit
spur *v.* urge, incite, induce, provoke, goad, press
spurious *adj.* false, fake, deceptive, phony, feigned
spurn *v.* reject, shun, slight, snub, scorn, disdain
spurt *v.* burst, gush, spout, issue, spring
spy *v.* see, discover, glimpse
squabble *v.* wrangle, quarrel, bicker, argue, feud
squalid *adj.* filthy, foul, dirty, unclean, seedy
squalor *n.* filth, poverty, misery
squander *v.* waste, dissipate, expend, lavish, misuse
square *adj.* fair, just, honest, straight, level, true
squeamish *adj.* queasy, modest, prudish, finicky
squeeze *v.* compress, crush, squash, press, pinch
squelch *v.* subdue, crush, squash, thwart, suppress
squirm *v.* wriggle, writhe, fidget, twist, shift
stab *n.* wound, cut, puncture, thrust
stabilize *v.* steady, secure, brace, poise
stable *adj.* fixed, firm, steady, sturdy, enduring, perpetual, steadfast, sound, reliable, solid

staff *n.* personnel, employees, crew, cast
stage *n.* platform, dais, scaffold
stagger *v.* **WEAVE:** falter, waver; **ASTONISH:** astound, amaze, dumbfound, shock, surprise
stagnant *adj.* inert, stale, dirty, filthy, fetid
stagnate *v.* decay, rot, decompose, taint
staid *adj.* steady, sober, sedate, quiet, solemn
stake *v.* wager, risk, imperil, hazard, venture, bet
stale *adj.* dry, trite, common, dull, humdrum
stalk *v.* hunt, track, chase, pursue
stall *v.* delay, obstruct, hamper, hinder, impede
stalwart *adj.* stout, sturdy, strong, rugged, robust, vigorous, bold, gallant, steadfast, formidable
stamina *n.* endurance, strength, vigor, vitality, power
stammer *v.* sputter, falter, stumble, hesitate, stutter
stand *n.* position, attitude, belief, opinion
stand *v.* endure, resist, oppose, confront, withstand
standard *n.* **MODEL:** measure, gauge, example; **BANNER:** symbol, flag, pennant
staple *adj.* basic, necessary, essential, fundamental
stare *v.* gaze, gawk, gape, glare, look, watch
stark *adj.* simple, desolate, dreary, grim, harsh
start *n.* beginning, origin, onset, outset, initiation
start *v.* initiate, begin, commence, establish
startle *v.* surprise, alarm, scare, frighten, disturb
state *n.* condition, situation, circumstances, status, position, standing, station
state *v.* recite, declare, pronounce, assert, affirm
statement *n.* declaration, allegation, assertion, remark, report, account
stately *adj.* majestic, dignified, regal, grand, elegant
static *adj.* immobile, stationary, fixed, rigid

station *n.* rank, standing, position
stationary *adj.* fixed, static, permanent, rooted, stable
statue *n.* sculpture, bust, image, icon, figurine
stature *n.* height, bulk, build, status, standing
status *n.* state, condition, position, rank, standing
statute *n.* law, decree, act, bill, rule, ordinance, edict
stay *n.* prop, support, brace, prop
stay *v.* remain, continue, wait, linger, pause, detain, hinder, suspend, curb
steadfast *adj.* resolute, unwavering, constant, faithful, dependable, firm
steal *v.* rob, thieve, filch, pilfer, swindle, embezzle
steep *adj.* precipitous, sheer, abrupt
steeple *n.* spire, tower, minaret
steer *v.* guide, direct, pilot, conduct, lead, navigate
stellar *adj.* remarkable, phenomenal, outstanding
stem *v.* stop, check, curb, halt
stereotype *v.* classify, categorize, typecast, label
sterling *adj.* genuine, flawless, noble, perfect, excellent, superior, exceptional
stern *adj.* severe, rigid, hard, strict, austere, rigorous
stiff *adj.* rigid, formal, inflexible, firm, stubborn, obstinate, unyielding, formal, uncompromising, severe
stiffen *v.* harden, congeal, thicken, coagulate
stifle *v.* suppress, repress, restrain, stop
stigma *n.* disgrace, shame, infamy, blemish, blot, stain, taint
stigmatize *v.* disgrace, discredit, dishonor, defame, shame, brand, humiliate
still *adj.* silent, motionless, inert, stationary, hushed, calm, serene, tranquil
still *v.* silence, hush, calm, soothe, stop, stall, arrest

stilted *adj.* awkward, affected, unnatural, strained, contrived, artificial, labored, stiff

stimulate *v.* excite, arouse, activate, rouse, provoke

stingy *adj.* niggardly, miserly, tight, closefisted

stint *v.* limit, confine, restrict, restrain

stipulate *v.* specify, determine, designate, indicate

stipulation *n.* prerequisite, condition, qualification, term, requirement, clause

stir *n.* tumult, bustle, excitement, commotion, disorder, uproar, furor, agitation, fuss

stir *v.* agitate, rouse, excite, incite, provoke, stimulate

stock *v.* store, supply, hoard, equip, fill, furnish

stockpile *n.* reserve, supply, deposit, hoard, store

stoic *n.* impassive, apathetic, indifferent, nonchalant, composed, poised

stolid *adj.* impassive, unemotional, dispassionate, indifferent, imperturbable

stomach *n.* belly, paunch, abdomen

stoop *v.* bend, bow, crouch

stop *v.* halt, end, terminate, discontinue, arrest, restrain, hinder, impede, prevent, thwart

store *v.* hoard, gather, collect, stash, stockpile

storm *n.* tempest, blizzard, gale, squall, commotion, turmoil, outbreak, disturbance

stormy *adj.* tempestuous, wild, blustering, tumultuous, raging, turbulent, boisterous

story *n.* TALE: anecdote, yarn, parable, fable, legend, report, account; LEVEL: floor, landing

stout *adj.* PLUMP: portly, heavy, bulky, corpulent; RESOLUTE: brave, courageous, bold, fearless, dauntless, indomitable, firm, strong, robust, hardy

straggler *n.* dawdler, lingerer, laggard, slowpoke

straight *adj.* direct, honest, fair, just, virtuous, open
straighten *v.* adjust, align, rectify, correct
strain *n.* effort, exertion, force, pressure, anxiety, tension, stress
strait *n.* difficulty, distress, predicament, plight
strange *adj.* unusual, abnormal, bizarre, peculiar, extraordinary, outlandish, unfamiliar, unknown
stranger *n.* foreigner, alien, outsider
stratagem *n.* trick, deception, ruse, wile, scheme, plan, contrivance, device
strategy *n.* tactics, scheme, system, approach
stray *v.* wander, drift, roam, deviate, digress
stream *n.* flow, emit, issue, pour, run
streamer *n.* flag, banner, pennant, standard, ensign
strength *n.* power, force, might
strengthen *v.* fortify, reinforce, restore, invigorate
strenuous *adj.* vigorous, spirited, laborious
stress *n.* **EMPHASIS:** weight, significance, accent; **APPREHENSION:** trepidation, misgiving
stretch *n.* expanse, range, reach, extent
strew *v.* scatter, spread, disseminate, broadcast
strict *adj.* demanding, exacting, rigid, inflexible
strident *adj.* raucous, shrill, harsh, piercing, grating
strife *n.* conflict, fight, discord, clash
strike *v.* **HIT:** slap, cuff; **UNEARTH:** find, uncover
stringent *adj.* strict, harsh, severe
stripling *n.* youth, child, lad, lass, youngster
strive *v.* endeavor, attempt, compete, contend
stroll *v.* walk, saunter, meander, wander, roam
strong *adj.* muscular, potent, solid, impregnable
struggle *n.* battle, clash, conflict, exertion, endeavor
struggle *v.* grapple, contend, strive, toil, labor

strut *n.* support, brace, prop, mainstay
stubborn *adj.* obstinate, headstrong, stiff, resolute, inflexible, intractable
student *n.* pupil, scholar, disciple, apprentice
study *v.* investigate, analyze, scrutinize, examine, ponder, consider, reflect
stump *v.* perplex, confuse, confound, baffle, mystify
stun *v.* shock, confound, amaze, astonish, astound, bewilder, overwhelm, stupefy
stupendous *adj.* amazing, astounding, marvelous, extraordinary, incredible, spectacular, wondrous
stupid *adj.* dull, boring, tedious, vapid, tiresome, foolish, absurd, inane, senseless
stupor *n.* daze, trance, numbness, lethargy
sturdy *adj.* robust, rugged, stalwart, strong, strapping, muscular, firm, indomitable, stout
stutter *v.* stammer, stumble, falter
stylish *adj.* fashionable, chic, smart, modish
suave *adj.* sophisticated, smooth, cultured, worldly
subdue *v.* defeat, conquer, overpower, tame
subjective *adj.* biased, prejudiced, individual
subjugate *v.* conquer, enslave, subdue, defeat
sublime *adj.* lofty, inspiring, imposing, majestic
submerge *v.* immerse, engulf, plunge, sink
submission *n.* surrender, resignation, compliance
submit *v.* **ACCEDE:** comply, obey; **SUGGEST:** volunteer, propose, present, tender
subordinate *adj.* inferior, lower, junior, subservient
subscribe *v.* support, donate, authorize, sanction
subsequent *adj.* following, ensuing, succeeding, later
subservient *adj.* subordinate, servile, deferential
subside *v.* decline, dwindle, diminish, lessen, wane

subsidize *v.* support, sponsor, fund, back, assist
subsidy *n.* endowment, allowance, grant, bequest
substance *n.* object, element, essence, basis, meaning, import, gist, significance
substantial *adj.* plentiful, abundant, ample, considerable, wealthy affluent, influential, valuable
substantiate *v.* authenticate, confirm, validate, prove, verify, corroborate, attest, document
substitute *adj.* alternative, surrogate, tentative
subterfuge *n.* ploy, scheme, stratagem, device, expedient, deceit, deception
subtle *adj.* delicate, understated, refined, elusive, deceptive, inferred, insinuated, artful, insidious
subtract *v.* deduct, decrease, diminish, lessen, lower
succeed *v.* FLOURISH: thrive, prevail, triumph; REPLACE: supersede
success *n.* achievement, mastery, victory, attainment
successful *adj.* triumphant, flourishing, thriving
succession *n.* sequence, order, continuation
succinct *adj.* brief, concise, terse, abbreviated
succor *n.* aid, help, sustenance, assistance
succumb *v.* submit, concede, relent, capitulate, die, collapse, fail
sudden *adj.* abrupt, quick, unexpected, impromptu
suffer *v.* endure, tolerate, bear, undergo, agonize
sufficient *adj.* plenty, ample, enough
suffuse *v.* saturate, pervade, soak, impregnate
suggest *v.* propose, submit, imply, insinuate
suit *v.* satisfy, please, gratify, shape, accommodate
suitor *n.* wooer, admirer, gallant, beau
sulk *v.* pout, scowl, frown, glower
sullen *adj.* moody, morose, gloomy, somber

sully *v.* shame, dishonor, stain, taint, tarnish, blemish, defile, corrupt, besmirch

sultry *adj.* sweltering, muggy, humid, sticky

sum *n.* quantity, value, aggregate, total, tally

summary *n.* condensation, digest, abridgment, brief

summit *n.* peak, pinnacle, apex, crown, culmination

summon *v.* call, invite, invoke, request, petition

sumptuous *adj.* luxurious, elegant, lavish, opulent

sundry *adj.* various, several, divers

superb *adj.* outstanding, exquisite, grand, magnificent, luxurious

supersede *v.* replace, supplant, succeed

supervise *v.* superintend, chaperon, manage, control

supervision *n.* management, guidance, surveillance

supplant *v.* replace, displace, succeed, supersede

supple *adj.* elastic, pliable, compliant, limber

supplement *n.* addition, subsidiary, extension

supplement *v.* augment, enhance, fortify

supplicate *v.* implore, beseech, beg, entreat

supply *v.* equip, stock, replenish

support *n.* **AID:** assistance, help, relief, succor; **BRACE:** prop, column, buttress, strut

suppose *v.* assume, infer, presume, believe, think

suppress *v.* **OVERPOWER:** repress, curb, quell, crush; **CONCEAL:** bury, cover

supreme *adj.* preeminent, superior, greatest

supremacy *n.* dominion, dominance, preeminence

surcharge *n.* tax, duty, surtax, tariff, levy, toll

sure *adj.* trusty, reliable, infallible, certain, safe, solid, precise, accurate, unerring, inevitable

surface *n.* rise, appear, emerge

surge *v.* gush, rush, pour, rise, heave, oscillate

surly *adj.* cantankerous, rude, irritable, sullen, hostile
surmise *v.* speculate, guess, infer, imagine, suppose
surmount *v.* conquer, transcend, hurdle, overcome
surpass *v.* exceed, transcend, excel
surplus *n.* excess, abundance, remainder, residue
surprise *n.* astonishment, amazement, shock, wonder
surprise *n.* astound, bewilder, dumbfound, startle
surrender *v.* submit, abandon, capitulate, yield
surreptitious *adj.* furtive, clandestine, stealthy
surrogate *adj.* substitute, backup, alternative
surround *v.* encompass, enclose, circle
survey *n.* poll, study, review, outline, critique
survey *v.* scrutinize, scan, examine, inspect, observe
survive *v.* endure, persist, remain, continue
survival *n.* subsistence, continuation, durability
susceptible *adj.* receptive, impressionable, responsive, vulnerable
suspect *v.* DISTRUST: mistrust, doubt; BELIEVE: suppose, imagine, conjecture
suspend *v.* postpone, delay, defer, interrupt
suspense *n.* apprehension, indecision, anxiety
suspension *n.* delay, deferment, postponement
suspicion *n.* skepticism, misgiving, mistrust, cynicism, notion, impression
suspicious *adj.* DUBIOUS: shady, untrustworthy, doubtful; WARY: skeptical
sustenance *n.* food, nourishment, provisions
swagger *v.* strut, prance, boast, brag, gloat
swallow *v.* drink, eat, gulp, consume, devour
swamp *n.* bayou, marsh, mire, morass, slough
swarm *n.* horde, mass, flock, multitude, host
sway *n.* dominion, dominance, control, influence

swear *v.* **PROMISE:** declare, testify, affirm; **BLASPHEME:** damn, curse

sweet *adj.* luscious, aromatic, fragrant, clean, fresh, melodious, harmonious, mellow

swell *v.* increase, inflate, bloat, bulge, grow

swift *adj.* fast, rapid, expeditious, fleet, prompt, quick

swig *v.* drink, swallow, quaff, gulp, guzzle

swindle *v.* trick, deceive, dupe, defraud, victimize

swing *v.* hang, dangle, flap, oscillate, wave

switch *v.* swap, trade, exchange, replace, substitute

sycophant *n.* flatterer, flunky, parasite, toady

sylvan *adj.* picturesque, pastoral, idyllic, bucolic

symbol *n.* character, letter, numeral, representation

symbolize *v.* signify, connote, mean, represent

sympathetic *adj.* considerate, compassionate

sympathize *v.* commiserate, console, pity

sympathy *n.* compassion, understanding, warmth, consolation, solace, comfort

symptom *n.* clue, trait, characteristic, feature, sign

synchronize *v.* accommodate, adjust, attune

syndicate *n.* coalition, alliance, company, association

syndicate *v.* affiliate, connect, consolidate, merge

synopsis *n.* summary, abridgment, condensation

synthesis *n.* combination, integration, formation

system *n.* strategy, plan, scheme, method,

systematic *adj.* methodical, orderly, precise, regular

table *v.* postpone, delay, defer, shelve

tabloid *n.* newspaper, periodical, publication

taboo *adj.* forbidden, banned, prohibited

tacit *adj.* implied, understood, assumed, inferred

taciturn *adj.* reserved, quiet

tact *n.* subtlety, discretion, finesse, style

tactics

tactics *n.* scheme, stratagem, procedure, system
tag *v.* label, ticket, designate, identify
tailor *v.* customize, adapt, adjust, conform
taint *v.* corrupt, infect, defile, contaminate
take *v.* obtain, get, procure, seize, grasp, capture, adopt, select, accept, choose, pick
tale *n.* **YARN:** narrative, account; **FALSEHOOD:** fib, lie
talent *n.* aptitude, genius, gift
talisman *n.* amulet, charm
talk *n.* conversation, dialogue, discourse, speech
talk *v.* converse, speak, discuss, chatter, gossip
talkative *adj.* loquacious, garrulous, chatty, gabby
tall *adj.* towering, high, big, rangy, lanky
tally *n.* count, reckoning, sum, calculation
tame *adj.* docile, gentle, obedient
tamper *v.* alter, change, meddle, damage
tangible *adj.* material, corporeal, tactile, discernible, evident, actual, real, genuine
tantalize *v.* tease, provoke, torment, frustrate, vex
tantamount *adj.* equivalent, parallel, identical
tape *n.* bind, wrap, seal, mend
tarnish *n.* blemish, blot, stain, taint
tarnish *v.* defame, disgrace embarrass
tarry *v.* stall, linger, loiter, dally, dawdle, stay
task *n.* job, labor, assignment, duty, chore
taste *n.* partiality, liking, bias, preference
taste *v.* sample, try, sip, savor, relish, enjoy
taunt *v.* insult, jeer, mock, provoke
tavern *n.* bar, saloon, pub, cafe, inn, lodge, hostelry
tawdry *adj.* cheap, sleazy, flashy, ostentatious
tax *n.* levy, assessment, tariff, toll, duty, obligation
teach *v.* instruct, inform, train, enlighten, guide

tear *v.* rip, split, sever, cleave, rend

tease *v.* annoy, taunt, torment, harass, irritate, vex

technique *n.* **METHOD:** procedure, system, approach, methodology; **ABILITY:** skill, aptitude, knack

tedious *adj.* monotonous, tiresome, dull, boring

tell *v.* recount, describe, report, speak, mention, explain, reveal, declare, divulge

temper *n.* disposition, temperament, humor, composure, poise

temper *v.* calm, soothe, pacify, mollify

temperament *n.* disposition, attitude, mood, emotion

temperance *n.* restraint, sobriety, abstinence

temperate *adj.* calm, composed, cool, reasonable

tempestuous *adj.* stormy, raging, tumultuous

temporary *adj.* transitory, fleeting, interim

tenable *adj.* defensible, justifiable, maintainable

tenacious *adj.* resolute, persistent, obstinate

tenant *n.* renter, leaseholder, inhabitant

tend *v.* guard, protect, keep, manage

tendency *n.* inclination, partiality, bias, penchant

tender *adj.* **DELICATE:** fragile, frail; **COMPASSIONATE:** sympathetic, kindhearted considerate

tenet *n.* belief, conviction, dogma, creed, doctrine

tenor *n.* drift, trend, tone, course

tense *adj.* taut, nervous, agitated, strained, drawn

tension *n.* pressure, strain, stress, unease

tentative *adj.* provisional, probationary, experimental, indefinite

tenuous *adj.* fine, narrow, insubstantial, flimsy, feeble

tepid *adj.* lukewarm, indifferent, halfhearted, languid

terminal *adj.* boundary, limit, extremity

terminate *v.* complete, conclude, eliminate, cancel

termination *n.* close, finish, cessation, completion
terminology *n.* vocabulary, language, jargon
terminus *n.* extremity, objective, conclusion
terrible *adj.* frightful, appalling, dreadful, horrible, horrendous, disastrous, disturbing, extreme
terrific *adj.* splendid, marvelous, wonderful, outstanding, super
terrify *v.* terrorize, appall, paralyze, horrify, frighten
territory *n.* area, region, dominion
terror *n.* fright, horror, alarm, dismay, consternation
terse *adj.* brief, succinct, concise, precise, curt
test *n.* inspection, experiment, examination, quiz
testify *v.* swear, certify, demonstrate, indicate, argue
testimony *n.* statement, declaration, confirmation, testament, affidavit
testy *adj.* irritable, cranky, grouchy, edgy, short-tempered, touchy, peevish
thank *v.* acknowledge, appreciate, recognize, credit
thaw *v.* warm, melt, dissolve, liquefy, loosen
theft *n.* burglary, robbery, thievery, looting
theology *n.* religion, faith, belief, scripture, dogma, convictions, creed
theorem *n.* principle, hypothesis, postulate, premise
theory *n.* conjecture, speculation, rationale, explanation, view, conception, outlook
theoretical *adj.* abstract, academic, hypothetical
theorize *v.* speculate, postulate, presume, suppose
therapeutic *adj.* restorative, curative, recuperative, remedial, corrective
thesis *n.* opinion, contention, argument, assumption, assertion, hypothesis
thick *adj.* abundant, dense, packed, crowded

thicken v. jell, congeal, stiffen, harden, intensify
thin adj. lean, gaunt, scanty, meager, scarce
thin v. dilute, weaken, reduce
think v. contemplate meditate, consider, remember, recall, recollect, believe, suppose
thirst n. longing, desire, yearning, eagerness
thorough adj. total, meticulous, precise, painstaking
thoroughfare n. artery, highway, expressway, boulevard, concourse, freeway
thought v. concept, conviction, notion, opinion, theory, hypothesis, supposition
thoughtful adj. considerate, caring, attentive, concerned, discreet, tender
threadbare adj. worn, shabby, tattered, frayed, seedy
threat n. risk, hazard, danger, jeopardy, menace
threaten v. endanger, menace, terrorize, scare
threshold n. start, beginning, outset, commencement
thrift n. economy, husbandry, conservation
thrifty adj. frugal, sparing, provident
thrill n. excitement, stimulation
thrill v. delight, electrify, rouse
thrive v. flourish, succeed, increase, grow
throb v. pulse, pound, thump, pulsate
throng n. mass, multitude, horde, swarm, host, assemblage, crowd
through adj. completed, done, finished
throw v. fling, hurl, pitch, heave, toss
thrust v. shove, plunge, jab, push
thug n. hoodlum, goon, heavy, gangster, criminal
tiara n. crown, diadem, coronet
tidings n. news, information, gossip, lowdown
tidy adj. neat, orderly, spruce, trim

tie

tie *n.* **ROPE:** band, strap, cord, **NECKTIE:** bow, scarf, cravat, choker, **CONNECTION:** relation, bond, link, knot, **STANDOFF:** draw, deadlock, stalemate

tie *v.* fasten, secure attach, connect, join, link

tier *n.* line, row, array, bank

tiff *n.* quarrel, dispute, disagreement, scrap, spat

tighten *v.* squeeze, compress, constrict, clench

tilt *n.* tip, list, slant, incline, slope, angle, pitch

time *n.* **AGE:** epoch, generation, cycle; **INTERVAL:** duration, span; **RHYTHM:** tempo, beat, cadence

timely *adj.* auspicious, propitious, favorable, prompt

timetable *n.* schedule, program, calendar, agenda

timid *adj.* shy, retiring, fearful, withdrawn, reticent, indecisive, vacillating

timorous *adj.* timid, fearful, apprehensive, anxious, scared, afraid

tinge *n.* trace, hint, trifle, dab, nuance

tinker *v.* dabble, putter, potter, trifle

tint *v.* stain, color, tinge

tiny *adj.* small, diminutive, minute, microscopic

tip *n.* **PEAK:** pinnacle, summit; **GRATUITY:** compensation, consideration; **ADVICE:** pointer, hint, clue

tirade *n.* harangue, denunciation, outburst

tire *v.* exhaust, fatigue, drain, irk, bore

title *n.* **DESIGNATION:** name, appellation, epithet; **CLAIM:** interest, holding, ownership

titter *v.* laugh, giggle, snicker, chuckle

toil *v.* labor, work, strive, slave, sweat

token *adj.* nominal, superficial, minimal

token *n.* sign, emblem, mark

tolerable *adj.* **ENDURABLE:** sufferable, bearable; **ADEQUATE:** decent, average

tolerance *n.* **STAMINA:** forbearance, toleration; **IM-PARTIALITY:** magnanimity, compassion

tolerant *adj.* unprejudiced, moderate, merciful

tolerate *v.* **ALLOW:** oblige, indulge; **SUFFER:** abide, accept, bear

tomb *n.* grave, vault, crypt, sepulcher, mausoleum

tonic *adj.* refresher, restorative, stimulant

tool *n.* implement, appliance, utensil, gadget

top *n.* pinnacle, crest, summit, zenith, crown

topical *adj.* local, isolated, provincial, regional

topple *v.* fall, tumble, collapse, overturn, upset

torment *n.* anguish, suffering, distress, misery

torment *v.* distress, vex, afflict, annoy, tease, harass, irritate, pester, provoke, needle

torpid *adj.* inactive, inert, lethargic, sluggish, motionless, dormant, hibernating

torpor *n.* idleness, inactivity, indolence, sluggishness

torrent *n.* cloudburst, deluge, flood

tortuous *adj.* winding serpentine, twisted, snaky, crooked, bent

toss *v.* throw, fling, pitch, cast, hurl, chuck

total *adj.* entire, utter, whole, gross

totter *v.* stumble, falter, weave, reel, lurch

touchy *adj.* irritable, peevish, grouchy, testy

tough *adj.* rugged, hardy, durable, sturdy, hardy, unyielding, incorrigible

tourist *n.* visitor, sightseer, wayfarer

tournament *n.* competition, rivalry, contest, match

tousle *v.* dishevel, disarray, ruffle, muss

tout *v.* vaunt, plug, promote, herald, extol

town *n.* community, municipality, village, hamlct

toxic *adj.* poisonous, deadly, lethal, virulent

trace n. vestige, indication, hint, suggestion
track v. hunt, trail, pursue, trace
tractable adj. docile, compliant, pliable, flexible
trade n. vocation, profession, livelihood, craft
trade v. exchange, swap, barter, buy, sell
tragedy n. disaster, calamity, catastrophe, affliction, suffering, tribulation
tragic adj. disastrous, dreadful, distressing
train v. tutor, teach, enlighten, educate, inform, instruct, guide
trait n. characteristic, quality, property, attribute, mannerism, habit
tramp n. hobo, vagabond, vagrant, gypsy
tramp v. roam, rove, hike, tromp, march
tranquil adj. peaceful, serene, placid, still, pleasant
tranquillity n. quiet, calm, serenity
transform v. alter, transfigure, convert, commute
transgress n. overstep, infringe, violate, trespass
transient adj. brief, transitory, passing, fleeting
translate v. reword, explain, interpret, decipher
translucent adj. transparent, clear
transmit v. send, transfer, convey, dispatch
transparent adj. translucent, diaphanous, lucid, clear, thin, sheer
transpire v. happen, occur, ensue, result
transpose v. switch, swap, exchange, transfer
trap n. snare, trick, stratagem, maneuver, artifice
traumatic adj. alarming, upsetting, frightful
travel v. journey, tour, roam, expedition, excursion
travesty n. parody, satire, spoof burlesque, lampoon, caricature, farce
treacherous adj. unfaithful, deceitful, deceptive,

insidious, disloyal, treasonous, difficult, unstable
treatise *n.* dissertation, thesis, essay, discourse
treaty *n.* agreement, settlement, covenant, pact
tremble *v.* shiver, quiver, shake
tremendous *adj.* colossal, huge, immense
tribulation *n.* distress, suffering, hardship
tribute *n.* accolade, homage, recognition, applause
trick *n.* deception, artifice, ruse
trim *adj.* neat, orderly, tidy, groomed, natty
trinket *n.* bauble, adornment, decoration, ornament
trip *n.* voyage, excursion, jaunt, pilgrimage
trite *adj.* ordinary, commonplace, hackneyed, stale
triumph *v.* prevail, conquer, overwhelm, overpower
trivial *adj.* insignificant, inconsequential, unimportant, irrelevant, frivolous
troll *v.* goblin, gremlin, hobgoblin, demon
trophy *n.* award, citation, medal
trot *v.* canter, jog, lope, amble
trouble *n.* calamity, distress, misfortune, tribulation
trouble *v.* distress, harass, harry, irritate, pester
troublesome *adj.* pesky, bothersome, trying, perplexing, galling, burdensome, disturbing
trough *n.* channel, furrow, rut, crater, ditch
truce *n.* armistice, reprieve, amnesty, cease–fire
truculent *adj.* fierce, mean, malevolent, pugnacious, belligerent, contentious, hostile
true *adj.* real, genuine, truthful, undistorted, authentic, just, honest, faithful, reliable
trunk *n.* chest, strongbox, coffer, case
trust *n.* confidence, dependence, reliance, faith,
try *v.* endeavor, strive, test, examine
tryst *n.* meeting, rendezvous, assignation

tumble *v.* fall, slip, descend, decline, totter, drop

tumor *n.* growth, cyst, polyp, sarcoma, melanoma

tumult *n.* disorder, commotion, turmoil, melee, agitation, ferment

tumultuous *adj.* riotous, violent, restive, uneasy, boisterous, disorderly, obstreperous

turbulent *adj.* violent, blustery, disorderly

turbulence *n.* commotion, excitement, uproar, tumult, disturbance

turmoil *n.* chaos, commotion, disorder, tumult, turbulence, uproar

turn *v.* **ROTATE:** spin, gyrate; **CONVERT:** transform, change, alter, transmute,

turnout *n.* attendance, audience, crowd, spectators

turpitude *n.* depravity, baseness, perversion, vileness, evil, sinfulness, corruption

tussle *v.* scuffle, grapple, struggle, fracas, brawl

tutor *n.* instructor, trainer, coach, teacher

tweak *v.* nip, pinch, grasp, squeeze, pull, twist

twine *n.* rope, cord, strand, string, braid

twinge *n.* twitch, tingle, spasm, crick, stitch, throb

twinkle *v.* shimmer, glitter, flicker, glint, glimmer

twirl *v.* twist, gyrate, turn, rotate, pivot

type *n.* kind, class, breed, group, family, genus

typical *adj.* characteristic, representative, ideal

typify *v.* represent, personify, epitomize, exemplify

tyrannical *adj.* oppressive, despotic, arbitrary, domineering, unjust, cruel

tyro *n.* amateur, novice, apprentice, neophyte

ubiquity *n.* prevalence, pervasiveness, commonness, omnipresence, universality

ugly *adj.* homely, unsightly, displeasing, monstrous,

objectionable, nasty

ulcer *n.* abscess, infection, boil

ulterior *adj.* concealed, shrouded, obscured

ultimate *adj.* extreme, final, decisive, concluding, eventual, maximum, utmost, preeminent

ultimatum *n.* warning, mandate, demand, order

umpire *v.* mediate, arbitrate, judge, decide, settle

unaffected *adj.* **NATURAL:** simple, sincere, genuine, real, artless; **UNMOVED:** indifferent, unemotional, unresponsive, disinterested

unassuming *adj.* modest, unpretentious, humble, simple, plain, diffident

unauthorized *adj.* unsanctioned, prohibited, illicit, forbidden, banned

unbalanced *adj.* unstable, maladjusted, biased, untrustworthy, treacherous

unbearable *adj.* intolerable, insufferable, obnoxious

unbecoming *adj.* inappropriate, unsuitable, indecent, unseemly, rough, improper, unfit

unbend *v.* relax, rest, soften, ease, relent

unbiased *adj.* impartial, objective, neutral, unprejudiced, tolerant, disinterested

unbounded *adj.* **IMMENSE:** endless, vast, boundless; **UNCONFINED:** free, unbridled, unfettered

uncanny *adj.* strange, odd, weird, mysterious, eerie

unceasing *adj.* continual, incessant, chronic, perpetual, persistent

uncivilized *adj.* primitive, barbarous, crude, uncouth

unclean *adj.* dirty, grimy, soiled, squalid, foul, vile, impure, defiled, adulterated, profaned

uncommon *adj.* exceptional, extraordinary, unique, remarkable, rare, scarce

uncompromising *adj.* obstinate, inflexible, unyielding, immovable, steadfast,

unconditional *adj.* absolute, certain, unrestricted

unconscionable *adj.* unscrupulous, unprincipled, wicked, wanton, dishonest, unholy

unconscious *adj.* senseless, oblivious, benumbed

uncouth *adj.* rude, ill–mannered, vulgar, crass

uncover *v.* reveal, expose, disclose, unearth

undaunted *adj.* fearless, courageous, valiant, intrepid, audacious

underestimate *v.* misjudge, miscalculate, slight

undergo *v.* endure, tolerate, suffer, bear, abide

underhanded *adj.* sly, furtive, deceitful, dishonest, traitorous, unscrupulous

undermine *v.* weaken, erode, corrode, decay, threaten

underrate *v.* devaluate, lessen, downgrade, depreciate

underscore *v.* emphasize, accentuate, accent

understand *v.* comprehend, grasp, perceive, discern, interpret, hear, accept, conclude

understanding *adj.* sympathetic, accepting, tolerant

understanding *n.* comprehension, grasp, awareness

undervalue *v.* minimize, cheapen, misjudge, belittle, discredit, underrate

underwrite *v.* guarantee, support, endorse

undetermined *adj.* dubious, obscure, enigmatic, doubtful, unsettled

undo *v.* cancel, efface, erase, expunge, obliterate

undress *n.* disrobe, undrape, shed, peel

undulate *v.* wave, surge, heave, flap, pulsate, billow

unduly *adj.* excessively, inordinately, exceedingly

undying *adj.* eternal, permanent, everlasting, unending, unceasing, persistent

uneasy *adj.* restless, perplexed, troubled, apprehensive, fidgety, nervous, jittery, uncomfortable

unencumbered *adj.* free, unobstructed, unhampered, unhindered, unfettered

unequal *adj.* disparate, unlike, uneven, odd

unequaled *adj.* matchless, incomparable, unparalleled, distinct, peerless, dissimilar, special

unequivocal *adj.* definite, unmistakable, incontestable, evident, absolute, explicit, clear, plain

unerring *adj.* accurate, exact, precise, perfect, correct, definite, unfailing, infallible

uneven *adj.* jagged, coarse, rugged, lumpy, serrated, intermittent, spasmodic, irregular, rough

unfailing *adj.* certain, absolute, sure, reliable, sure-fire, dependable

unfair *adj.* unjust, prejudiced, discriminatory, biased, inequitable, despotic, wrongful, arbitrary

unfaltering *adj.* steadfast, resolute, untiring, unfailing, unflagging, tireless, persistent, firm, constant

unfasten *v.* uncouple, detach, free, separate, undo

unfathomable *adj.* incomprehensible, enigmatic, mysterious, inscrutable, profound, baffling, puzzling

unfeeling *adj.* callous, merciless, cold-hearted, unsympathetic, hard, brutal, cruel

unfeigned *adj.* genuine, real, natural, unaffected, truthful, candid, sincere

unflagging *adj.* tireless, unrelenting, persisting, assiduous, devoted, consistent

unfold *v.* evolve, reveal, show, unravel, unearth, resolve, open, extend, expand

unfortunate *adj.* unlucky, hapless, doomed, ill–fated, inept, cursed, condemned

unfounded *adj.* groundless, baseless, unsupported, unsound, idle, vain, erroneous, untrue

unfurl *v.* unfold, open, uncoil, extend, expand

ungainly *adj.* clumsy, awkward, ungraceful, lumbering, maladroit, inept, ponderous, bulky

ungovernable *adj.* uncontrollable, headstrong, unruly

unguarded *adj.* open, undefended, unprotected, imprudent, incautious

unguent *n.* ointment, salve, lotion, balm, dressing, poultice, dressing

uniform *adj.* regular, routine, normal, unwavering, invariable, consistent, steady

uniformity *n.* regularity, similarity, accord, steadiness, order, concord

unify *v.* combine, integrate, consolidate, compact, concentrate, arrange, blend, integrate, synthesize

unimpeachable *adj.* irrefutable, obvious, conclusive, unassailable, adequate, satisfactory

unintentional *adj.* involuntary, accidental, inadvertent, unplanned, unconscious

union *n.* coalition, merger, melding, alliance, confederacy, association, order, league, brotherhood, society, matrimony, juncture, connection

unique *adj.* singular, particular, peerless, unrivaled, unequaled, matchless, unusual, uncommon, odd, peculiar, rare

unison *n.* coincidence, agreement, concord

unit *n.* element, constituent, component, part, section, piece, member

unite *v.* combine, join, link, couple, connect, associate, incorporate, blend, consolidate, compound, fuse, weld, marry, join, couple

unity *n.* union, harmony, agreement, concert, unison, concord, rapport, congruity

universal *adj.* general, widespread, extensive, entire, whole, sweeping

universe *n.* creation, cosmos, world, totality

unjust *adj.* unfair, partial, prejudiced, biased, inequitable, shabby, undeserved, unjustified, unmerited

unkempt *adj.* disorderly, disheveled, messy, tousled, untidy, crude, vulgar

unkind *adj.* cruel, harsh, unfeeling, callous, cold-hearted, hard, brutal, heartless

unlettered *adj.* untaught, ignorant, uneducated, illiterate, unenlightened, untutored

unlike *adj.* different, dissimilar, incompatible, mismatched, disparate, divergent, diverse

unlimited *adj.* boundless, infinite, immense, vast, extensive, endless, unconstrained, unrestricted, total, complete, totalitarian

unmanageable *adj.* difficult, unruly, ungovernable, uncooperative, stubborn, obstinate, balky, rebellious, uncontrollable, wild, irrepressible

unmoved *adj.* determined, decided, solid, unshaken, unaffected, collected, firm, steadfast, indifferent, resolute, unemotional

unnerve *v.* upset, unsettle, disarm, aggravate, fluster, discourage, disconcert

unparalleled *adj.* uncommon, rare, singular, unequaled, unrivaled, unique, peerless, matchless

unprecedented *adj.* unparalleled, unique, unequal, unusual, uncommon, untoward

unprepared *adj.* surprised, unaware, dumfounded, unguarded, careless, imprudent, unwary

unprincipled *adj.* amoral, corrupt, wanton, unscrupulous, unethical, dishonest

unqualified *adj.* incompetent, unable, inept, unskilled, untrained, unsatisfactory, unsuitable, incapable, unfit, ineligible,

unravel *v.* explain, elucidate, clarify, justify, resolve, interpret, solve, untangle, unwind, disengage

unremitting *n.* constant, ceaseless, endless, incessant, constant, perpetual, unending, continuous,

unrest *n.* agitation, disquiet, trouble, disturbance, bickering, confusion, crisis, quarrel, turbulence

unscathed *adj.* unharmed, safe, unimpaired, sound, uninjured

unseemly *adj.* indecent, improper, unbecoming, inappropriate, wrong, incorrect,

unsettle *v.* confuse, disturb, disrupt, perturb, bother, trouble, upset, fluster, ruffle, rattle

unsightly *adj.* unattractive, homely, plain, disagreeable, repulsive, hideous

unsophisticated *adj.* naive, provincial, callow, unrefined, simple, coarse, crude, harsh, vulgar, artless, guileless, ingenuous, pure, natural, genuine

unspeakable *adj.* unutterable, indescribable, astonishing, incredible, offensive, abusive, nasty, coarse, repulsive, odious, ineffable

untiring *adj.* inexhaustible, constant, powerful, resolute, strong, unflagging

unveil *v.* reveal, show, expose, divulge, announce

upbraid *v.* censure, scold, admonish, chide, reproach, reprove, berate, condemn,

upheaval *n.* eruption, earthquake, volcano, blowup, outbreak, explosion, outburst

uphold *v.* maintain, support, champion, sustain, endorse, sanction, bolster, help

uppermost *adj.* topmost, foremost, highest, predominant, supreme, loftiest

upright *adj.* upstanding, honest, good, outstanding, moral, ethical, principled, just, righteous, pure, true

uprising *n.* revolt, insurrection, rebellion, revolution, demonstration, skirmish

uproar *n.* clamor, commotion, disturbance, fracas, furor, hubbub, melee

uproarious *adj.* hilarious, funny, noisy, tumultuous, turbulent, frenzied, confused, disorderly

uproot *v.* remove, transport, liquidate, excavate, extirpate, eradicate, eliminate, dislodge

upset *adj.* irritated, worried, uneasy, shaky, troubled, unsettled, disturbed, aggravated, concerned, perturbed, disconcerted

upset *v.* capsize, overturn, topple, founder, upend, invert, flip

upshot *n.* outcome, consequence, conclusion, result

upstart *n.* opportunist, pretender, snob, phony, fraud, rogue, impostor

urban *adj.* city, metropolitan, municipal, civic

urbane *adj.* suave, poised, polished, refined, smooth, elegant, gracious, courteous

urchin *n.* waif, stray, foundling, orphan, ragamuffin, child, infant

urge *n.* drive, desire, impulse, craving, passion, push, influence, stimulus, impulse

urge *v.* drive, impel, press, spur, incite, goad, stimulate, implore, beg, beseech, entreat, persuade, induce, advise, advocate, recommend

urgent *adj.* pressing, compelling, demanding, driving, forcing, imperative, anxious, insistent, earnest

urgency *n.* seriousness, need, insistence, gravity, exigency, emergency, crisis, necessity

usable *adj.* useful, employable, applicable, functional

usage *n.* custom, practice, acceptance, habit, convention, fashion, form

use *n.* application, help, habit, custom, way

use *v.* employ, utilize, operated, apply, exploit

useful *adj.* beneficial, helpful, serviceable, effective, practical, functional, handy

usual *adj.* common, customary, ordinary, familiar

usurp *v.* capture, commandeer, appropriate, assume

usury *n.* greed, avarice, rapacity, loansharking

utensil *n.* instrument, device, implement, gadget

utility *n.* usefulness, value, advantage

utilize *v.* use, employ, exploit, operate

utmost *adj.* ultimate, maximum, maximal, entire, greatest, undiminished, unlimited

utopian *adj.* idealistic, ideological, visionary, perfect, ideal, fanciful, theoretical

utter *adj.* complete, entire, total, unconditional, unqualified, thorough

utter *v.* speak, articulate, vocalize, voice, say, remark, express, announce, proclaim, state,

utterance *n.* assertion, declaration, enunciation, proclamation, pronouncement

vacant *adj.* empty, uninhabited, abandoned, deserted, expressionless, vacuous, vapid

vacate *v.* leave, abandon, depart, quit

vacation *n.* holiday, furlough, respite, sabbatical

vaccinate *v.* immunize, inoculate, inject

vacillate *v.* waver, hesitate, fluctuate, alternate, sway

vacuum *n.* void, emptiness, vacuity, nothingness

vagary *n.* caprice, whim, urge, notion, impulse, fancy, quirk, eccentricity

vagrant *n.* beggar, tramp, hobo, idler, loafer, rascal

vague *adj.* obscure, indistinct, indefinite, imprecise, unspecified, uncertain, loose, unclear

vain *adj.* FUTILE: unavailing, fruitless, ineffective, inefficient, hollow; CONCEITED: egotistical, smug, arrogant, proud, narcissistic

valet *n.* manservant, attendant, butler, steward

valiant *adj.* valorous, brave, bold, courageous, intrepid, stouthearted, fearless, chivalrous

valid *adj.* logical, well–founded, sensible, sound, convincing, authoritative, legal, lawful

valley *n.* glen, dale, hollow, basin, lowland, vale

valor *n.* bravery, courage, boldness, spirit

valorous *adj.* brave, valiant, courageous, fearless

valuable *adj.* expensive, precious, rare, priceless, useful, beneficial, profitable, serviceable

value *n.* worth, importance, cost, price, significance

value *v.* appraise, assess, estimate, evaluate, rate, judge, weigh, consider, reckon

vandalism *n.* defacement, damage, mutilation, disfiguration, marring, spoiling

vanguard *n.* forefront, leaders, precursors, spearhead

vanish *v.* disappear, depart, evaporate, fade, dissolve

vanity *n.* conceit, pretension, self–esteem, pride, folly

vanquish *v.* conquer, overwhelm, overpower, defeat, quell, quash, subdue, suppress, subjugate, crush

vapid *adj.* dull, lifeless, insipid, uninteresting, tiresome, spiritless, vacuous, prosaic, mundane

vapor *n.* fog, haze, mist, gas, smog, condensation

vaporize *v.* evaporate, vanish, dissolve, disappear

variable *adj.* fluctuating, inconstant, wavering

variance *n.* difference, divergence, discrepancy, incongruity, disagreement, discord

variation *n.* alteration, modification, deviation, difference, discrepancy, diversity, dissimilarity, irregularity, inequality, aberration, departure

variety *n.* category, group, classification, division

various *adj.* miscellaneous, assorted, divers, diverse, diversified, varied, sundry

varnish *v.* embellish, disguise, mask, veil, falsify

vary *v.* change, alter, modify, diversify, deviate, differ, fluctuate, alternate

vast *adj.* boundless, large, limitless, unbounded, extensive, immense, widespread

vat *n.* container, keg, barrel, cask, tub

vault *n.* crypt, tomb, mausoleum, sepulcher

vault *v.* jump, hurdle, bound, leap, spring

vaunt *v.* boast, gloat, brag, strut, swagger, flaunt

veer *v.* swerve, deviate, diverge, curve, deflect, bend

vehement *adj.* fervent, energetic, impassioned

vehemence *n.* ardor, eagerness, energy, enthusiasm, passion, zeal, spirit, determination

vehicle *n.* conveyance, transportation, medium, means, agency, instrumentality

veil *v.* conceal, mask, cover, shroud, cloud, obscure

velocity *n.* speed, swiftness, dispatch, quickness

venal *adj.* corrupt, unscrupulous, treacherous, dishonorable, mercenary, corruptible

vend *v.* sell, merchandise, market, retail

veneer *n.* facing, cover, coating, surfacing, facade,

front, pretension, display

venerable *adj.* esteemed, revered, distinguished, honorable, ancient, respected

venerate *v.* admire, worship, revere, esteem, respect

vengeance *n.* revenge, retaliation, retribution

vengeful *adj.* vindictive, unforgiving, unrelenting, spiteful, rancorous, intractable, malicious

venial *adj.* excusable, justifiable, forgivable

venom *n.* bitterness, virulence, malice anger, contempt, spitefulness, malevolence, hate

vent *v.* express, air, assert, verbalize, articulate, expound, release, unleash, discharge

venture *n.* undertaking, enterprise, adventure, investment, speculation, endeavor attempt

venture *v.* chance, wager, risk, gamble, hazard, dare, plunge, imperil, jeopardize, endanger, hazard

veracious *adj.* truthful, accurate, precise, honest, sincere, trustworthy, righteous

veracity *n.* truth honesty, sincerity, accuracy, precision, exactness, correctness

verandah *n.* terrace, porch, deck, patio, courtyard

verbal *adj.* oral, spoken, stated

verbose *adj.* wordy, windy, loquacious, tedious, garrulous, talkative, chatty

verdant *adj.* green, flourishing, thriving, dense, lush

verdict *n.* decision, judgment, ruling, finding, adjudication, decree, determination, sentence

verge *n.* edge, brink, border, limit, margin, rim, brim

verify *v.* confirm, prove, authenticate, corroborate, substantiate, validate

verification *n.* evidence, proof, validation, documentation, support, confirmation

veritable *adj.* real, genuine, actual, positive, true, virtual, authentic

vernacular *adj.* native, indigenous, regional, informal, colloquial, everyday, ordinary, familiar

vernacular *n.* dialect, argot, jargon, idiom

versatile *adj.* flexible, pliable, adaptable, tractable, docile, pliant, yielding

versatility *n.* flexibility, pliancy, agility, compliance, adaptability, amenity, amiability

versed *adj.* experienced, seasoned, competent, adept, capable, skilled, practiced, trained

version *n.* rendition, interpretation, rendition

vertical *adj.* erect, upright, perpendicular, plumb

vestibule *n.* foyer, hallway, entry, lobby

vestige *n.* trace, indication, shred, fragment, remainder, hint, suggestion

veteran *adj.* experienced, seasoned, skilled, versed

veto *v.* reject, discard, eliminate, refuse, void, nullify, invalidate, forbid, dismiss

vex *v.* annoy, harass, irk, bother, disturb, irritate, plague, torment, agitate

viaduct *n.* bridge, overpass, trestle, scaffold, catwalk

vibrate *v.* shake, flutter, tremble, quiver, undulate, fluctuate, oscillate, reverberate

vicarious *adj.* substituted, delegated, sympathetic

vice *n.* wickedness, corruption, evil, depravity, immorality, depravity, iniquity, malignancy

vicinity *n* area, locality, neighborhood, environment, proximity, nearness

vicious *adj.* immoral, corrupt, base, degenerate, vile, depraved, reprehensible, wrong, malicious, malevolent, spiteful, malignant, unruly

victim *n.* casualty, dupe, gull, prey, sucker, fool
victor *n.* winner, champion, vanquisher, conqueror
victory *n.* triumph, conquest, success, achievement
victorious *adj.* triumphant, successful
vie *v.* compete, oppose, contend, clash, rival, strive
view *n.* scene, sight, spectacle, vision, glimpse, aspect, object, purpose, intention, description, notion, opinion, judgment, assessment
view *v.* observe, regard, behold, survey, witness, inspect, examine, study, scrutinize
vigil *n.* watchfulness, wakefulness, surveillance
vigilant *adj.* watchful, alert, observant, attentive, careful, wary
vigor *n.* strength power, potency, stamina, energy, endurance, vitality, soundness
vile *adj.* evil depraved, wretched, repulsive, contemptible, revolting, disgusting, offensive, vulgar
vilify *v.* malign, slander, slur, defame
village *n.* town, community, hamlet, municipality
villain *n.* miscreant, cad, rascal, rogue, scoundrel
vindicate *v.* exonerate, acquit, absolve, clear, defend, justify, support, uphold, corroborate, assert
vindictive *adj.* vengeful, unforgiving, spiteful
vintage *adj.* classic, choice, old, excellent
violate *v.* breach, infringe, transgress, trespass
violation *n.* transgression infringement, breach, defilement, debasement, assault, outrage
violent *adj.* intense, fierce, furious, rough, vicious, brutal, barbarous, savage, fierce
virgin *n.* pure, undefiled, unsullied, unadulterated, unmixed, fresh, unspoiled
virile *adj.* vibrant, strong, forceful, vigorous, robust

virtue *n.* integrity, justice, temperance, purity, decency, merit, distinction, excellence

virtuous *adj.* moral, ethical, honest, noble, right, pure, good, chaste

virulent *adj.* **LETHAL:** malignant, venomous, poisonous; **HATEFUL:** bitter, malicious, antagonistic

virus *n.* infection, disease, germ, microbe

visa *n.* endorsement, permit, authorization

visage *n.* countenance, appearance, aspect

viscous *adj.* sticky, thick, sticky, gummy

visible *adj.* discernible, perceptible, perceivable, obvious, apparent, clear, evident, conspicuous

visibility *n.* distinctness, perceptibility, prominence

vision *n.* **PERCEPTION:** sight, understanding, discernment, intuition; **CONCEPT:** image, imagination, view, **HALLUCINATION:** apparition, ghost, phantom

visit *n.* call, appointment, interview, talk, sojourn

visitor *n.* guest, caller, company

visor *n.* shield, sunshade, bill, peak

vista *n.* view, perspective, prospect, outlook

visual *adj.* visible, perceptible, obvious; ocular

vital *adj.* **ESSENTIAL:** necessary, important, critical, requisite; **VIGOROUS:** lively, energetic, active

vivacious *adj.* lively, animated, brisk, spirited, sprightly, energetic, spry

vivid *adj.* **BRIGHT:** shining, intense, lucid, lively, spirited, energetic, vivacious, realistic, picturesque, distinct, graphic, striking, clear, discernible

vocabulary *n.* lexicon, glossary, dictionary

vocal *adj.* **UTTERED:** spoken, oral, expressed, articulated, verbalized; **OUTSPOKEN:** open, honest, assertive, candid, blunt, frank

vocation *n.* occupation, profession, trade, business, pursuit, calling

vociferous *adj.* noisy, boisterous, uproarious, blatant

vogue *n.* fashion, style, custom, trend, fad, popularity, acceptance, rage

voice *n.* expression, utterance, assertion, declaration, preference, opinion, say, vote, view

void *adj.* useless, empty, barren, destitute, vacant, abandoned, unoccupied

void *n.* nothingness, emptiness, space, vacuum

volatile *adj.* explosive, unstable, fickle, erratic, frivolous, passing, transient, ephemeral

volition *n.* will, choosing, choice, preference, election, discretion, determination

voluble *adj.* talkative, loquacious, fluent, articulate, verbose, wordy, garrulous

volume *n.* **EDITION:** book, manuscript; **MASS:** size, magnitude, bulk; **LOUDNESS:** intensity, strength

voluntary *adj.* willing, disposed, inclined, prone, deliberate, intended, intentional, planned, willful

volunteer *v.* offer, extend, render, submit, proffer, tender, propose, suggest, recommend

voluptuous *adj.* sensual, indulgent, carnal, erotic, lustful, licentious

voracious *adj.* greedy, insatiable, ravenous, hungry, rapacious, grasping

vote *v.* elect, choose, enact, legislate, select, decide

vouch *v.* certify, attest, swear, state, assure

vow *n.* promise, pledge, covenant, contract

vow *v.* swear, promise, assure, attest, certify, affirm

voyage *n.* journey, excursion, trip, tour

vulgar *adj.* coarse tasteless, gross, crude, unrefined

vulgarity *n* obscenity, rudeness, indelicacy, coarseness, crassness, impropriety, immodesty

vulnerable *adj.* unprotected, unguarded, defenseless, exposed, susceptible, unsafe

waft *v.* float, hover, drift, skim flit flutter

wage *v.* conduct, undertake, pursue, execute

wages *n.* pay, compensation, stipend, remuneration

wager *v.* bet, stake, risk, gamble, speculate, hazard

waif *n.* stray, foundling, orphan, urchin, ragamuffin

wail *v.* lament, bemoan, sob, whine, mourn

wait *v.* abide, delay, linger, remain, tarry, stay

waive *v.* forgo, sacrifice, relinquish, renounce, resign, postpone, defer, shelve, table

wake *v.* arouse, rise, awaken, stir, rouse, call, prod, activate, provoke, stimulate, motivate, kindle

walk *n.* path, lane, passageway, promenade

wan *adj.* pallid, sickly, pale, pasty, ashen, blanched

wand *n.* baton, staff, stick, scepter

wander *v.* roam, drift, ramble, meander, rove, range, stroll, saunter, digress, stray, shift, veer

wane *v.* diminish, subside, abate, decline, weaken, dwindle, decrease, fade, sink, fail

want *n.* **NECESSITY:** requirement, demand, lack, deficiency, inadequacy, **POVERTY:** impoverishment, indigence, privation, need

want *v.* desire, crave, long, covet, wish, fancy

wanton *adj.* **MALICIOUS:** hateful, spiteful, reckless, willful, unruly; **LEWD:** lascivious, lustful, dissolute

ward *n.* **DEPENDENT:** child, minor, orphan; **DISTRICT:** territory, precinct, parish

warden *n.* guard, jailer, guardian, caretaker, custodian, watchman

wariness *n.* caution, alertness, vigilance

warm *adj.* gracious, amiable, pleasant, kind, intimate, amicable, sympathetic, close

warn *v.* caution, advise, admonish, counsel, forewarn, alert inform, apprise

warrant *n.* guarantee insurance, assurance, pledge, certificate, authorization commission, license, permit, order, writ

warrant *v.* certify, approve, authorize, sanction

wary *adj.* alert, attentive, wary, cautious, circumspect, vigilant, watchful

wash *v.* clean, cleanse, scrub, swab, lave, bathe

waste *adj.* superfluous, excess, useless, extra, unused

waste *n.* **DEVASTATION:** ruin, blight, destruction; **TRASH:** garbage, debris, refuse, rubbish; **SQUANDER:** consume, expend, misuse, dissipate

watch *v.* observe, view, see, regard, scrutinize, inspect, guard, patrol, protect

watchful *adj.* vigilant, alert, careful, mindful, attentive, observant, wary

water *v.* irrigate, sprinkle, douse, drench, wet, soak, flood, shower, rain

waterlogged *adj.* soaked, sodden, sopping, saturated

waver *v.* fluctuate, vacillate, hesitate

wax *v.* increase, grow, enlarge, expand, flourish

way *n.* method, style, custom, technique, system

waylay *v.* ambush, assail, lurk, trap

weak *adj.* delicate, dainty, feeble, puny, infirm, powerless, flimsy, slight, wobbly

wealth *n.* riches, affluence, assets, abundance

wear *n.* deterioration, erosion, fraying, fatigue

weary *adj.* tired, exhausted, drained, fatigued, spent

weary *v.* harass, annoy, bother, badger, pester, irk, vex, distress, harry, torment

weep *v.* cry, sob, whimper, bawl, moan, wail, lament

weigh *v.* consider, contemplate, ponder, study

weight *n.* **SIGNIFICANCE:** import, importance, gravity, consequence, influence; **MASS:** density, heft, heaviness, tonnage

weird *adj.* mysterious, eerie, spooky, uncanny, unnatural, ghostly, puzzling, arcane

welcome *adj.* appreciated, desirable, delightful

welcome *v.* greet, salute, hail, embrace

weld *v.* join, connect, bind, bond

well *adj.* healthy, strong, hardy, robust, fit, sound

wet *v.* soak, drench, saturate, douse, dampen

wheedle *v.* coax, wangle, entreat, appeal, beg, cajole

whereabouts *n.* location, position, situation, locale, place, spot, site

whet *v.* sharpen, hone, strop, file, grind, taper

whim *n.* impulse, inclination, urge, impulse, desire, craving, caprice, whimsy, notion, fancy, quirk

whimper *v.* cry, whine, sniffle, snivel, weep

whimsical *adj.* capricious, fanciful, playful, impulsive

whine *v.* cry, complain, grumble, snivel, whimper

whip *v.* beat, lash, flog, scourge, switch, punish

whirl *n.* revolve, rotate, spin, gyrate

whittle *v.* form, fashion, sculpt, carve, chisel, shape

whole *adj.* entire, unbroken, undivided, complete

wholesome *adj.* nourishing, healthy, nutritious, beneficial, advantageous, good

whoop *v.* holler, howl, shout, cheer, scream, yell

wicked *adj.* evil, depraved, immoral, nefarious

wide *adj.* extensive, comprehensive, universal

widen *v.* broaden, increase, expand, extend, spread, extend, enlarge, augment, stretch

width *n.* breadth, expanse, amplitude, scope

wield *v.* handle, utilize, operate, use, control, manage

wild *adj.* untamed, uncivilized, unrestrained

wile *n.* trickery, deception, deceit, artifice, ruse

will *n.* **COMMAND:** decree, order, bidding, **DECISION:** choice, determination, **DESIRE:** purpose, fancy, pleasure, wish

will *v.* **COMMAND:** order, decree, proclaim, direct; **BEQUEATH:** grant, give, leave

willful *adj.* **DELIBERATE:** intended, meant, voluntary, willed; **STUBBORN:** obstinate, headstrong, inflexible, adamant, resolute

wilt *v.* droop, wither, shrivel, decay, slump

wily *adj.* deceitful, artful, cunning, skillful, crafty, sly, treacherous, tricky

win *v.* **TRIUMPH:** prevail; **ACHIEVE:** secure, persuade, influence, convert

wince *v.* flinch, recoil, cringe, falter, twitch

wind *v.* curve, twist, swerve, snake, meander, curl, twist, twine, encircle

windfall *n.* blessing, godsend, boon, bonanza

winning *adj.* **ENGAGING:** captivating, charming, pleasant, likable, dazzling, winsome; **VICTORIOUS:** triumphant, conquering, successful

winnings *n.* accumulation, profits, gain

winnow *v.* sift, separate, sieve, extract, eliminate

winsome *adj.* winning, beautiful, charming, captivating, lovely, cute, engaging, comely, delightful

wisdom *n.* sagacity, understanding, discretion, insight, tact, diplomacy, intelligence, knowledge

wise *adj.* intelligent, scholarly, learned, educated, sagacious, rational, sensible, prudent, insightful, discerning, smart

wish *n.* desire, craving, inclination, ambition, aspiration, goal, promise

wish *v.* **CRAVE:** yearn, want, need; **DIRECT:** order, bid, instruct; **REQUEST:** beg, , entreat, solicit

wisp *n.* tuft, clump, shred, shock

wistful *adj.* melancholy, longing, yearning, sentimental, nostalgic, wishful, plaintive

wit *n.* intellect, reason, sagacity, sense, wisdom

witch *n.* sorceress, enchantress, hag, crone, hex

witchcraft *n.* sorcery, wizardry, divination, magic

withdraw *v.* retract, revoke, recant, abrogate

wither *v.* shrivel, wilt, shrink, atrophy, languish

withhold *v.* repress, restrain, check, retain

withstand *v.* oppose, defy, confront, resist, endure

witness *n.* spectator, bystander, onlooker, eyewitness

witness *v.* observe, see, watch, perceive, notice

witticism *n.* quip, jest, pun, gag, joke, wisecrack

witty *adj.* humorous, amusing, bright, keen, droll

wizard *n.* magician, conjurer, soothsayer, sorcerer

wizened *adj.* withered, shriveled, dry, dehydrated

woe *n.* sorrow, anguish, grief, misery, agony

woeful *adj.* mournful, sad, sorrowful, doleful

wonder *n.* amazement, astonishment, shock, awe

wonder *v.* **QUESTION:** ponder, doubt, speculate; **MARVEL:** gape, stare

wonderful *adj.* extraordinary, marvelous, astounding, awesome, remarkable, startling, excellent, superb

wondrous *adj.* amazing, astonishing, striking, astounding, extraordinary, miraculous